Reconciling Trade and Climate

ELGAR INTERNATIONAL ECONOMIC LAW

Series Editors: Alan O. Sykes, *Frank and Bernice J. Greenberg Professor of Law, University of Chicago Law School, USA,* and Mary E. Footer, *Professor of International Economic Law, University of Nottingham, UK*

This new monograph series is intended to provide a point of convergence for high quality, original work on various aspects of international economic and WTO law, ranging from established subject matter, such as international agricultural trade or the application of core trade disciplines such as MFN, to cross-cutting issues involving the interaction of international standards in the fields of investment, tax, competition, food safety and consumer protection with international trade law or the relationship of horizontal exceptions such as the general exception to domestic regulatory barriers. Theoretically rigorous, these books will take an analytical and discursive approach to the field, wherever possible drawing on insights from disciplines other than law, such as economics and politics, in an attempt to arrive at a genuinely inter-disciplinary perspective. Proposals are encouraged that primarily engage with new and previously under-developed themes in the field, or alternatively offer an innovative analysis of areas of uncertainty in the existing law.

Bringing together work both from established authors – academics and practitioners alike – and from a new generation of scholars, the *Elgar International Economic Law Series* aims to play an important role in the development of thinking in the field.

Reconciling Trade and Climate

How the WTO Can Help Address Climate Change

Tracey Epps

Senior Trade Law Adviser, New Zealand Ministry of Foreign Affairs and Trade

Andrew Green

Faculty of Law, University of Toronto, Canada

ELGAR INTERNATIONAL ECONOMIC LAW

Edward Elgar
Cheltenham, UK • Northampton, MA, USA

Published by
Edward Elgar Publishing Limited
The Lypiatts
15 Lansdown Road
Cheltenham
Glos GL50 2JA
UK

Edward Elgar Publishing, Inc.
William Pratt House
9 Dewey Court
Northampton
Massachusetts 01060
USA

A catalogue record for this book
is available from the British Library

Library of Congress Control Number: 2010926001

ISBN 978 1 84980 006 8

Typeset by Servis Filmsetting Ltd, Stockport, Cheshire
Printed and bound by CPI Group (UK) Ltd, Croydon, CR0 4YY

Contents

PART VI CONCLUSION

Abbreviations

AB	Appellate Body
BTA	border tax adjustment
CITES	Convention on International Trade in Endangered Species of Wild Flora and Fauna
COP	Conference of the Parties
CTE	Committee for Trade and Environment
DSB	Dispute Settlement Body
DSU	Dispute Settlement Understanding
GATT	General Agreement on Tariffs and Trade
GHG	greenhouse gas
GSP	Generalized System of Preferences
LDC	least developed country
MEA	multilateral environmental agreement
MFN	most-favoured-nation
PPM	process and production method
SCM Agreement	Agreement on Subsidies and Countervailing Measures
TBT Agreement	Technical Barriers to Trade Agreement
UNCTAD	United Nations Conference on Trade and Development
UNFCCC	United Nations Framework Convention on Climate Change
WTO	World Trade Organization

PART I

Introduction

1. Reconciling trade rules and climate policies

1.1 THE PROBLEM OF TRADE AND CLIMATE CHANGE

It seems that new reports come out monthly about the urgency with which climate change must be addressed. The reports of the Intergovernmental Panel on Climate Change (IPCC) are perhaps the most famous calls to action but certainly not the only, or most extreme, ones. Climate change is already negatively affecting species and natural systems.[1] These reports suggest major acceleration of such effects if action is not taken. Leaders of large and small countries recently converged on Copenhagen, citing the need for policies and plans and some form of multilateral agreement to replace the Kyoto Protocol. The current debate is about how quickly action is needed and what will be most effective in reducing greenhouse gas (GHG) concentrations and the impact of climate change on the environment, including humans. Unfortunately, despite the scientific consensus and the apparent political recognition of the need to cooperate to reach a solution, action has fallen far short of what scientists claim is needed to reduce the probability of dangerous impacts on the planet and human civilization.

In this debate international trade and 'globalization' seem often characterized as a key source of the problem. However, we believe that this is both wrong and unhelpful – that there are important ways in which both trade and action on climate policy can work together to reduce the risks from climate change and to foster development. Most obviously perhaps, the movement of goods itself by ships, rail and truck creates GHG emissions. Moreover, the extent of economic growth and the emissions attendant on growth, such as from the production of electricity or other forms

---

[1] IPCC, *Climate Change 2007: Synthesis Report. Contribution of Working Groups I, II and III to the Fourth Assessment Report of the Intergovernmental Panel on Climate Change* (Geneva: IPCC, 2007) (IPCC FAR (2007)). See also International Scientific Steering Committee, *Avoiding Dangerous Climate Change: International Symposium on the Stabilization of Greenhouse Gas Concentrations* (Exeter, 2005).

of energy, are seen as the source of the rise in GHG emissions and a major obstacle to their reduction. International trade has led to increased economic growth and emissions in developed countries. Economic growth from trade by developing countries, and particularly large countries such as China and India, threatens to cause increasing emissions in the future. To the extent that World Trade Organization (WTO) rules support continued liberalization and growth of international trade, these rules have come to be seen as part of the problem.

At the same time, however, climate change policies are seen as harming trade and economic growth. Climate policies may impose high costs on industry, potentially reducing the competitiveness of these industries in an increasingly integrated global economy. This concern also implicates developing countries. They worry that while developed countries grew rich through carbon-intensive economies, they themselves will be denied the ability to grow and help their citizens out of poverty by strictures on GHG emissions. These concerns about the fairness of climate policies have been obstacles to international action.

In this book, we take a more optimistic view of the connection between international trade and action on climate change. We seek to find solutions that both foster trade (and a rules-based trading system) and support the goal of tackling climate change. The theme of this book is that there are *synergies* between trade and climate policies that can lead to more efficiently addressing climate change. In fact, we see three inter-related goals that policy-makers must focus on and which, through the manner in which they reinforce each other, have the potential to increase social welfare. These goals are mitigating climate change, deterring protectionism, and furthering the development goals of developing countries.

1.2   CLIMATE CHANGE, PROTECTIONISM AND DEVELOPMENT

The first goal of *mitigating climate change* arises because of the nature of the causes of climate change.[2] The global average temperature has been rising over the past century with most of this increase 'very likely' due to man-made increases in GHG emissions.[3] The impacts of climate change depend on the size of the increase in average temperatures. The policy goal

---

[2]   See Chapter 2 for a more detailed discussion of the theory relating to mitigating climate change and fostering trade and development.
[3]   IPCC, *supra* note 1.

of maintaining an average temperature rise of below 2 degrees Celsius has been set by scientists and is reflected in the 2009 Copenhagen Accord.[4]

In order to restrict temperature increases to this level, policies will have to address the key causes of GHG emissions. Climate change is a large-scale externality – a market failure in which individuals who create GHG emissions through such activities as driving cars or using electricity generated from coal obtain the benefits from the activities.[5] However, the costs in terms of climate change are imposed on others – largely either future generations or individuals in other countries. Governments need to choose instruments to address this market failure, such as taxes, regulations, emissions trading, or even informational remedies.

The second goal – that of *deterring protectionism* – relates to the nature of trade and its connection to social welfare. Economic efficiency is maximized with liberal trade as goods are supplied by the most efficient producers regardless of where they are located. However, governments may put in place tariffs and other protectionist measures in order to placate concentrated interests such as import competing industries.[6] One goal of trade rules then is to reduce protectionism to the extent possible in order to maximize economic efficiency.[7]

---

[4] Available online at http://unfccc.int/resource/docs/2009/cop15/eng/o7.pdf (date accessed: 22 January 2010). It should be noted that 193 signatories to the UN climate convention – those represented in the Alliance of Small Island States, the Least Developed Countries, and the Africa Group – all warned at the Copenhagen Conference of the Parties in December 2009 that 1.5 degrees is the absolute limit and that 2 degrees would mean hardship, mass migrations, and even death for many of their citizens. Bridges Copenhagen Update, 'High-level Politics Meets Low Ambition: Taking Stock of COP15' (International Centre for Trade and Sustainable Development, Geneva, 2009).

[5] N. Stern, *The Economics of Climate Change: The Stern Review* (Cambridge: Cambridge University Press, 2007).

[6] As discussed in Chapter 2, there are some potentially welfare enhancing rationales for trade barriers or measures but the general case is that trade barriers reduce economic efficiency. See Michael Trebilcock and Robert Howse, *The Regulation of International Trade*, 3rd edn (London: Routledge, 2005).

[7] Protectionism, as noted by Levy, tends to be seen as anything other than advocacy of free trade. Levy suggests treating protectionism as the advocacy of policies that are intended to favour domestic producers over foreign exporters. He classifies three types of protectionist measures: (1) intentional protectionism, where measures are explicitly intended to favour domestic industry over imports; (2) incidental protectionism, where measures can be justified on other grounds but also have the effect of obstructing import competition; and (3) instrumental protectionism, which describes a growing set of policies in which trade actions are used as a lever to change another country's policies. Philip I. Levy, 'Protectionism in the Global Economy' (2009) *Georgetown Journal of International Affairs*.

Finally, economic prosperity and growth in standards of living have not been evenly distributed around the world. There is clear inequality in income and standards of living both in and across countries, with many countries' citizens living in abject poverty.[8] The third goal we want to emphasize is therefore the need for *further development* in order to raise standards of living around the world. The standard of living can and should be measured in a range of ways beyond mere income per capita, such as through examining whether individuals have the capabilities necessary to live lives they have reason to value.[9] Development cannot therefore be equated directly with economic growth or trade but economic activity is an aspect of human freedom, particularly as a means of fostering other goals (such as health and education).

Synergies between trade rules and climate change policies arise from the interactions of trade rules, economic growth and measures to address climate change. Trade rules not only provide scope for individual countries to meet their own targets for mitigating climate change but may also help governments facing domestic opposition. For example, a key concern with government action addressing climate change is that it will impose costs on domestic industry, making them uncompetitive compared with industries in countries that have not taken action. Under WTO rules, the cost of some of these measures can be imposed on imports and rebated to exports, helping to overcome domestic opposition to climate policies. There are, of course, difficulties with these measures; they are difficult to apply fairly and can harm relations with the countries facing the measures.[10] However, they can play some role in addressing domestic political economy concerns.

Further, trade rules attempt to ensure that countries do not put in place measures that are ostensibly aimed at addressing climate change but instead, in whole or in part, are intended to protect domestic industry at the expense of foreign producers. Countries' climate policies are in theory constrained by WTO rules from harming trade flows that may provide not only economic growth but also greater environmental benefits. For example, to the extent Brazilian ethanol is cheaper and more environmentally beneficial over its life cycle than US corn-based ethanol, WTO restrictions on protectionist measures that deny Brazilian access to US markets can aid economic growth and the effort to address climate change.[11]

---

[8]   Jeffrey D. Sachs, *The End of Poverty: Economic Possibilities for Our Time* (New York: The Penguin Press, 2005).
[9]   Amartya Sen, *Development as Freedom* (New York: Knopf, 1999).
[10]   See Chapters 8 and 13.
[11]   See, for example, Doaa Abdel Motaal, 'The Biofuels Landscape: Is There a Role for the WTO?' (2008) 42 (1) *Journal of World Trade* 61.

Trade rules therefore need not constrain efficient domestic action and may help governments to overcome political economy constraints on action. They can also address climate change by providing scope for countries to take measures to deter other countries that are not addressing climate change. Addressing climate change is an additive public good – that is, a public good that results from reducing the combined emissions of countries.[12] The more countries (and especially large emitters) take action, the greater the public good. However, like all public goods, parties may try to 'free-ride' on the actions of others. They want to benefit from other countries' emission reductions but do not want to bear the costs of taking action themselves (for example, sacrifices in lifestyle or economic activity). Such free-riding could manifest itself as countries not joining up to climate change regimes or not complying with commitments made under such regimes. As discussed further in Chapter 3, while there are only two countries that did not ratify the Kyoto Protocol (the US and San Marino), there are many others that have no emission reduction commitments or are unlikely to meet the commitments they do have. Trade measures such as border adjustments and even import bans can reduce both non-participation and non-compliance, leading to increases in the public good. These measures can be taken unilaterally by individual countries or be part of a multilateral agreement. Regardless of their source, they can be an effective tool in reducing free-riding. Current trade rules provide scope for their use, but, as with the use of measures to address domestic political economy barriers to climate action, they raise tensions and potential fairness issues with respect to the target countries.[13]

Trade measures therefore can help countries meet their own domestic targets and induce others to participate in the effort to address climate change. Trade can also help overcome concerns about the impacts of climate change measures on developing countries. This theme ties in with concerns about the fairness of any attempts to address climate change. A sticking point in the international climate change negotiations has been

---

[12] Scott Barrett, *Why Cooperate? The Incentive to Supply Global Public Goods* (Oxford: Oxford University Press, 2007). A public good is one whose benefit is shared by either the public as a whole or a sub-group thereof. It has two characteristics that are the opposite of those defining private goods: (i) it is impossible or too expensive for the supplier to exclude those who do not pay for the benefit (non-excludability); and (ii) consumption by one person does not leave less for others to consume (non-rivalrous competition). Richard D. Smith et al., *Global Public Goods for Health: Health Economics and Public Health Perspectives* (New York: Oxford University Press, 2003) at 4.
[13] See Chapters 13 and 14.

that developed countries argue that, as noted above, addressing climate change is an additive public good so all countries, including developing countries, need to take action. Developing countries, on the other hand, argue it is unfair that developed countries grew economically on the basis of GHG emissions, whereas now developing countries are being asked to constrain their own growth by the need to reduce emissions.

WTO rules, in theory at least, hamper attempts by developed countries to use climate change measures in a manner that protects their own industries at the expense of industries in developing countries. Limiting such protectionism can at a minimum ensure that any action to address climate change is taken with the least possible impact on developing countries. Further, trade rules can provide for positive measures to benefit developing countries. Developed countries can, for example, provide preferences to imports from developing countries as an incentive for developing countries to take climate change action. Such measures can be used to enhance the economic opportunities for developing countries in the context of climate change.

1.3   KEY INTERACTIONS

These themes, of synergies and of fairness and development, implicate the current WTO rules including both how they are drafted and how they should be interpreted. We will discuss these rules in the context of three key ways in which trade and climate change policy interact: (i) in countries' use of climate policies to address their own emissions; (ii) in countries' use of unilateral action to induce other countries to take action on climate change; and (iii) in multilateral solutions to climate change.

1.3.1   Implications of Trade Rules for Domestic Climate Policy

Any domestic policy that imposes costs on or provides benefits to domestic industries, or provides some barriers to imports, raises concerns about conflicts with WTO rules, as one of the main roles of the WTO rules is to reduce unnecessary barriers to trade. These domestic policies do not have to favour domestic industry explicitly or intentionally harm foreign producers. Much of the conflict between trade rules and domestic policies will arise in the context of policies that appear neutral as between domestic and foreign producers but which other countries argue implicitly harm their producers. For example, a tax on all high emission cars, whether domestic or foreign, appears neutral but what if the rule results in the domestic cars facing a much lower average tax than imports? Depending on how

WTO rules are interpreted, governments may be limited in the policies they can adopt. The first set of issues relates to this interaction of domestic climate policies and trade rules: do trade rules constrain countries' ability to address climate change? Conversely, can trade measures help countries implement climate change policies (such as by helping overcome domestic opposition by addressing competitiveness concerns)?

1.3.2 Unilateral Measures to Induce Other Countries to Take Action on Climate Change

Given that addressing climate change is a public good, countries will be concerned that if they take action, other countries will simply free-ride on their efforts and take no action themselves. Countries may therefore wish to use trade measures to either force or provide incentives to these other countries to take action. For example, countries could impose a tax on imports from countries which have not adopted climate policies. Alternatively, they could afford tariff preferences to countries that do take climate action. Trade rules will determine the scope for such unilateral action. The second set of interactions therefore relates to the extent to which unilateral trade measures can be used for this purpose. If they can, should they?

1.3.3 Multilateral Solutions

The final set of issues concerns multilateral solutions. The Kyoto Protocol was an attempt to build multilateral action on climate change. However, it did not initially include any means to force countries that are not signatories to adopt the Protocol or, indeed, even to ensure parties that did adopt the Protocol meet their commitments. The enforcement mechanisms that were eventually adopted have been described as too weak to be effective.[14] Other multilateral environmental agreements such as the Montreal Protocol on Ozone Depleting Substances have used trade measures to back commitments or to induce non-participants to join the agreement. Such measures include bans on the trade in products from these non-parties that have been made with ozone depleting substances. This last set of issues therefore asks whether trade measures can and should be built into any post-Kyoto climate change regime.

---

[14] Barrett, *supra* note 12, and Robert N. Stavins and Scott Barrett 'Increasing Participation and Compliance in International Climate Change Agreements' (Fondazione Eni Enrico Mattei Working Paper No. 94.2002; Kennedy School of Government Working Paper No. RWP02-031, 2002).

1.4   THE ROLE OF INSTITUTIONS

Institutional design issues are central to any discussion of the relationship between trade rules and climate change. Domestic climate policies are made by governments that are more or less representative of their citizens. WTO rules are made and interpreted under a set of international institutional rules. The content of any international climate change agreement will depend on the institutional arrangements for its negotiation. Each of these sets of institutions confers power on different groups or individuals.

Decisions about which climate policies to adopt involve complex economic, political and ethical choices. The set of institutions making these decisions in large part determines how these choices will be made, and whose preferences and values prevail. Allowing domestic governments alone to decide on the appropriate policy raises the spectre of the use of such policies to protect domestic industry at the expense of foreigners. Allowing the WTO dispute resolution body to decide raises fears that it will not adequately consider the views and values of different countries or of the environment. Permitting decisions to be made in multilateral negotiations potentially allows broad deliberation about the appropriate approach to a global issue, but gives rise to concerns about consideration of the interests of under-represented or non-represented countries or groups such as developing countries.

This book will therefore focus on how WTO rules and the interpretation of those rules by panels and the WTO Appellate Body determine whose values prevail and possibly the quality of the resulting decisions. Not all bodies have the same information or the same ability to assess the information – domestic governments, for example, may have a greater ability to assess local values and conditions. Each type of institution (domestic government, multilateral international body, international dispute resolution body) therefore puts a different emphasis on legitimacy and competency. We will discuss how the choice of institutions impacts the potential synergies of trade and climate policies as well as the possibilities for using trade to enhance fairness and development opportunities in the climate change context.

1.5   OUTLINE OF THE BOOK

The framework of this book generally flows from the three key interactions between trade and climate change set out above. Before getting to these interactions, however, Part II sets the stage for the discussion. Chapter 2 discusses in greater detail the underlying concerns about both climate change and international trade. It focuses on the 'public goods' nature of climate change and the free-riding to which it gives rise. It also discusses how trade agreements arise because of an underlying prisoners' dilemma in which countries that would benefit from more liberal trade need to reach some form of credible agreement to ensure that other parties do not cheat on their commitments. We then use this discussion of the nature of climate change and trade to address why countries enter into international agreements and the underlying constraints on such agreements. International agreements must be self-enforcing as there is no overarching authority or government to make and enforce these agreements. This self-enforcing nature gives rise to a difficult balance between participation and enforcement – stronger enforcement may, in certain circumstances, lead to fewer countries being willing to participate or, if they do participate, to take on significant obligations.[15] Who makes the agreements, how free countries are to make their own policies, and how these agreements are enforced all raise difficult institutional questions of legitimacy and competence.

Chapter 3 then provides a basic overview of the current WTO and climate regimes. Following this, Chapter 4 discusses the three main interactions between these regimes and between these regimes and domestic policies: (i) the relationship between international trade rules and domestic climate policies; (ii) the scope for unilateral action by countries against countries they feel are not meeting their responsibilities to address climate change; and (iii) the potential inclusion of trade measures in a multilateral climate agreement.

Part III begins the analysis of these interactions by focusing on the relationship between WTO rules and domestic climate policies. Governments can use a range of policies to address climate change including regulatory measures or emissions trading schemes, taxes, subsidies and border measures. This part is largely structured around these instrument choices. Each chapter begins with a discussion of why the instrument may be useful in addressing climate change and then analyses the interactions between these instruments and WTO rules. Chapters 5 and 6 primarily discuss the potential constraints of WTO non-discrimination rules on the use of regulatory measures and emissions trading or taxes, respectively. The WTO Appellate Body has altered its interpretation of these rules over time, most recently potentially increasing scope for domestic environmental policies. Chapter 7 focuses on subsidies that fall under a different, much more stringent set of rules. These rules significantly constrain the ability of countries to use subsidies to address climate change. Finally, Chapter 8 addresses

---

[15]   Barrett, *supra* note 12.

border measures such as applying taxes to imports or rebating taxes on exports. While there is some scope for the use of such border measures, the WTO rules in this area are unclear, giving rise to potential conflicts in the future if countries attempt to use them to address concerns about the competitiveness of their industry. There are also significant fairness concerns as regards their use with respect to developing countries.

While WTO rules might constrain certain uses of these instruments, there are some exceptions to these rules under WTO agreements. Chapter 9 focuses on the ability of countries to use these exceptions to justify their climate policies. In particular, it discusses the scope of Article XX of the GATT, which provides a list of grounds on which countries can base policies that otherwise violate WTO rules (such as those requiring non-discrimination). While Article XX does not provide an explicit broad environmental exception, it does permit measures that are 'necessary' to protect human or animal life or health, as well as measures relating to the conservation of exhaustible natural resources. The WTO Appellate Body has recently interpreted these provisions, along with the provisions of Article XX relating to how the measures are applied, in a manner that provides greater scope for domestic climate policies.

Chapter 10 draws together these discussions of instruments, rules and exceptions and their implications for which set of institutions should prevail. It discusses the lack of flexibility and certainty under current interpretations. It also sets out the concerns with the fairness and accessibility of the dispute settlement system. There is evidence that developing countries have difficulty effectively using the process because of the nature of the system and the available remedies. These difficulties impact not only the connection between WTO rules and domestic policies but also the other interactions discussed in Parts IV and V. This chapter then addresses the approach panels and the Appellate Body can and should take to reviewing decisions made by domestic governments. To what extent do they defer to domestic decisions or, conversely, do they second-guess these decisions and make the ultimate decisions themselves? The Appellate Body has struggled, and continues to struggle, to find the appropriate balance between deference and review.

Part IV turns to the second interaction between trade rules and climate policies – the extent to which countries can use unilateral measures to induce other countries to take action on climate change. Chapter 11 examines whether countries can use trade measures to provide positive incentives to other countries to take action on climate change. Such measures could include trade preferences to imports from countries not currently taking action as well as investment and subsidies or technology transfers to these countries. There is some scope for these measures under WTO rules, although less than perhaps commonly believed. Chapter 12 briefly turns to removing roadblocks that may be preventing countries taking climate change action. To the extent countries are concerned about loss of competitiveness of their industries relative to countries not taking action on climate change, the rules initially discussed in Part III (for example those relating to border adjustments) have a role to play. Chapter 13 discusses the thorny issue of using unilateral measures as 'sticks' to force other countries to adopt climate policies. These unilateral measures include bans on imports and punitive tariffs. They also encompass one of the most controversial issues in the trade and environment area – the ability of countries to put in place internal or border measures that relate not to the product itself (for example, the emissions from a car) but to how the product was made (for example, the GHG emissions from the electricity generation facility used to power the factory where the other country's car was manufactured). Part of the difficulty comes from the challenge of designing trade measures that are severe enough to cause action by other countries and yet not so severe to the country imposing them that they cannot be credibly threatened. There is also a concern about forcing countries to follow the values of citizens of other countries.

Part V addresses the final area of interaction between trade rules and climate change policies – multilateral solutions to climate change. Chapter 14 analyses the desirability of recent calls to include trade measures in a post-Kyoto multilateral climate change agreement. Trade measures can reduce both non-participation in and non-compliance with international agreements. Using trade measures in a multilateral agreement may also increase the fairness of attempts to induce participation in addressing climate change internationally as compared with the unilateral measures discussed in Part IV. However, there are risks, including that those inside the regime will use the measures in a manner that unnecessarily harms those on the outside. Chapter 15 will examine the other approach – that is, rather than trade measures being included in a climate change agreement, trade agreements could take greater account of climate change. For example, trade agreements could provide greater scope for trade in environmental goods and services or transfers of environmental technologies.

Part VI draws out the lessons we take from the prior chapters and the institutional reforms they point towards. We argue that the discussion of the interactions between climate change policies and trade rules supports our themes of synergies and of fairness. The stark characterization of trade as antithetical to the global struggle against climate change is inappropriate and, moreover, unhelpful. In order to combat climate change in the most effective and fair manner, trade is essential. Trade rules and institutions must continue to adapt to ensure environmental values are not lost in the search for more liberalized trade – but not to use them to foster climate action would be to neglect an important lever at a time when urgent action is needed.

PART II

Linkages between trade and climate change

2. Climate change, trade and international agreements

2.1 CLIMATE CHANGE AS AN ADDITIVE PUBLIC GOOD

Climate change is occurring. In its 2007 Fourth Assessment Report, the Intergovernmental Panel on Climate Change (IPCC) adopted a very strong statement concerning the existence and cause of climate change. It stated that 'Warming of the climate system is unequivocal, as is now evident from observations of increases in global average air and ocean temperatures, widespread melting of snow and ice, and rising global average sea level.'[1] These findings have since been confirmed and extended by further studies, including updated observations of recent changes in climate, better attribution of observed climate change to human and natural causal factors, improved understanding of carbon-cycle feedbacks, and new projections of future changes in extreme weather events and the potential for catastrophic climate change.[2] The increase in greenhouse gases (GHGs) in the industrial era is unprecedented in more than 10 000 years. The global average atmospheric concentration of carbon dioxide has increased enormously since the beginning of the Industrial

---

[1] Intergovernmental Panel on Climate Change (IPCC), *Climate Change 2007: Synthesis Report: Summary for Policymakers* (Fourth Assessment Report, available online at: www.ipcc.ch).

[2] The *World Development Report 2010* cites H.M. Füssel, 'The Risks of Climate Change: A Synthesis of New Scientific Knowledge Since the Finalization of the IPCC Fourth Assessment Report', Background note for the WDR 2010, and V. Ramanathan and Y. Feng, 'On Avoiding Dangerous Anthropogenic Interference with the Climate System: Formidable Challenges Ahead' (2008) 105(38) *Proceedings of the National Academy of Sciences* 14245–50. In the World Bank, *World Development Report 2010: Development and Climate Change* (Washington, DC: The World Bank, 2010) at 76. There has been a recent backlash against the finding of human-induced climate change, in part fuelled by a set of emails relating to climate change data. For a sceptical view, see, for example, Bjorn Lomborg, *Cool It* (New York: Knopf, 2007) (arguing that while humans are responsible for climate change, many claims of climate activists are 'wildly exaggerated').

Revolution. In the twentieth century alone, the carbon dioxide concentration increased from around 280 parts per million (ppm) to 387 ppm.[3] Moreover, it is 'very likely' (that is, greater than 90 per cent certainty) that this increase is attributable to human activity, mostly from the burning of fossil fuels, but also due to deforestation and changes in land use.[4] The question is: why is it happening?

2.1.1   Emissions and Externalities

GHG emissions arise because of what Sir Nicholas Stern has called 'the greatest and widest ranging market failure ever seen'.[5] For markets to work efficiently, individuals must make choices based on all the costs and benefits of their actions. They maximize their own welfare taking into account their preferences (such as for driving) along with these costs and benefits. With full information, overall welfare will increase as individuals take actions for which the benefits are greater than the costs.

In the climate change context, individuals receive the benefits of activities which emit GHGs such as driving cars, using electricity generated with fossil fuels, and flying in airplanes. They do not, however, bear the full costs of these activities.[6] Climate change is occurring but it is not occurring everywhere to the same degree. Some areas of the world, particularly those in the developing world, are being hit harder than others. They are experiencing droughts or floods, loss of species and other harms. Many developed countries, on the other hand, are experiencing fewer directly apparent impacts.[7] Individuals, particularly in developed countries,

---

[3]   *World Development Report*, ibid.
[4]   IPPC, *supra* note 1. The combustion of coal, oil, and natural gas contributes around 80% of the carbon dioxide emitted annually, with land-use changes and deforestation accounting for the remaining 20%. In 1950 the contributions from fossil fuels and land use were almost equal but since then energy use has grown by a factor of 18. Concentrations of other GHGs, including methane and nitrous oxide, have also increased significantly as a result of fossil fuel combustion, farming and industrial activities, and land-use changes. *World Development Report*, ibid. at 71–2.
[5]   N. Stern, *The Economics of Climate Change: The Stern Review* (Cambridge: Cambridge University Press, 2007).
[6]   Costs in this sense include not only financial but also social and environmental costs.
[7]   Of course, developed countries also are experiencing and will experience the direct and indirect effects of climate change. See, for example, Andrew T. Guzman and Jody Freeman, 'Sea Walls Are Not Enough: Climate Change and U.S. Interests' (2009) *Columbia Law Review*.

obtain the benefits of driving or flying but the cost is shifted to others. The result is that they engage in too much of these types of activities.

There is a further aspect to the externality that makes it even more troublesome. GHGs are emitted into the atmosphere and remain there for a long time. The atmospheric lifetime of carbon dioxide is estimated to be between 50 and 200 years. This means that carbon dioxide entering the atmosphere today could remain there until 2210.[8] The emissions today, therefore, will impact individuals in the future – perhaps many generations in the future. Individuals receive the benefit of flying or driving today but the costs are spread far out into the future, making the externality even worse. Again, since they do not face the cost, they will over-indulge in GHG-emitting activities.

Climate change can therefore be seen as the result of a negative externality. Individuals making choices receive the benefits but impose the costs on others – in their own and other countries and in future generations. Markets and individual choice do not work efficiently if individuals act in a purely self-interested and self-centred fashion and if some costs are not fully borne by the individual making the decision.[9] Individuals may act in a non-self-interested fashion in some cases. For example, they may act because of norms or values such as a concern for the fairness of their choices or for the environment itself.[10] These norms may be enforced by others, such as where neighbours express disapproval of someone who drives an SUV. Norms or values may also be internally enforced, where an individual has a feeling of guilt at not making climate friendly choices. If these norms or values are insufficient or non-existent, governments may

---

[8]   Climate and Ozone Depletion Teaching Pack, Atmosphere, Climate and Environment Information Programme, Teaching Pack, aric, Manchester Metropolitan University (available online at: www.ace.mmu.ac.uk, date accessed: 1 February 2010). By contrast, the warming effect of methane emissions lasts for only a few decades, while that of aerosols lasts for only days to weeks. *World Development Report, supra* note 2 at 72.

[9]   An individual is self-centred and self-interested if she chooses to maximize her own welfare in a way that is not affected either by the interests of others or by moral values such as fairness. See, for example, A. Sen, *Rationality and Freedom* (2002), at 30 and 213. Sen argues that rational choice has tended to view individuals as having three types of private reasons for acting: (i) self-centred welfare (an individual's welfare depends on her own consumption); (ii) self-welfare goal (the individual's goal is to maximize her own welfare); and (iii) self-goal choice (an individual's choices are guided by meeting her own goals).

[10]   See A. Green 'You Can't Pay Them Enough: Subsidies, Environmental Law and Social Norms' (2006) 30 (2) *Harvard Environmental Law Review* 407, which discusses the relationship between rational choice theory and social norms and values in individuals' choices relating to climate change.

take action to overcome the externality. For example, governments may impose a tax on individuals that makes them face the full cost of their choices or put in place regulatory measures that limit choices.

2.1.2 Why Do Countries Act?

If individuals choose activities that emit too much GHG, why do countries choose to adopt or not adopt either domestic or international policies about climate change? What determines whether or not they act to address the externality? To understand countries' choices about climate change, we need to take a step back and briefly discuss why countries take any action. One view of why countries act is that they make choices in the same way as individuals; they choose policies that are in their own best interests based on a rational balancing of the relevant costs and benefits of different policies.[11]

However, it is clearly not so simple. Even on this rational choice view of state action, there are different possible notions of 'self-interest' and questions as to whose self-interest is relevant to the particular policy choice. One view is that government policy-makers make choices that foster the welfare of their country and its citizens as a whole. These policy-makers choose what they perceive to be in the public interest for the country.[12] There are of course different ways that this 'public interest' can be ascertained. Policy-makers may simply make decisions technocratically based on their own view of the benefits and costs and what is in the best interests of the nation. Alternatively, they may aggregate the preferences of all the citizens of the country over the particular issue and make the choice that maximizes the net benefits. They may even undertake a deliberative process in which citizens discuss the policy options and come to some set of shared preferences and choices. The process and institutional arrangements that are used to determine the public interest will be important to the legitimacy of the choice and, as we will see in subsequent parts, the strength of the arguments for WTO decision-makers to defer to these choices.

Conversely, instead of policy-makers aiming to foster the national

---

[11] See, for example, Alan O. Sykes, 'International Law', in A. Mitchell Polinsky and Steven Shavell (eds), *Handbook of Law and Economics*, Vol. I (Amsterdam: Elsevier, 2007), discussing the rational actor model of state behaviour. For the strong form rational choice view of state action, see Jack L. Goldsmith and Eric A. Posner, *The Limits of International Law* (Oxford: Oxford University Press, 2005).

[12] See Robert Baldwin and Martin Cave, *Understanding Regulation: Theory, Strategy, and Practice* (New York: Oxford University Press, 1999) at 19.

welfare, they may be seeking to further their own welfare.[13] For example, legislators may make policy decisions based on which interest groups are more willing to provide them with rewards for those decisions. These may come in the form of funds for re-election or future job opportunities. This 'public choice' or political economy view of state decisions raises concerns about the relative power or resources of groups within a state.[14] Concentrated groups sharing a common interest, such as industrial associations, are often argued to have greater power than more diffuse groups such as consumers or citizens more generally. Concentrated groups face greater costs from any policy (such as the costs of complying with an emissions regulation) and tend to have greater resources to organize and provide incentives to policy-makers. Further, these concentrated interest groups generally have lower costs of organizing because they have fewer members than more diffuse groups. As a result, concentrated groups may be better positioned to steer policy in their favour and away from the public interest. This political economy view of how states make decisions raises concerns about the WTO decision-makers deferring to government decisions. It is not clear that deferring to such decisions will be in the best interests of the members of the WTO as a whole, let alone the individual member making the policy choice (or its citizens).

On this view, then, states take actions that are in their own self-interest, in whatever manner that is defined. However, states may also act for other reasons, including the values of their citizens. They may act against their narrowly defined self-interest in order to fulfil other objectives such as a concern for fairness or for abiding by the 'law'. In one sense this may be viewed as an expanded form of self-interest to the extent that individuals within the state have preferences for other-regarding action. Constructivist theories of international law take a broader approach to these preferences, finding a norm-creating function in the formation and processes of international law.[15]

---

[13]   Sykes, *supra* note 11.

[14]   In 1971, Stigler wrote a seminal article in which he stated that, as a rule, regulation is acquired by industry and is designed and operated primarily for its benefit. That is, industry 'captures' the regulatory agency and uses regulation to prevent competition. George J. Stigler, 'The Theory of Economic Regulation' (1971) 1 *Bell Journal of Economics* 3. For other material related to public choice theory, see Mancur Olson, *The Logic of Collective Action* (Cambridge, MA: Harvard University Press, 1971), Anthony Downs, *The Economic Theory of Democracy* (New York: Harper, 1957) and Dennis Mueller, *Public Choice III* (Cambridge: Cambridge University Press, 2003).

[15]   See Jutta Brunnée and Stephen J. Toope, *Legitimacy and Persuasion in International Law* (Cambridge: Cambridge University Press, forthcoming).

A rational choice model and a norm-based model of why countries act have some similarities. Self-interest may manifest not only through the direct welfare of the state (such as the impact on the economy or the well-being of its citizens) but also through the reputational effects of its actions.[16] A country may, for example, have made a commitment to reduce its GHG emissions by a certain amount. To the extent it does not do so, it may not gain the benefits of the agreement (since other countries may fail to live up to their commitments once the non-complying state's commitment is no longer credible). Further, non-compliance may have impacts in other areas of international cooperation – to the extent the state is seen as not trustworthy in one area, other states may not wish to enter into agreements with it on other issues or may seek a higher price for cooperation. Thus, while under the self-interested model there is generally not seen to be a 'norm' of abiding by law, reputational effects may induce compliance.

In this book, we will primarily take the view that countries are self-interested as it provides a useful framework for analysing the causes and breakdown of cooperation.[17] We will examine self-interest in the sense of both national welfare and public choice. This focus will assist the institutional analysis relating to WTO rules and domestic policies. We will, however, also consider other potential motivations for both countries and individuals throughout the course of the analysis and the connection between processes and norms. Given these potential reasons for why countries take action, we will now return to the question we asked earlier – why do countries take or not take action on climate change?

2.1.3 Climate Change, Public Goods, and Free-riders

As with individuals, GHG emissions from countries arise because of an externality – the country obtains the benefits of the GHG emitting activity but does not bear the full costs and therefore engages in too much of the activity. There is more to this problem unfortunately. Addressing these emissions and the impacts of climate change is a global public good. As

---

[16] A. Guzman, 'The Promise of International Law' (2006) 92 *Virginia Law Review* 533 (noting that reputation turns one-shot games into repeat games and allows cooperative solutions to problems) and Andrew T. Guzman, 'Reputation and International Law' (2006) 34 *Georgia Journal of International and Comparative Law* 379.

[17] A. Guzman, ibid. at 538 (arguing that the rational choice 'offers the most fruitful strategy for studying state behavior and that it should be the dominant (though not the exclusive) approach to international law'). For a strong form of the argument that states only act in their own self-interest, see *supra*, note 11.

noted above, a public good is a good that one party cannot stop others from enjoying (that is, it is non-excludible), and one party's enjoyment does not reduce the amount for others (that is, it is non-rivalrous). Barrett notes that there are different types of public goods. He argues that addressing climate change through reducing GHG emissions is an 'additive public good' – a public good that depends on the aggregate reductions of GHG emissions by countries.[18]

As with other public goods, the risk with additive public goods is that some parties will 'free-ride' on the efforts of others. If countries are essentially self-interested, they will not reduce emissions, in the hope that they can continue to obtain the benefits of emissions while others bear the costs of addressing climate change. The difficulty is, of course, if all countries act this way, the public good (addressing climate change) will not be produced. Each country will attempt to allow the others to act, resulting in no action. Such behaviour is called free-riding.

This free-riding may occur if government policy-makers are focused on maximizing national welfare. They may attempt to avoid the costs of taking action on climate change and yet still gain the benefits. It may also occur under political economy or public choice scenarios in which the policy-makers are seeking to enhance their own welfare by putting in place policies that favour GHG emitters. Policies may not be adopted which, though collectively rational, are not individually rational for each country.

If the public goods problem arises within a country (such as where individuals are attempting to free-ride on the GHG reducing actions of others), there are a variety of ways in which these problems can be overcome. For example, governments can force individuals to take actions that are in their best interests but which they would not take if left to their own devices, such as through a tax on GHG emissions. Alternatively, individuals in small cohesive groups can rely on norms of behaviour and reputation to overcome these problems. As we will discuss, at the global level, producing public goods can be even more difficult as there is no international government with power to take such action.

---

[18] See Scott Barrett, *Why Cooperate? The Incentive to Supply Global Public Goods* (Oxford: Oxford University Press, 2007) (describing reducing concentrations of GHG in the atmosphere as an additive or 'aggregate efforts' public good as opposed to a 'single best efforts' public good (such as stopping an asteroid from hitting the earth), which can rely on unilateral action, or a 'weakest link' public good (such as stopping the spread of a disease), which depends on every country being involved).

2.2 TRADE AGREEMENTS, PRISONERS' DILEMMAS, AND PROTECTIONISM

It is not sufficient to discuss only the effects of climate change and the need to address them. The ultimate goal should not be simply to address climate change but to maximize social welfare, however defined. The environment is a central part of any discussion of social welfare. However, there are other elements as well. As Sen points out, there are various aspects or 'freedoms' that make up a fulfilled life – 'a life one has reason to value'[19]. He points in particular to political freedoms, economic facilities, social opportunities, transparency guarantees, and protective security. These freedoms encompass 'both the processes that allow freedom of actions and decisions, and the actual opportunities that people have, given their personal and social circumstances.'[20] They are closely related and depend on the physical environment and individuals' relationship to it. They also encompass economic freedoms. Sen argues that markets are tied to economic growth and increase living standards and '[p]olicies that restrict market opportunities can have the effect of restricting the expansion of substantive freedoms that would have been generated through the market system, mainly through overall economic prosperity'.[21] Economic freedoms help generate the prosperity needed for other freedoms or social facilities such as education or health services. Sen also notes that restricting people's ability to transact is itself a form of 'unfreedom'. It is not that markets are the font of all good, nor should they be without restriction. Instead, Sen is pointing to a broader view of how to foster lives that individuals have reason to want to lead.

International trade fits within these freedoms in the sense of fostering economic opportunities. Increasing trade can increase the economic growth of the parties. Trade can, in particular, be beneficial for developing countries. The WTO's current Doha Round of negotiations (the so-called 'Doha Development Round') has been estimated to have the potential to increase global economic activity by $100 billion, with developing countries obtaining approximately 80 per cent of the gains.[22] Further, develop-

---

[19] Amartya Sen, *Development as Freedom* (New York: Anchor Books, 1999), at 74.
[20] Ibid. at 17.
[21] Ibid. at 26.
[22] K. Anderson and William Martin, *Agricultural Trade Reform and the Doha Development Agenda* (Washington, DC: World Bank, 2005). There is a need to attend to the distributional impacts related to the gains from trade. See Jeffrey Sachs, *The End of Poverty* (New York: Penguin, 2005) (arguing that while trade is

ing countries are provided in some instances with special preferences that allow them access to developed country markets at a lower tariff rate than for developed countries. The hope is that such preferences can bolster economic growth for developing countries.[23] Again, the argument is not that trade or economic growth are ends in themselves but that they are important for both developed and developing countries in providing the conditions for improving the lives of their people.

Like climate change, trade raises concerns about cooperation between countries. Regan writes of two principal 'stories' about why trade agreements are necessary – one about externalities and the other about protectionism.[24] The externality story concerns a terms of trade effect of one country's actions on another.[25] In this story, a country can change its terms of trade (the relative price of its goods on the world market) by imposing an import tariff – that is, making the world price of the imported goods fall relative to that of the goods that the country exports. The country, in effect, benefits from lower priced imports and higher priced exports. The result is a form of the 'prisoners' dilemma'. If all countries acted this way, they would all be better off if they could credibly commit to

---

important to provide growth to developing countries, there is still a need for other measures (including aid and institutional reform) to ensure that developing countries benefit from the economic activity arising from more liberalized trade). See also Paul Krugman, 'Trade and Inequality, Revisited' *Vox* (15 June 2007) (arguing for the importance of taking into account the distributional impacts of freer trade even in developed countries).

23 There is a debate about whether these permissive policies for trade barriers aid developing countries. See, for example, T. Epps and M.J. Trebilcock, 'Special and Differential Treatment in Agricultural Trade: Breaking the Impasse' in Chantel Thomas and Joel P. Trachtman (eds), *Developing Countries in the WTO Legal System* (Oxford: Oxford University Press, 2009).

24 Donald Regan, 'What Are Trade Agreements For? – Two Conflicting Stories Told by Economists, With a Lesson for Lawyers' (2006) 9 (4) *Journal of International Economic Law* 951. For other discussions of why countries enter into trade agreements, see Kyle Bagwell and Robert Staiger, *The Economics of the World Trading System* (Cambridge, MA: MIT Press, 2002) and Douglas Irwin, Petros Mavroidis and Alan Sykes, *The Genesis of the GATT* (Cambridge: Cambridge University Press, 2008).

25 Bagwell and Staiger argue for viewing trade and trade agreements through a terms of trade lens. For example, see Bagwell and Staiger (2002). For the terms of trade story to apply, the country applying the tariff must be a 'large' country in relation to the good such that its tariff policy impacts the world price. However, Bagwell argues that countries may be 'large' for some goods and 'small' for others. K. Bagwell, 'Remedies in the WTO: An Economic Perspective', in Merit E. Janow, Victoria J. Donaldson and Alan Yanovich (eds), *The WTO: Governance, Dispute Settlement & Developing Countries* (Huntington, NY: Juris Publishing, 2008).

not imposing tariffs to improve their terms of trade. However, it is difficult for countries to make such a commitment where there is no international body to enforce it.

The second story relates to protectionism.[26] Each country would be better off by unilaterally adopting a policy of free trade. A tariff raises the price of imports and provides gains to domestic producers of goods along with revenue for the government. However, when a tariff is put in place, there is also a loss to consumers of imports, who must now pay more for the goods and in some cases are priced out of the market. The losses to consumers from a tariff exceed the gain to the producers of the good plus the government revenue.[27] As a result, in theory countries should unilaterally move to free trade. However, the protectionist story is based on the political economy model of why countries act. Domestic producers and their workers have the resources and the incentive to induce government policy-makers to put in place tariffs which favour the producers despite the loss to the country as a whole. While consumers lose, they are a diffuse group with greater costs of organizing and lower individual stakes in the issue than the producers. Political officials adopt tariffs as they have the most to gain (including, for example, funds for re-election, promises of votes, or future job opportunities) from complying with the wishes of producers.

In these stories, trade agreements are a means of overcoming a prisoners' dilemma, allowing countries to commit to lowering tariffs and raising trade volumes.[28] This objective explains why agreements tend to constrain the use of tariffs. It can also explain some of the non-tariff-related features of trade agreements. Once negotiations were successful in bringing down

---

[26]   See, for example, Warren Schwartz and Alan O. Sykes, 'The Economic Structure of Renegotiation and Dispute Resolution in the World Trade Organization' (2002) 31 *Journal of Legal Studies* S179. Bagwell and Staiger argue that the terms of trade story can encompass protectionist objectives of governments as the political factors can be captured through the local price of goods: Bagwell and Staiger, *supra* note 24 and Bagwell, ibid.

[27]   Paul Krugman and M. Obstfeld, *International Economics: Theory and Policy*, 7th edn (London: Pearson, 2005).

[28]   Bagwell, *supra* note 25. Alternatively, trade agreements could be viewed as allowing countries to maximize the member governments' welfare and, in particular, the welfare of their political officials. The terms of the agreements, under this view, should be seen as political bargains to allow political officials to gain from seeking favours from concentrated interests: Sykes, *supra* note 11. A third possibility is that trade agreements could be viewed as allowing countries to credibly commit to their domestic constituencies not to engage in protectionism – that is, as a form of 'tying themselves to the mast' so they cannot be pressured into protecting domestic industries.

tariffs on goods, there was a concern that countries would shift protectionism from tariffs to other 'behind-the-border' measures such as discriminatory regulations or taxes.[29] Trade agreements were seen as a means of
policing such 'behind-the-border' measures.

As we will see, the potential conflict between trade and climate policies
arises in the form of both tariff and non-tariff barriers to trade. Countries
may raise tariffs to attempt to force another country to take action on
climate change, or to mitigate the impacts of domestic climate measures
on the competitiveness of their own industry. They may also use measures
that appear to be aimed at GHG emissions but, in fact, are in whole or in
part designed to provide an advantage to domestic industry. Trade agreements and dispute resolution panels attempt to constrain these conflicts.
The fear is that in doing so they will also constrain the ability of countries
to address climate change.

2.3   THE DESIGN OF INTERNATIONAL
AGREEMENTS

Trade agreements therefore are similar to international climate change
agreements. Each attempts to provide gains to countries that would not
otherwise arise, because of self-interested, non-cooperative behaviour. In
the climate change context, the agreement overcomes the unwillingness of
countries to contribute to an aggregate public good. In the trade context,
trade agreements may overcome a prisoners' dilemma under which countries are better off acting cooperatively but cannot credibly commit to
doing so. They may also provide a credible means to commit either internationally or domestically not to engage in protectionism.

The design of international agreements is therefore central to any
discussion of both international trade and climate change policy. This
design is influenced by two key factors. First, countries cannot be forced
to sign onto any agreement or accept any particular level of commitments
under an agreement. Countries must willingly agree to be bound by an
agreement. Further, even if they do agree to participate in an agreement
and adopt commitments, no general international body exists to enforce
compliance with an agreement. Countries must willingly agree both to be
bound by the agreement and to any enforcement mechanism under the
agreement. Such enforcement includes not only the formal enforcement

---

[29]   Michael J. Trebilcock and Robert Howse, *The Regulation of International
Trade*, 3rd edn (London: Routledge, 2005).

mechanisms under the particular agreement but also the potential reputational loss from failing to comply with a treaty. Entering into the agreement signals a commitment the strength of which depends on the history of compliance by the state.[30]

This self-enforcing nature of international agreements makes for difficult trade-offs in designing effective treaties.[31] Countries must balance the level of commitments they accept under the agreement and the strength of the enforcement mechanisms. It may be that countries will either not participate in an agreement or not accept significant commitments if the agreement contains strong enforcement provisions.

The second factor is that international agreements often deal with complex, uncertain issues that cannot be fully specified in advance. For example, negotiations to reduce tariffs may be difficult given uncertainty about future economic conditions. It may be even more difficult to set out in advance rules concerning non-tariff barriers. There are many different products, many measures which can impact trade and uncertainty about future economic and political conditions. As a result, Horn and Mavroidis argue that trade agreements can be viewed as incomplete contracts.[32] They leave a number of matters unspecified because of the cost (or impossibility) of negotiating each potential rule.

These two factors help explain why certain treaties exist and the nature of their dispute settlement systems. Designing treaties requires determining what should be in the treaty (that is, what it should cover and how detailed the requirements should be) and how conflicts under the treaty should be resolved. These issues are necessarily connected. If international agreements are incomplete, there is a need for a body to fill in the gaps. For example, if countries cannot (or decide not to) agree on detailed rules on what are permissible non-tariff barriers to trade, they may instead insert a general provision in the agreement (as they did in the GATT) that no measure can discriminate in favour of domestic products at the

---

30   Guzman, 'Reputation and International Law', *supra* note 16.
31   For a discussion of this trade-off in environmental agreements, see Barrett, *supra* note 18, and Scott Barrett, *Environment and Statecraft: The Strategy of Environmental Treaty-Making* (Oxford: Oxford University Press, 2003). In the context of trade agreements, see Henrik Horn and Petros Mavroidis, 'International Trade – Dispute Settlement', in Alan O. Sykes and Alan Guzman (eds), *Research Handbook in International Economic Law* (Cheltenham, UK and Northampton, MA, USA: Edward Elgar, 2008).
32   See, for example, Horn and Mavroidis, ibid. at 183, and Henrik Horn, Giovanni Maggi and Robert W. Staiger, 'Trade Agreements as Endogenously Incomplete Contracts' (NBER Working Paper 12745, December 2006). See also Sykes, *supra* note 11.

expense of imports.[33] The parties may then agree to a dispute resolution body that has the power to interpret the provision and apply it to particular measures. At the same time, these tribunals may have the power to directly enforce the agreement such as by authorizing trade sanctions (as in the case of the WTO) and/or more indirectly enforce it such as by announcing non-compliance in order to trigger reputational penalties for the violators (as may be the case for violations of the Kyoto Protocol). The lack of an international equivalent of a domestic government requires the parties to agree on how much power to give these tribunals and what sanctions they may impose. There can be complex processes of deciding what commitments countries are willing to undertake, how detailed they are willing to make these commitments ex ante, what the remedies are for non-compliance with the agreement, and what institutions should be established to interpret and enforce the agreement.

2.4   RULES, STANDARDS AND INSTITUTIONS

This discussion of the nature of the appropriate content of international agreements and the appropriate dispute settlement system raises issues about who actually decides the questions of what actions are permissible. The institutional arrangements will determine who makes the decision about what is the most efficient or most fair solution. An international agreement with few commitments or strictures on domestic policy allows domestic governments to decide the scope of their permissible policies. Such an agreement allows greater domestic policy control but potentially at the expense of gains from cooperative action on some issues. For example, if there are few commitments as to the appropriate level of GHG reductions for countries, there is a greater range of permissible climate policies for each country but a lack of control of the free-rider problem. If, on the other hand, the agreement contains very detailed commitments, in one sense each domestic government has control over its policy (since it had to agree to be bound by the agreement) but the actual scope of policies will depend on such factors as the process of negotiation of the agreements, trade-offs across issues, who is involved in the negotiations, and the ex ante information required. Further, to the extent the agreement is incomplete and the actual application of particular rules is left to a tribunal, the tribunal may have power to decide which policies are appropriate.

How then to decide on the content and enforcement mechanism of an

---

[33]   Horn, Maggi and Staiger, ibid.

agreement? With the variety of activities, economic conditions, industries and potential measures covered by any agreement relating to trade or to climate change, agreements concerning trade and climate are likely to be incomplete. Horn et al. argue that in the trade context the incompleteness will depend on the level of uncertainty about different circumstances and contracting costs (such as the costs of negotiating the agreement).[34] As contracting costs increase, the optimal contract may become more rigid (with contractual obligations more detailed and less sensitive to changing economic or political conditions) or more discretionary (providing governments with leeway to set policies). Horn et al. argue that the context matters for the choice between rigidity and discretion. For example, discretion will be better where domestic instruments (such as taxes or regulatory policies) are less useful at manipulating the terms of trade as the importing countries then are less able to use these instruments to protect their domestic industries. Similarly, if the importing country has less power in the market for the imported good, it has less incentive to use protectionist measures and therefore can be provided with greater discretion.

These factors raised by Horn et al. are in effect a subset of a larger concern about the costs and benefits of different types of agreements. In the broadest terms, institutions and agreements should be designed to maximize social welfare. Maximizing social welfare in this sense must encompass both economic efficiency and fairness including any preferences over the fair allocation of costs and benefits of society. In this way, efficiency and fairness are intimately tied and in the broadest sense efficiency encompasses a society's view of fairness.[35] A choice cannot be efficient unless it maximizes welfare, including distributing its subsequent burdens and benefits fairly across members of the society. This connection between efficiency and fairness raises difficult questions about how to decide what is 'fair', how you can tell whether social welfare is maximized and who are the relevant members of a society. Are they the citizens of a particular state? All people in all countries? Future generations?

Different institutions will generate different answers to these questions. This, in part, returns us to the issue of who decides. Each institutional

---

[34]   Horn, Maggi and Staiger, ibid.

[35]   Kaplow and Shavell argue that there can be no consideration of fairness separate from social welfare where social welfare includes preferences of individuals or society over distributional fairness (see, for example, Louis Kaplow and Steven Shavell, *Fairness versus Welfare* (Cambridge, MA: Harvard University Press, 2002). This argument spawned a large debate over whether efficiency and fairness were necessarily separate or whether efficiency in the broadest sense encompasses fairness. For our purposes, it is not necessary to attempt to resolve this debate.

arrangement provides different concerns related to the effectiveness of the agreements and institutions from an environmental perspective, the costs of adopting a particular agreement and dispute resolution form (including negotiating costs, enforcement costs and information costs), equity and the political feasibility of particular forms of agreements or dispute settlement systems. For our purposes, we will focus on two particular categories of variables for choosing the optimal form of agreement and dispute resolution system: flexibility and cost.[36]

2.4.1 Flexibility

Flexibility refers to how detailed the requirements are in an agreement. A central question is how much completeness is optimal and, if there are gaps in the agreement, how they are to be filled in the case of conflict. The flexibility in an agreement can in part be thought of in terms of whether the agreement should be based on rules or standards. Rules are detailed prescriptions of how particular issues are to be resolved. For example, a rule in an agreement could specify that carbon taxes at a particular level on specified goods are permissible. Standards, on the other hand, are more general statements of what is required, leaving a tribunal to decide whether a particular measure falls within the requirements of the standard. In the trade context, the national treatment principle (requiring that imports be treated no less favourably than domestically produced goods) is a standard as states must comply with this principle and a tribunal decides if a particular regulation satisfies the principle. Both rules and standards can be more or less flexible but these terms are useful as broad categories.

Flexibility, or conversely complexity, raises a variety of issues related to the efficiency and fairness of an agreement or set of institutions. These issues include:

- *Variation in costs and benefits* Increasing flexibility permits better tailoring of requirements to differences in costs and benefits. These differences could arise, for example, across different countries. Each country will have different costs for different methods of addressing climate change. Moreover, different countries will have greater or lesser costs of climate change over time. A flexible requirement would take these differences into account to allow countries to respond to

---

[36] For a seminal discussion of the trade-offs inherent in choosing the optimal form of legal requirements, see Louis Kaplow, 'Rules Versus Standards: An Economic Analysis' (1992) 42 (3) *Duke Law Journal* 557.

climate change optimally for their particular circumstances. This flexibility could come from very detailed rules about what measures are permissible in particular circumstances. Alternatively, flexibility could arise where a tribunal takes into account differences in costs and benefits across countries. Finally, flexibility could arise by allowing countries to make determinations about the appropriate measure in their circumstances, absent tribunal oversight.

- *Variation in development*   The flexibility must encompass the differences between developed countries as well as between developed and developing countries and between different developing countries. For example, Sari divides developing countries into five categories: (i) the large rapidly industrializing countries, being predominantly Brazil, India and China (and to some extent Indonesia); (ii) the oil producing countries, a number of which are OPEC countries; (iii) forested countries, primarily Latin American countries (other than Brazil and Peru), which have promoted forests as sinks to reduce carbon dioxide levels in the atmosphere; (iv) small island countries that are generally vulnerable to climate change; and (v) the Least Developed Countries, which are 49 countries identified by the United Nations as the 'least developed'.[37]

- *Variation in values*   As noted above, responding to climate change is at its core an ethical issue – how much do we owe to people in other countries and to future generations? People's values will vary both across and within countries.[38] Differences in values could lead to variations in the speed at which different countries feel they should address climate change and different decisions about the appropriateness of a particular measure. For example, a stringent tax on emissions may be viewed differently in a country that has a very high preference for intergenerational equity as opposed to a state that does not value the welfare of future generations as highly. There may be some merit in flexibility where the rule or standard

---

[37]   Agus Sari, 'Developing Country Participation: The Kyoto–Marrakech Politics' (Hamburg Institute of International Economics, Discussion Paper 333, 2005).

[38]   This difference may arise under various visions of how a country decides on its policy, whether it is a mere aggregation of the preferences of those related to a particular state (or a subset of those people) or results from a more deliberative process in which the decisions of the state determine its policy. See Sen, *supra* note 9.

allows countries to respond to the preferences of their own citizens, as opposed to requiring all measures to conform to a particular vision of the appropriate equitable distribution. Again flexibility could come from a detailed agreement, through a tribunal determining whether a measure falls within a standard, or by leaving the choice of measures to particular states.

- *Information and uncertainty* There is little debate now that climate change is actually occurring. However, there is debate about such issues as when the impacts will appear, what is the optimal path to emissions reductions, and what types of instruments will bring about emission reductions.[39] Moreover, some of the information about these issues will be revealed over time – we will know more in the future about how severe the change will be than we know now. There is value to retaining some flexibility to adjust to new information over time.

- *Innovation* Two types of innovation will be important to addressing climate change. First, a key factor in addressing climate change will be finding new ways to do things that we do now without emitting as much GHG – new means of creating electricity, new production processes, new forms of transportation. Whatever agreement relates to trade and climate change, it should be designed in a manner that fosters rather than hinders innovation across goods and services. In part, this simply means not allowing barriers to trade in new forms of goods, to the extent they are more environmentally friendly than existing goods. Diffusion of new climate friendly goods will be critical to global reductions in GHGs. Second, countries may innovate in how they address climate change. As noted above, there is uncertainty about what instruments will work best to reduce GHGs to stave off catastrophic global warming. Any institutions or agreements aimed at addressing the interaction of climate change and trade need to provide space for such innovation.

2.4.2 Cost

There are large benefits to flexibility. It allows tailoring to the circumstances of particular countries, to new information as it arises, and to new ways of taking action. Such flexibility increases not only the efficiency of

---

[39]   See, for example, Lomborg, *supra* note 2.

the system but also its fairness as it allows a more nuanced determination of who gets to decide which policies are permissible and legitimate. However, there are also costs to flexibility, otherwise states could simply design agreements that take all possible contingencies into account. It will be the interaction of the benefits of flexibility and the costs of different forms of institutions and agreements that will determine how best to address the different issues related to the overlap of trade and climate change. The costs will differ across parties and institutions. These costs include:[40]

- the costs of promulgating a requirement and, in particular, the information costs related to identifying the various aspects of a rule prior to its being applied and the bargaining costs of specifying the particular rule;[41]
- the costs of parties subject to the legal command obtaining information about what the command requires;
- enforcement costs including the costs of monitoring compliance and litigating any enforcement action;
- costs from bargaining between the affected parties after a violation has occurred.[42]

These costs depend in part on the various institutions and parties that are involved in trade disputes. For example, if the WTO membership acting as a body attempts to negotiate and draft agreements relating to climate change and trade, the large number of parties and variety of circumstances may lead to high bargaining and information costs as parties attempt to ascertain up front what measures are reasonable for other parties to take. If an agreement can be reached, however, the enforcement costs may be lower as there may be fewer complaints brought (since the rules are clearer in a wider variety of circumstances) and the complaints that are brought may be easier to decide. Conversely, if the WTO relies mainly on less detailed standards (as is the case presently), the upfront

---

[40]   Kaplow argues that the optimal form and content of legal commands will depend on relative costs and benefits. Louis Kaplow, 'Rules Versus Standards: An Economic Analysis' (1992) 42 (3) *Duke Law Journal* 557.
[41]   See, for example, in the trade context Horn, Maggi and Staiger, *supra* note 32 at 2–3 (formalizing the costs of contracting and discussing WTO agreements as incomplete contracts) and Warren Schwartz and Alan O. Sykes, 'The Economic Structure of Renegotiation and Dispute Resolution in the World Trade Organization' (2002) 31 *Journal of Legal Studies* S179.
[42]   See, for example, Schwartz and Sykes, ibid. and Joel P. Trachtman, 'Building the WTO Cathedral' (SSRN) http://ssrn.com/abstract=815844 (updated 17 February 2006).

costs of information and bargaining are lower but the enforcement costs may be very high. States may be more likely (especially in the near term) to bring complaints to determine whether they fall within the standard and the panels and/or Appellate Body hearing complaints will have more difficulty in deciding the complaints.

2.5 CHOOSING THE RIGHT BALANCE

Choosing which set of institutions to use to address the overlap of climate change and trade (and how to design those institutions) will depend on balancing these costs and benefits. The ultimate goal is to increase global social welfare – allowing people the freedom to live the lives they want to live to the extent possible. This goal requires that strong action be taken on climate change because of its potential impacts both now and in the future. It also points to the necessity of liberalized trade, in particular to help those in developing countries to attain the freedoms (such as access to health care, education and other goods) enjoyed by the developed world. Both efficiency and fairness will need to be taken into account in finding the right institutional framework to aid in achieving this goal.

In large part, the institutional framework (including whatever form of agreement is chosen) will determine or at least strongly influence who decides which policy (whether it be a climate policy or trade policy) is permissible. The concerns about flexibility and cost point to two important considerations about this choice of who decides which we will focus on in subsequent chapters. They help determine the right balance in terms of efficiency and fairness and the appropriate institutional reforms for the future. First, what is the relative institutional *competence* of the different potential decision-makers? Relative competence will depend in part on who has the relevant information. If the domestic government has better information about the effects of climate policies in a particular jurisdiction or about the concerns of its citizens about climate change, it will be important to take this into account in designing the dispute resolution system. Guzman, for example, argues that domestic governments have better information about their citizens' preferences concerning health risks and therefore the WTO should defer to judgments in these areas or risk large error costs.[43] This is then a question of who is more competent to make decisions.

The second key factor is the *legitimacy* of the different decision-makers.

---

[43] Andrew T. Guzman, 'Food Fears: Health and Safety at the WTO' (2004) 45 *Virginia Journal of International Law* 1. See also Kaplow, *supra* note 40 at

To a certain extent, the legitimacy of the decision-maker will depend on whose values are incorporated into the decision. For example, one argument against WTO decision-making in social policy areas (such as health and environmental policy) is that the individuals who sit on WTO panels and the Appellate Body tend to be steeped in trade values. They are often individuals who have worked for some time in the trade area and, it is argued, tend to prioritize trade over other values. Domestic government officials, on the other hand, are argued to take account of the broader social concerns of their citizens. These arguments must of course be tempered by political economy concerns about the decision-making of domestic officials. They may not be attempting even to maximize national social welfare in the sense of taking into account the preferences of all the citizens. They may instead be attempting to garner returns from particular interest groups. Thus the question: who has greater legitimacy to make decisions?

These choices about who decides certain issues will pervade all our discussions of the interactions of trade and climate change policies. They form the basis for other factors such as the independence of decision-makers, the process of decision-making and who gets to be heard in the process. In terms of WTO review of domestic policies, the stringency of WTO review will determine whether the domestic government's information and values about climate change will prevail or those of trade panels or the Appellate Body. We will discuss various ways in which these concerns may be addressed including through adjusting the standard of review by the WTO, incorporation of information from international environmental treaties or acceptance of amicus briefs. These issues also underlie the discussion of unilateral and multilateral solutions to the free-rider problem at the core of the climate change issue. For unilateral solutions, the concern lies in part in the ability of some countries to force others to take action – the ability to impose their values (in particular, developed country values) on others (particularly developing countries). The same concerns may arise under multilateral solutions – different negotiating structures will favour the interests of different groups or countries.

Before we discuss the way forward with respect to agreements and institutions, we must first set out where we are now – in terms of both climate change and trade agreements. It is to this task we turn in Chapter 3.

608–11, discussing the issue of the likelihood of error by the party exercising the discretion.

3. The existing trade and climate change frameworks

This chapter provides an overview of the range of agreements and the basic institutional arrangements and structure of both the WTO and the international climate change regime. The climate change regime in particular is in a state of flux following the 15th Conference of the Parties in Copenhagen in December 2009. Rather than attempting a comprehensive and up-to-date description of the regime, we focus here on the core principles that date from the initiation of the UNFCCC and what we consider to be some of its enduring characteristics. The overview forms the foundation for the ensuing chapters that examine the linkages between trade and climate change. We focus on those institutional features of each regime that lay the groundwork for their interactions.

3.1 THE WTO

3.1.1 Overview of the WTO

The WTO, like its predecessor the General Agreement on Tariffs and Trade (GATT), was established to provide a common institutional framework within which its members can conduct trade relations. The organization provides a forum for negotiations between its members, for dispute settlement, and facilitates implementation, administration and operation of the various covered agreements as annexed to the Marrakesh Agreement Establishing the WTO.[1] While the predominant thrust of the WTO is to support trade liberalization,[2] the Preamble to the Agreement

---

[1] There are approximately 60 agreements, decisions, annexes, and understandings. These cover trade in goods, services, and intellectual property. The full text of the agreements can be found in World Trade Organization, *The Legal Texts: The Results of the Uruguay Round of Multilateral Negotiations* (Cambridge/ Geneva: Cambridge University Press/World Trade Organization, 1999).

[2] The Preamble to the Agreement Establishing the WTO notes the objectives of raising standards of living, ensuring full employment and growing real income

Establishing the WTO also refers explicitly to the environment, recording that Members wish to allow for 'the optimal use of the world's resources in accordance with the objective of sustainable development, seeking to protect and preserve the environment and to enhance the means for doing so in a manner consistent with their respective needs and concerns at different levels of development'. Despite the grand rhetoric, there is little consensus on what the Preamble's practical implementation ought to involve, not least with regard to climate change. As the WTO's Director-General, Pascal Lamy, has stated, 'WTO Members have very different perceptions of what the trading system ought to do on climate change'.[3] The question has not been addressed systematically within the WTO system, falling instead to climate change negotiators who have identified a number of issues but – as we discuss – failed to date to reach any comprehensive agreement.

3.1.2   The Key Agreements

A number of the covered agreements bear direct relevance to climate change and form the heart of the linkages between the trade and climate change regimes identified in this book. Their relevance stems from obligations that countries must abide by when enacting domestic climate change measures, and that will have a bearing on the ability to invoke trade measures as sanctions to force participation and/or compliance with reduction commitments, whether unilaterally or as part of a multilateral climate change agreement. The most important agreements are the General Agreement on Tariffs and Trade (GATT), the Agreement on Technical Barriers to Trade (TBT Agreement), and the Agreement on Subsidies and Counterveiling Measures (SCM Agreement). The most pertinent provisions of these agreements are outlined briefly below.

GATT
The GATT, signed in 1947, establishes the basic legal framework for international trade in goods and commits countries to agreed-upon tariff levels. Key provisions include: a prohibition on quantitative restrictions such as

---

and effective demand, and expanding the production of and trade in goods and services and to this end states the desire of Members to enter into 'reciprocal and mutually advantageous arrangements directed to the substantial reduction of tariffs and other barriers to trade and to the elimination of discriminatory treatment in international trade relations'.

3   Pascal Lamy, Speech to the European Parliament, 29 May 2008, available at: www.wto.org/english/news_e/sppl91_e.htm (date accessed: 15 August 2008).

quotas or bans (Article XI); tariff concession commitments (Article II); rules against discrimination both in favour of some Members and against others (the most-favoured-nation or MFN obligation in Article I) and in favour of domestic industry (the national treatment obligation in Article III); and disciplines on government subsidies (Article XVI). Exceptions in Article XX allow countries to justify measures that would otherwise violate one of its provisions. The two most relevant to climate change policy are those that exempt measures 'necessary to protect human, animal or plant life or health' (Article XX(b)) and those 'relating to the conservation of exhaustible natural resources' (Article XX(g)). Measures that fit one of these exceptions must be applied in a manner that ensures they do not constitute arbitrary or unjustifiable discrimination, or a disguised trade restriction.

TBT Agreement
The TBT Agreement addresses the possibility that technical regulations and standards, marking and labelling requirements, and procedures for assessment of conformity with regulations and standards might be designed and applied in such a manner that they create obstacles to international trade. The Agreement covers both mandatory 'technical regulations' and voluntary 'standards'. It seeks to prevent discrimination by placing procedural constraints on steps that countries must take in creating technical regulations or voluntary standards. It also includes (in Article 2.1) a national treatment provision that prohibits discrimination in favour of domestic products. In addition, Article 2.2 requires Members to ensure that their mandatory technical regulations (as well as the voluntary standards under their control) 'are not prepared, adopted or applied with a view to or with the effect of creating unnecessary obstacles to international trade'.

There are no provisions in the TBT Agreement that clarify its relationship with the GATT, although generally its provisions can be seen to add to those of GATT Article III. Any climate change agreement will have to comply with the provisions of both agreements. Marceau and Trachtman suggest that while it is possible that a measure might be in violation of the TBT Agreement while compatible with the GATT, it is less probable that a technical regulation complying with the TBT Agreement would violate the GATT.[4]

---

[4] For a full discussion of the relationship between the TBT Agreement and the GATT, see Gabrielle Marceau and Joel Trachtman, 'The Technical Barriers to Trade Agreement, the Sanitary and Phytosanitary Measures Agreement, and the General Agreement on Tariffs and Trade' (2002) 36 (5) *Journal of World Trade* 811 at 873.

SCM Agreement

Subsidies have long been disciplined by GATT Article XVI, which provides for notification and, if serious prejudice was caused or threatened, consultations regarding the possibility of limiting the subsidization. This provision was much strengthened by the introduction of the SCM Agreement in the Uruguay Round. It supplements GATT Article XVI by regulating the use of subsidies in order to reduce their adverse effects. Subsidies are defined in Article 1.1 as 'financial contributions by a government or any public body' such that 'a benefit is thereby conferred' on the recipient. The Agreement distinguishes between prohibited and actionable subsidies. The former are prohibited outright, while the latter may violate the Agreement depending upon their effect. *Prohibited* subsidies are those that are contingent on either (a) export performance or (b) the use of domestic goods over imported goods. *Actionable* subsidies are those that (a) cause injury to the domestic industry of another Member; (b) nullify or impair the benefits that Members accrue directly or indirectly under the GATT; or (c) cause serious prejudice to another Member's interests.

If an industry in one country is negatively affected by either a prohibited or actionable subsidy provided by another Member to its domestic industry, the affected Member may use the WTO's dispute settlement procedure to seek withdrawal of the subsidy or removal of its adverse effects. Alternatively, it can launch its own investigation and impose countervailing duties on subsidized imports found to be hurting domestic producers.

3.1.3   Dispute Settlement, Compliance, and Enforcement

The feature of the international trading regime that sets it apart from other international legal regimes is its dispute settlement mechanism, governed by the Dispute Settlement Understanding (DSU). This mechanism has been described by some commentators as the most important and most powerful of any international law tribunal.[5] Where one Member has a complaint against another, the DSU stipulates that they must first seek to resolve the matter through consultations. If consultations fail, the complaining Member may request the establishment of a Panel to hear the complaint. Panels are composed of three individuals who must make an 'objective assessment' of the facts and provide a report to the Members.[6]

---

[5]   John H. Jackson, *Sovereignty, the WTO, and Changing Fundamentals of International Law* (Cambridge: Cambridge University Press, 2006) 135. Jackson notes that some commentators, however, maintain that the International Court of Justice ought to take this title.

[6]   Article 11 of the Dispute Settlement Understanding requires a panel to

The unsuccessful Member may appeal the Panel's decision to the Appellate Body (which is a standing body of trade law experts). The decisions under the DSU have been well supported by Members. In the WTO's first decade, it adopted 97 panel reports and 61 Appellate Body reports.[7]

The losing Member will usually be asked to bring their policies into compliance with WTO rules, and where they fail to do so within a reasonable period of time, the complaining Member may negotiate compensation or, subject to consent of the Dispute Settlement Body (DSB),[8] suspend concessions to the losing party. While such consent is not difficult to obtain, there are questions surrounding the effectiveness of suspending concessions. In particular, smaller economies are likely to have difficulty using suspension of concessions to force compliance by a larger trading partner and so such suspension may not be important enough from the larger country's perspective to encourage compliance.[9]

3.1.4 Developing Countries in the WTO

Treatment of developing countries in the international trading regime has evolved considerably since the GATT was established in 1947. While the GATT's original 23 signatories included 11 developing countries, the Agreement did not initially recognize them as a group and made no special provision for their benefit. By the 1950s, however, they had made a case for special and differential treatment (SDT) based largely on notions of fairness and the belief that trade policies that maximize welfare in the rich industrialized countries may not be the same as those which do the most to promote development in the poorest countries.[10] They argued that it was not realistic to expect them to compete on a level playing field with industrialized countries and that free trade would only entrench a legacy of colonialism and dependence on primary commodities.[11]

---

make an 'objective assessment of the matter before it'.

[7]   Jackson, *supra* note 5 at 135.

[8]   The DSB is the WTO General Council – being a body composed of all WTO members – when it convenes to settle disputes arising between members.

[9]   See William J. Davey, 'The Sutherland Report on Dispute Settlement: A Comment' (2005) 8 (2) *Journal of International Economic Law* 321.

[10]   Joseph E. Stiglitz and Andrew Charlton, *Fair Trade For All: How Trade Can Promote Development* (New York: Oxford University Press, 2005) at 88.

[11]   Elizabeth Acorn, *Learning from Experience: Special and Differential Treatment in the World Trade Organization* (2006) [unpublished, Toronto]. For a succinct description of the history of SDT, see Hunter Nottage, 'Trade and Competition in the WTO: Pondering the Applicability of Special and Differential Treatment' (2003) 6 (1) *Journal of International Economic Law* 23 at 24.

This push by developing countries led to the redrafting of Article XVIII (Government Assistance to Economic Development) at the 1954–55 GATT Review Session. The redrafted Article gave developing countries policy space and flexibility to protect their import-competing infant industries, including by derogating from scheduled tariff commitments (Article XVIII, Section A) and by the use of export subsidies for manufactured goods (Article XVI.4). A decade later, at the conclusion of the Kennedy Round, Members adopted Part IV of the GATT. Part IV specifically addressed 'Trade and Development' and encouraged developed countries to recognize the importance of market access for developing countries. Most importantly, however, Part IV formalized the principle of 'non-reciprocity', exempting developing countries from having to make reciprocal tariff concessions, stating that 'the developed contracting parties do not expect reciprocity for commitments made by them in trade negotiations to reduce or remove tariffs and other barriers to trade of less-developed contracting parties'.[12] This move to improve market access for developing countries was built upon with the adoption in 1979 of the 'Enabling Clause' which created a permanent legal basis for preferential tariff treatment to exports from developing countries (pursuant to the Generalized System of Preferences or GSP)[13] as well as greater flexibility in the formation of preferential trade regimes between developing countries.

The Uruguay Round, which concluded in 1994, saw a shift in focus away from the notion of treating developing countries as exceptional, to an attempt to further their integration into the world trading system by asking them to take on the same substantive rights and obligations as developed countries.[14] SDT provisions were intended to assist in the integration process. Thus, the Uruguay Round Agreements introduced provisions giving developing countries extended time periods to comply with various obligations, and also sought to increase trade opportunities for developing countries through increased market access. In addition, they added a new layer of SDT provisions aiming to assist developing countries adjust to the liberalization required of them by having developed countries provide them with technical assistance.

The evidence available shows that, despite these commitments, developing countries continue to face serious trade-related impediments across various sectors. Scholars generally and governments of developing

---

[12]   Article XXXVI.8.

[13]   The GSP was implemented under the auspices of UNCTAD in 1971: Resolution 21(II) of the Second UNCTAD Conference, in UNCTAD, *Proceedings of the Conference of 1968, Report and Annexes* (United Nations, TD/97).

[14]   Acorn, *supra* note 11 at 16.

countries have criticized the Uruguay Round's SDT initiatives.[15] For example, Ostry writes that the Uruguay Round Agreements provide arbitrary implementation periods, inadequate technical assistance and 'seem[ingly] little more than tokenesque compensation'.[16]

All other factors aside, this history surely justifies reluctance on the part of developing countries to accept promises of trade-related 'carrots' to induce them to participate in any given climate change mitigation endeavour. Equally, it will deepen antagonism likely to be caused by any use of trade sanctions or other measures designed to compel developing countries to take climate change mitigation measures. Developed countries therefore face major challenges in overcoming this well-justified cynicism on the part of developing countries.

3.1.5 Trade and Environment in the WTO

The WTO maintains a Committee on Trade and Environment (CTE) which was established pursuant to the Ministerial Decision on Trade and the Environment, adopted in Marrakesh in 1994. While the CTE has a broad-ranging work program, it does not include any specific reference to climate change. However, several of its mandated tasks are highly relevant to the issues raised by climate change, including examination of the relationship between:

- the provisions of the multilateral trading system and trade measures for environmental purposes, including those pursuant to multilateral environmental agreements (MEAs);
- environmental policies relevant to trade and environmental measures with significant trade effects and the provisions of the multilateral trading system;
- the provisions of the multilateral trading system and charges and taxes for environmental purposes; and
- the provisions of the multilateral trading system and requirements

---

[15] See for example, Joel Trachtman, 'Legal Aspects of a Poverty Agenda at the WTO: Trade Law and "Global Apartheid"' (2003) 6 (1) *Journal of International Economic Law* 3.

[16] Sylvia Ostry, 'The Uruguay Round North–South Grand Bargain: Implications for Future Negotiations' (2000) *Political Economy of International Trade Law*. See also Joseph E. Stiglitz and Andrew Charlton, *Fair Trade for All* (New York: Oxford University Press, 2005); and Joseph E. Stiglitz, *Globalization and its Discontents* (New York: W.W. Norton & Company, 2003).

for environmental purposes relating to products, including standards and technical regulations, packaging, labelling, and recycling.

To date, there has been little progress on achieving any kind of agreement
on these issues and much remains uncertain and susceptible to interpretation by a panel or the Appellate Body should a dispute arise. Throughout
this book, we analyse how the dispute settlement system has dealt with, or
would be likely to deal with, the issues raised in the context of these relationships. The analysis reveals a significant degree of uncertainty across
each set of linkages. As we discuss, this uncertainty has both positive and
negative implications: it provides flexibility in an area where it is critical
that countries are able to react to changing information over time and
to experiment with different domestic approaches to achieving emission
reductions. However, it may also mean there is a certain regulatory 'chill'
effect if governments fear possible WTO challenges or trade sanctions,
and it may add to the administrative costs of trying to determine the likely
WTO-consistency or otherwise of a given measure.

3.1.6   On-going Trade Negotiations

In 2001, a new round of trade negotiations was launched at the Ministerial
Conference in Doha. The Ministerial Declaration adopted at Doha on
14 November 2001 set out the negotiating agenda for matters related to
trade and the environment in paragraph 31. It provided that the Agenda
is to cover, *inter alia*, the relationship between existing WTO rules and
specific trade obligations set out in multilateral environmental agreements (MEAs) and the reduction or, as appropriate, elimination of tariff
and non-tariff barriers to environmental goods and services. Again, these
negotiations were pending at the time of writing. There has been no
indication that, even if the negotiations are concluded, there will be any
substantial progress on clarifying the relationship between WTO rules and
multilateral environmental agreements. The specific issue of environmental goods and services is canvassed in Chapter 15.

3.2   THE INTERNATIONAL CLIMATE CHANGE
REGIME

3.2.1   History of Climate Change Negotiations

In 1979, the World Meteorological Organization (WMO) organized the
first World Climate Conference. It was here that climate change was

first internationally acknowledged as an 'urgent world problem'. The Conference called for global cooperation to examine the possible future course of the climate and to take the findings into account in planning for the future development of human society.[17] Together with the United Nations Environmental Programme (UNEP) and the International Council of Scientific Unions, the WMO subsequently established the World Climate Program.[18] A programme of scientific research and several intergovernmental conferences over the ensuing decade culminated in UN General Assembly Resolution 43/53 in 1988, which declared that 'climate change is a common concern of mankind'.[19] The Resolution endorsed the establishment of the Intergovernmental Panel on Climate Change (IPCC), which was established by the WMO and UNEP the same year.

The IPCC is a scientific body charged with providing an objective source of information about climate change. Its role is to 'assess on a comprehensive, objective, open and transparent basis the latest scientific, technical and socio-economic literature produced worldwide relevant to the understanding of the risk of human-induced climate change, its observed and projected impacts and options for adaptation and mitigation'.[20] In 1990, the IPCC produced its First Assessment Report in response to the General Assembly's request for a comprehensive review of and recommendations with respect to various aspects of climate change. The Report warned that, although there were many uncertainties, human activity was leading to increased atmospheric concentrations of carbon dioxide and rising temperatures.[21] This Report was invoked by the Ministerial Declaration produced at the Second World Climate Conference in 1990, which recommended that negotiations on a framework climate convention begin without delay.[22] The United Nations responded to this Declaration by launching negotiations on a framework convention on climate change. These negotiations were conducted under the auspices

---

[17]   See UNFCCC Secretariat, *United Nations Framework Convention on Climate Change Handbook* (2006), http://unfccc.int/resource/docs/publications/handbook. pdf at 17.

[18]   Ibid.

[19]   United Nations, General Assembly Resolution A/RES/43/53, 6 December 1988.

[20]   Intergovernmental Panel on Climate Change, www.ipcc.ch/about/index. htm (date accessed: 15 August 2008).

[21]   J.T. Houghton, G.J. Jenkins and J.J. Ephraums (eds), *Scientific Assessment of Climate Change – Report of Working Group I* (Cambridge: Cambridge University Press, 1990).

[22]   Ministerial Declaration contained in the report of the Conference in A/45/696/Add.1, Annex III (1990).

of an Intergovernmental Negotiating Committee formed under the UN General Assembly.[23]

3.2.2 The Current Agreements

The United Nations Framework Convention on Climate Change (UNFCCC) was opened for signature in June 1992 at the UN Conference on Environment and Development in Rio de Janeiro and entered into force just under two years later in March 1994. Its key goal is the stabilization of GHG concentrations in the atmosphere 'at a level that would prevent dangerous anthropogenic [human induced] interference with the climate system'.[24] The UNFCCC is a framework agreement and is designed to be amended and augmented over time. This occurs primarily through meetings of the Conference of the Parties (COP). The most significant addition to date is the Kyoto Protocol adopted by the COP-3 meeting in 1997.

The Kyoto Protocol sets binding targets for 37 industrialized countries and the EC for reducing GHG emissions. Several years and six meetings of the COP followed before the Kyoto Protocol finally reached the required number of signatures to achieve ratification in February 2005. As of 12 December 2007, a total of 176 countries and one regional integration organization (the European Economic Community) had ratified the Protocol. The US has not ratified the Kyoto Protocol, while Australia only did so following its 2007 federal elections. In the COP meetings following the conclusion of the Kyoto Protocol in 1997, the US made the 'meaningful participation' of developing countries a prerequisite for its ratification.[25] Following COP-6 in November 2000, the Bush administration officially stated that it would not be ratifying the Protocol.[26]

---

[23]   United Nations General Assembly, A/RES/45/212, 21 December 1990.

[24]   UNFCCC, Article 2.

[25]   Senate resolution 98 (proposed by Byrd-Hagel), adopted July 1997. Other contributing factors to the US refusal to ratify included that they would have to spend more than most other nations to comply with the commitments, despite having relatively little to gain. See Cass R. Sunstein, *The Complex Climate Change Incentives of China and the United States* (John M. Olin Law & Economics Working Paper No. 352 (2nd series), Public Law and Legal Theory Working Paper No. 176, The Law School, University of Chicago, 2007) 8. See also William Nordhaus, 'The Challenge of Global Warming: Economic Models and Environmental Policy' (2007), available online at: http://nordhaus.econ.yale.edu/dice_mss_072407_all. pdf (date accessed: 22 December 2009).

[26]   Farhanna Yamin and Joanna Depledge, *The International Climate Change Regime – A Guide to Rules, Institutions and Procedures* (Cambridge: Cambridge University Press, 2004) 27.

The Kyoto Protocol is based on the guiding principles contained in Article 3 of the UNFCCC, which include that the Parties should protect the climate system 'on the basis of equity and in accordance with their common but differentiated responsibilities and respective capabilities. Accordingly, the developed country Parties should take the lead in combating climate change and the adverse effects thereof.' This principle was strongly influenced by the fact that the largest share of historical and current global emissions of GHGs has originated in developed countries and that per capita emissions in developing countries are still relatively low.[27] Pursuant to the common but differentiated responsibilities principle, the UNFCCC divides countries into three groups: Annex I (industrialized countries that were members of the OECD in 1992, plus countries with economies in transition (EIT)); Annex II (the OECD members of Annex I but not EIT members); and non-Annex I (mostly developing countries).

This distinction is maintained in the Kyoto Protocol, where only Annex I countries have legally binding limits on their GHG emissions. Together, Annex I countries are required to reduce their combined emissions to 5 per cent below 1990 levels in the first commitment period of 2008–12. In order to achieve the 5 per cent reduction target, countries have their own specific targets (negotiators could not agree on a common emissions reduction goal), which range from 8 per cent reductions for the European Union (EU) to a 10 per cent allowable increase for Iceland. Annex II countries are required to provide financial resources to enable developing countries to undertake emission reductions and to help them adapt to the adverse effects of climate change. They also have to 'take all practicable steps' to promote the development and transfer of environmentally friendly technologies to EIT Parties and developing countries. Non-Annex I countries do not have to commit to specific targets, but must report their emission levels and develop national climate change mitigation programmes.

The Kyoto Protocol allows Annex I governments to determine what domestic policies and measures to take in order to achieve their targets, although possibilities are listed in Article 2. It also defines three flexibility

---

[27] Developed countries now contribute about half of annual GHG emissions, but have nearly 85% of the world's population. The energy-related carbon footprint of an average citizen of a low- or middle-income country is 1.3 or 4.5 metric tons of carbon dioxide equivalent respectively. This compares with 15.3 in developed countries. Further, the majority of past emissions (and thus the greatest percentage of the existing atmospheric stock of GHGs) is the responsibility of developed countries. World Bank, *World Development Report 2010: Development and Climate Change* (Washington, DC: The World Bank, 2010) at 44.

mechanisms (Emissions Trading,[28] the Clean Development Mechanism,[29] and Joint Implementation[30]) whereby Annex I countries can earn and trade emission credits through projects implemented in either other developed or developing countries, which they can use towards meeting their commitments.

While Annex I countries have significant flexibility in how they choose to meet their commitments, they are also subject to certain constraints. In particular, Article 2(3) requires that they strive to implement policies and measures in such a way as to minimize 'adverse effects', including effects on international trade and economic impacts on other countries, particularly developing country Members. In addition, Article 3(14) requires Annex I countries to strive to implement their emission reduction commitments in such a way as to minimize adverse social, environmental and economic impacts on developing country Parties, and the Conference of the Parties is charged with considering what actions are necessary to ensure this is the case.

3.2.3   Dispute Settlement, Compliance, and Enforcement

It has been stated that the procedures and mechanisms relating to compliance under the Kyoto Protocol are the strongest and institutionally most sophisticated non-compliance procedures adopted by any MEA to date.[31] However, in comparison with the WTO's dispute settlement mechanism, the mechanism remains fairly weak. It was negotiated and designed following adoption of the Kyoto Protocol.[32] The institutional centrepiece of the mechanism is the Compliance Committee, which was the last of the bodies established under the Protocol, by COP-7 in Marrakesh.[33]

The key enforcement mechanism, which is to be overseen by the Compliance Committee's Enforcement Branch, is known as the 1.3 penalty rule. If a party fails to meet its initial commitments under Article 3.1 of the Kyoto Protocol, its emissions cap in the subsequent commitment period will be reduced by 1.3 times the emissions it committed to but

---

[28]   Article 17.
[29]   Article 12.
[30]   Article 6.
[31]   Yamin and Depledge, *supra* note 26 at 386.
[32]   Pursuant to Article 18, which called upon the Conference of the Parties serving as the Meeting of the Parties to the Kyoto Protocol (CMP) to approve, at its first session, 'procedures and mechanisms' to determine and address cases of non-compliance with the Protocol.
[33]   In decision 24/CP.7 as confirmed by the CMP in decision 27/CMP.1.

failed to reduce.[34] Further, the non-complying party cannot participate in the flexibility mechanisms in order to meet its commitments until it meets its targets.[35] While this may appear to be a severe sanction, a country that is not in compliance may not enter into re-negotiations and, even if it does so, it may not be willing to take on such significant reductions.[36] Enforcement or motivation for compliance may therefore come largely from the damage to reputation from not complying with commitments. This will probably not be sufficient to ensure compliance given the high costs of addressing climate change and also the fact that in all likelihood other countries will also have failed to meet their commitments.

3.2.4 Developing Countries and the UNFCCC

As noted, application of the 'common but differentiated responsibilities' principle led to developing countries having no binding emission reduction commitments under the Kyoto Protocol. Three factors were key in the adoption of this approach: (i) their low per capita emissions; (ii) their need for development; and (iii) the fact that the currently high global concentration of GHGs is overwhelmingly due to past emissions from industrialized countries.[37] The approach has been criticized by those who argue that the climate change regime will never be effective until it includes the major developing countries, such as China and India.[38] This was a key theme

---

[34] Yamin and Depledge, *supra* note 26 at 394. See also Robert N. Stavins and Scott Barrett (2002), 'Increasing Participation and Compliance in International Climate Change Agreements' (Fondazione Eni Enrico Mattei Working Paper No. 94.2002; Kennedy School of Government Working Paper No. RWP02-031). They describe the penalty (at 20) as follows: 'If an Annex I party were to emit, for example, 100 tons more than allowed in the first compliance period (2008–2012), then the party's emission cap for the next compliance period (possibly 2013–2017) would be reduced by 130 tons – 100 tons to offset the excess plus an additional 30 tons as a penalty for non-compliance.'

[35] Ibid.

[36] Scott Barrett, *Environment and Statecraft: The Strategy of Environmental Treaty-Making* (New York: Oxford University Press, 2003) at 386. See also Stavins and Barrett, ibid. (arguing that the enforcement mechanism in the Kyoto Protocol can be expected to fail because it does not require sacrifice and punishment is forever delayed (the magnitude of punishment depends not just on an agreed penalty rate but on future emission limits and a country must agree to its future emission limits otherwise it would not choose to participate)).

[37] Agus Sari, 'Developing Country Participation: The Kyoto–Marrakech Politics' (Hamburg Institute of International Economics, Discussion Paper 333, 2005) 18.

[38] See, for example, Stavins and Barrett, *supra* note 34 at 12. See also generally

at the COP-15 in Copenhagen in December 2009. It was widely accepted going into the meeting that agreement would be not only politically impossible but also environmentally useless if the principle simply meant that developing countries had no responsibilities at all. The question thus became one of what those responsibilities ought to be. The Copenhagen Accord failed to clearly address this issue – it provides for non-Annex I countries to take mitigation action on a voluntary basis. Least developed countries (LDCs) and small island developing nations may 'undertake actions voluntarily and on the basis of support'.

3.3   CONCLUDING REMARKS

The international trade and climate change frameworks were developed and have evolved with only token reference to each other. This inter-action will not be sufficient in the future. The climate change regime directly implicates domestic and international consumption and production patterns and, hence, international trade rules.[39] It is critical therefore that trade rules support, rather than hinder, action on climate change. Similarly, climate change must not be allowed to provide a smokescreen for protectionist action that would threaten international trade liberalization and further threaten the economic progress of developing countries. The remainder of this book examines the linkages between the two regimes to assess where synergies lie and where risks arise that might threaten to derail the goals of trade liberalization and the climate change regime.

Albert Mumma and David Hodas, 'Designing a Global Post-Kyoto Climate Change Protocol that Advances Human Development' (Widener Law School Legal Studies Research Paper Series No. 08-67, 2008)
[39]   International Centre for Trade and Sustainable Development, Bridges Copenhagen Update, 21 December 2009, Issue 3.

4. The role of trade measures in addressing climate change

4.1 INTRODUCTION

The fundamental premise of this book is that the international trading regime and efforts to address climate change are not only inextricably linked but that synergies can be found between them that will enable achievement of environmental, trade and development goals. Understanding these linkages and possible synergies is critical for governments, policy-makers, academics, and others engaged with either endeavour. International trade is important to economic growth and prosperity in both developed and developing countries, whilst projections are that climate change will have significant impact on societies throughout the world (although current projections show that some countries will lose more than others and that there may, at least in the short term, even be some 'winners' from climate change). Linkages between the international trading regime and efforts to address climate change require governments and policy-makers in each area to take account of the other. Trade rules may both constrain and facilitate action to address climate change, while actions taken to address climate change will in some cases have important implications for trading relationships.

In this chapter, we introduce the three different types of linkages between trade and climate change to be examined. A key theme of the book is that international trade rules need not conflict with action on climate change. On the contrary, trade institutions and the rules they monitor can aid efforts to address climate change, both in terms of domestic actions to reduce emissions and in terms of encouraging participation and compliance with multilateral climate change agreements. Accordingly, while highlighting and examining areas of incompatibility between the two regimes, we seek to focus on ways in which they may complement each other, recognizing the benefits to be gained by countries exploiting comparative advantage through international trade, but equally the importance and urgency of taking action to mitigate (and adapt to) climate change.

4.2 IMPLICATIONS OF TRADE RULES FOR DOMESTIC CLIMATE CHANGE POLICY

4.2.1 Choosing Domestic Climate Policies

Governments could attempt to address climate change using a variety of tools. While economists tend to speak of the efficiency of taxes in causing parties to internalize externalities in some cases, it is important to take into account other factors such as whether it is possible to get the measure adopted. We will use four key criteria to discuss domestic policy instruments for addressing climate change: environmental effectiveness, efficiency, equity and political feasibility.[1]

Environmental effectiveness
The choice of policy instrument will obviously depend on the policy goal and how likely the instrument is to meet that goal. The goal could be a reduction in GHG emissions by a certain percentage or an increase in the generation of electricity by renewable energy or an increase in the use of public transit. Whatever the stated goal, one of the primary concerns will be how to measure whether the instrument is actually having an impact on the particular activity or whether any change is due to other factors. Is, for example, an increase in the generation of electricity from renewable sources due to a government subsidy or would it have occurred in any event?

In addition to the difficulty in determining whether the instrument is actually bringing about the desired end, there is a concern about environmental side-effects of the instrument.[2] A particular instrument may be very effective at achieving its primary goal but cause other, unintended

---

[1]   See R. Revesz and R. Stavins, 'Environmental Law', in A.M. Polinsky and S. Shavell (eds), *The Handbook of Law and Economics* vol. 1 (Amsterdam: Elsevier, 2007) arguing that instruments should be assessed based on cost-effectiveness, distributional equity and political feasibility. Cost-effectiveness includes whether the instrument achieves its goal, whether it does so at the lowest possible cost, whether it provides the relevant information to government and whether it provides adequate dynamic incentives (such as for research and development of new technology).

[2]   See D. Duff and A. Green, 'Market-Based Policies For Renewable Energy Source Electricity: A Comparative Evaluation', in N. Chalifour, J. Milne, H. Ashiabor, K. Deketelaere and L. Kreiser (eds), *Critical Issues in Environmental Taxation: International and Comparative Perspectives*, vol. V (Oxford: Oxford University Press, 2008) for a discussion of environmental side-effects and other aspects of instrument choice in the context of renewable sources of electricity.

environmental consequences. The most obvious example would be reducing GHG emissions through nuclear power, which causes its own environmental concerns. Other environmental effects may be less direct, such as where the use of the particular instrument changes the norms or values around the activity. For example, the imposition of a tax on some activity (such as gasoline) may influence individuals to see the goal (for example, driving less or driving smaller cars) as a function of the price to be paid for polluting the environment rather than a responsibility.[3] Such a shift in values or norms may offset some of the gains from the use of a tax. These other environmental effects may be worth bearing in some cases but it is important to consider all such impacts in the analysis.

Efficiency
Efficiency can be used in a broad or narrow sense. The broad sense of efficiency examines the impact of the policy on social welfare. Efficiency in this sense relates to how the measure affects all individuals in society and whether it leads to an overall improvement in their welfare.[4] Social welfare could be examined on a national basis, determining whether the policy improves welfare for the citizens of a particular country even if there are some costs that are imposed on individuals in other countries. It could also be examined on a global basis which would take into account not only the costs and benefits in the country imposing the measure but also any impacts (positive or negative) it would have in another country. This form of social welfare analysis can be controversial as it in general requires comparing the costs and benefits of particular policies. While it may be difficult (or impossible) to quantify all the costs and benefits of a particular policy, the process of analysing all the costs and benefits, even if they are not quantified, may help improve decision-making.[5]

---

[3]   For a discussion of instrument choice and norms or values, see C. Sunstein, 'Social Norms and Social Roles' (1996) *Columbia Law Review* 903, R. McAdams, 'The Origin, Development and Regulation of Norms' (1997) 96 (2) *Michigan Law Review* 338, and A. Green, 'You Can't Pay Them Enough: Subsidies, Environmental Law and Social Norms' (2006) 30 *Harvard Environmental Law Review* 407.

[4]   Note that the broader, social welfare version of efficiency encompasses the other factors as the social welfare function would include the costs and benefits to the environment from the policy and, depending on the weights of the social welfare function, could reflect the preferences of the society for equity.

[5]   Cass Sunstein, *Risk and Reason* (Cambridge: Cambridge University Press, 2002), Richard Revesz and Robert Stavins, *supra* note 1, and Richard Posner, *Catastrophe: Risk and Response* (Oxford: Oxford University Press, 2004). See Frank Ackerman and Lisa Heinzerling, *Priceless* (New York: New Press, 2004)

The narrower version of efficiency is, in essence, cost-effectiveness. It involves ensuring that whatever the environmental goal, it is met at least cost. All costs should be included, such as the costs of abatement equipment, the public costs of administering the regime (including the information costs of developing or monitoring the regulations and enforcement costs), and the private compliance costs. These costs can change over time and therefore it is important to consider the dynamic effects of a measure, such as the extent to which the measure fosters technological innovation.[6]

Equity
Policies can distribute the costs and benefits of addressing climate change very differently. For example, a carbon tax may provide benefits to society as a whole but impose a heavier burden on particular sectors such as low-income groups. It may be possible to offset potential negative distributional impacts; for example, through using the revenue from the tax to reduce the taxes on the lower-income groups. It is important to examine the extent to which measures designed to offset the distributional impacts actually end up reducing the environmental effectiveness or efficiency of the policy. Some tax designs will have this effect more than others. For example, a carbon tax could involve exemptions for particular groups in order to spare them the costs of the policy, but of course any such exemptions are likely to reduce the environmental effectiveness of the tax and may also reduce the efficiency of the measure for dealing with climate change (increasing the cost to achieve the same level of emission reductions). An alternative to the approach of providing exemptions that would preserve environmental benefits is a revenue-neutral tax such as that imposed in British Columbia in Canada, where the tax not only is revenue-neutral but achieves equity goals by including protection for lower-income individuals.[7] A particular society may decide that the costs of adjusting for distributional impacts may be warranted by the added fairness of the policy, but it is important to understand the trade-offs when choosing the optimal policy.

Political feasibility
The final factor we discuss is the political feasibility of the particular measure. As we have seen recently, environmental taxes may be difficult to

---

(arguing that cost–benefit analysis is inappropriate in environmental law as environmental impacts are not quantifiable or commensurable with monetary costs).

[6]   Revesz and Stavins, *supra* note 1.

[7]   British Columbia, Backgrounder: Balanced Budget 2008, online at: www. bcbudget.gov.bc.ca/2008/backgrounders/backgrounder_carbon_tax.htm   (date accessed: 3 March 2010).

put in place in many countries, such as the US and Canada (at least federally). Other countries have been able to put taxes in place but they contain significant exemptions to make them politically feasible. Conversely, governments may be able to put in place an emissions trading scheme even though such schemes are in effect very similar to taxes in terms of raising the costs of production.[8] Subsidies are often the most politically feasible measure as the benefits (at least the narrow economic benefits) are clearly visible whereas the costs (in terms of revenue raising) are more diffuse and less transparent. It therefore can be politically difficult to put in place an optimally effective, efficient and fair policy, although there is a connection between political feasibility and these other factors such as fairness. Political feasibility can be a particularly troublesome factor for the WTO to review if measures are challenged. We will discuss how WTO panels or the Appellate Body review a policy that has trade impacts where the government imposing the policy argues that a less trade restricting policy is not politically feasible.

Constraining and furthering policy   From the perspective of governments seeking to take action to address climate change, international trade rules may have both negative and positive implications. On the negative side, trade rules may constrain their ability to take optimal domestic measures to address climate change. On the positive side, trade agreements and institutions may be able to assist countries in meeting their obligations.

Constraints on actions   Member countries of the WTO are obliged to abide by the rules set out in the various covered Agreements. In particular, under the GATT, countries must refrain from taking actions that discriminate between their trading partners (the most-favoured-nation or MFN principle) and must also ensure that they do not discriminate against foreign producers in favour of their own domestic producers (the National Treatment principle). Similarly, the rules set out in the Subsidies and Countervailing Measures (SCM) Agreement seek to prevent discrimination by restraining the freedom of countries to provide subsidies to domestic producers. The broad categories of domestic measures that may be constrained pursuant to these various obligations are: (i) regulations and domestic emission trading systems, (ii) taxes, (iii) subsidies and (iv) border tax adjustments.

The potential problem with regulations is that, under WTO rules, they

---

[8] For a discussion of the characteristics of carbon taxes and emissions trading schemes, and the advantages and disadvantages of each, see Chapter 6.

might be considered trade restrictive and discriminatory if in fact they favour domestic companies at the expense of foreign competitors, or if they favour one trading partner over another. Whether or not they do so will depend on their design and manner of application and may be a source of controversy requiring resolution by the WTO Dispute Settlement Body.

Assisting countries to meet obligations   Trade agreements may support countries in meeting their emission reduction commitments. First, countries may be able to use trade sanctions to force others to participate in and/or comply with a climate change agreement. The use of trade sanctions or a credible threat of the same may help governments in the target country deal with domestic interest groups who oppose climate change measures. The government will be able to point to external rules that bind it, thus minimizing the opportunity for domestic interest groups to influence decisions. Second, countries may be able to use trade measures to allay the competitiveness concerns of domestic industries regarding climate change measures. If governments are able to assuage these concerns by taking measures to combat loss of competitiveness, then again trade rules may be a positive force in helping countries meet their emission reduction commitments. We pay particular attention to the possible use of border tax adjustments in this regard.

4.3   UNILATERAL ACTION TO FORCE OTHER COUNTRIES TO TAKE CLIMATE CHANGE ACTION

As noted in Chapter 2, a key difficulty in designing an international climate change regime is that addressing climate change through reducing GHG emissions is an 'additive public good', that is, a public good that depends on the aggregate reductions of GHG emissions by a large number of countries.[9] As with other public goods, the risk with additive public goods

---

[9]   As noted in Chapter 2, a public good is a good that is non-excludible (one party cannot stop others from enjoying the benefits of the good) and non-rivalrous (one party's enjoyment of the good does not reduce the amount for others). See Scott Barrett, 'Proposal for a New Climate Change Treaty System' (2007) 4 (3) *The Economists' Voice* Article 6. Barrett describes reducing concentrations of GHG in the atmosphere as an additive or 'aggregate efforts' public good as opposed to a 'single best efforts' public good (such as stopping an asteroid from hitting the earth), which can rely on unilateral action, or a 'weakest link' public good (such as stopping the spread of a disease), which depends on every country being involved.

is that some parties will free-ride on the efforts of others. For example, countries may refuse to sign on to a climate change agreement, may not make any substantial international commitments under the agreement, or may commit to reductions but fail to fulfil their commitments. The Kyoto Protocol provides an example of all of these types of free-riding. Some countries refused to sign on. Others, such as developing countries (many of which are major emitters) signed on but did not commit to any reductions. Still others, such as Canada, committed to reductions but will not meet their commitments.[10]

Trade measures taken by countries unilaterally may overcome the free-rider problem and foster both participation in a climate change agreement and compliance with commitments states have accepted under an agreement.[11] First, trade measures could be used as 'carrots' or positive incentives to countries to either join in a climate change agreement or comply with their commitments.[12] For example, parties to a climate change agreement could offer preferential trade concessions to non-joiners or non-compliers either on specific products related to climate change or more generally on all goods.[13] Such preferential access would be given on condition that the beneficiary country meets certain emission reduction commitments. An example of the type of model that might be used is the Generalized Scheme of Preferences (GSP) under the GATT, where developed countries act on a unilateral basis to provide preferential market access to goods from developing countries. Often, such access is only given where certain conditions are met, which might include certain

---

[10] See National Round Table on the Economy and the Environment (NRTEE), *Getting to 2050: Canada's Transition to a Low-emission Future* (Ottawa: NRTEE, 2007).

[11] A climate agreement could also allow parties to use trade measures as a means of meeting their climate objectives. For further discussion of this point, see Chapter 14.

[12] Howard Chang, 'An Economic Analysis of Trade Measures to Protect the Global Environment' (1994–95) 83 *Georgetown Law Journal* 2131 (discussing 'carrots' and 'sticks' in promoting environmental protection) and Scott Barrett, *Environment and Statecraft: The Strategy of Environmental Treaty-Making* (Oxford: Oxford University Press, 2003). See also Howard F. Chang, 'Carrots, Sticks, and International Externalities' (1997) 17 *International Review of Law and Economics* 309.

[13] These types of measures overlap with measures that are more specifically aimed at reducing environmental harm such as reducing subsidies for environmentally harmful industries or liberalizing trade in environmentally friendly goods and services (such as wind turbines). This chapter only examines these measures to the extent they relate to the objective of increasing participation in or compliance with an international climate change regime.

environmental standards or targets being met. This type of conditionality raises legality issues, however, and these are discussed in Chapter 11. Other 'carrots' might include increased investment, technology transfers, and capacity-building in environmental matters.

Second, measures could be taken that eliminate disincentives to participation or compliance. A primary disincentive for governments to take domestic climate change action comes from a loss of competitive advantage if their producers face costs that those in another state do not (because it is either not participating in or not complying with a climate change agreement). Measures to eliminate such disincentives might conceivably take the form of a tax placed on a product at the border when it is being imported from a non-joining or non-complying state or remitted on exports where they are destined for such a state (a 'border tax adjustment'). Regulations or internal taxes on certain characteristics of the product, such as its energy efficiency, might serve the same purpose.

Third, a state could ban the use of energy-intensive products or products that emit GHGs from non-joining or non-complying states. The ban could be implemented at the border, denying entry to any such product to the state but potentially allowing similar domestic goods to remain on the market (which is likely to be problematic under WTO rules). Alternatively, the ban could be imposed in the state for all such products, whether imported or domestically produced.

Finally, countries might wish to unilaterally use trade measures as a 'stick' to explicitly deter non-participation by forcing non-joining states to either sign on to a climate change agreement or to take equivalent efforts to address their emissions. They might also use trade measures to force parties to a climate change regime to comply with their commitments. As will be discussed in Part IV, in either case the trade measure must be severe enough to induce the non-joiner or non-complier to act – that is, the measure must raise the country's costs to such an extent that it provides an incentive for it to join or comply. In addition, the costs of the measure to the sanctioning state must not be so severe that the threat of imposing the measure lacks credibility.[14] These two conditions of severity and credibility will be central to designing an appropriate enforcement mechanism. Issues will also arise as to the political viability of using trade measures as a 'stick'.

---

[14] See Barrett, *supra* note 12, and Robert N. Stavins and Scott Barrett, *Increasing Participation and Compliance in International Trade Agreements* (Working Paper No. RWP02031, Kennedy School of Government, Harvard University, 2002).

4.4   MULTILATERAL SOLUTIONS

The third set of linkages between trade rules and climate change constitute what we refer to as 'multilateral solutions'. We identify two broad categories of multilateral solutions: first, the inclusion of trade measures within a multilateral environmental agreement (MEA); and second, increasing trade in environmentally beneficial goods and services.

With respect to the first, one potential way to harness trade measures to assist in meeting the goals of climate change is through a climate change agreement. That is, rather than relying on unilateral action by individual countries, the parties to a climate change agreement could incorporate trade measures against non-joiners or non-compliers in the agreement itself. Trade measures have been included in a number of MEAs in order to further the environmental protection objectives advanced by the agreement in question, including the Convention on International Trade in Endangered Species of Wild Fauna and Flora (CITES), the Basel Convention on the Control of Transboundary Movements of Hazardous Wastes and their Disposal, and the Montreal Protocol on Substances that Deplete the Ozone Layer. Each MEA uses trade measures differently to achieve its objectives. The most common is to use trade measures as a direct means of minimizing environmental damage by imposing restrictions or conditions on the ability of states to import or export certain products, whether they be harmful to the environment themselves (for example, hazardous chemicals) or where trade itself is harmful to the things sought to be conserved (for example, endangered species). The most extreme measures of this type are import or export prohibitions, while less stringent measures include packaging or labelling requirements that make it more difficult for states to export the goods in question.

A second way in which trade measures may be used in MEAs is to remove obstacles to non-compliance/participation so as to create a level playing field and thus deter free-riding. The Montreal Protocol, for example, provides for the prohibition of imports from and exports to states that are not party to the Protocol. The purpose is to promote broad participation in the Protocol and ensure that the environmental gains made are not undermined by activities in non-parties.[15]

Third, trade measures are used to enforce compliance (that is, as a 'stick' to sanction non-complying states). It should be noted, however, that the

---

[15]   Ludivine Tamiotti et al., *Trade and Climate Change*: A Report by the United Nations Environment Programme and the World Trade Organization (Geneva: WTO, 2009) at 13.

MEAs that have used trade measures in this manner have seen trade sanctions as a last resort; their focus has been on promoting and facilitating compliance rather than penalizing non-compliance.[16]

The questions that arise in the context of climate change revolve around the potential for including these types of trade measures in a climate change agreement. There are a number of uncertainties and difficulties associated with the legality of such measures under WTO law, including issues that arise when rules in an MEA and the WTO overlap or conflict.

The second multilateral solution that will be discussed is the scope for bringing the environment into trade agreements by reducing the barriers to trade in environmental goods (for example, more environmentally sustainable forms of biofuels) and services and to technology transfer. The WTO's Committee on the Environment (CTE) has been considering the issue of trade in environmental goods and services but has struggled to make progress as countries seek to reach agreement on a core list of environmental goods and services.

---

[16] *Ibid.* at 29.

PART III

Trade rules and domestic policies

5. Regulations and domestic emissions trading

5.1 WHEN SHOULD REGULATIONS OR DOMESTIC EMISSIONS TRADING BE USED?

Countries attempting to address climate change must find ways to deal with the negative externality that is at its core. As discussed in Chapter 2, individuals and industries obtain the benefits of activities that emit GHGs but do not bear all, or potentially even part, of the cost. Domestic policy must either explicitly impose this cost on individuals and industries or find another means of making them take actions that take these costs into account. There are a range of policy instruments that can potentially fulfil this function, including various types of taxes, subsidies to encourage particular choices and regulations that require individuals or industries to take certain actions. Countries vary in a number of ways, including in their values, priorities, susceptibility to the negative impacts of climate change, and policy preferences, and they need scope to use different policy instruments. Policy flexibility allows adaptation of the type of instrument to the country context.

Governments may use regulatory standards in an attempt to specify the type or level of behaviour that takes into account negative externalities. There are a range of different forms of regulatory measures. This chapter will focus on (i) standards, such as emissions levels, for particular goods or activities; (ii) the required disclosure of information, such as through product labelling; and (iii) domestic emissions trading programs. It then turns to how these measures may impact trade.

5.1.1 Types of Regulatory Measures

Setting standards
Governments may attempt to control GHG emissions by setting standards for different activities. These standards could be set for GHG emissions from particular products. For example, governments have set emission standards for cars and energy efficiency standards for different products, such as appliances. The standards could also relate to processes.

The government could, for example, set standards prescribing permissible emission levels from electricity generating facilities or oil production facilities. Governments can also set standards for the minimum proportion of electricity that must come from renewable sources of energy (so-called 'renewable portfolio standards').

These standards do not directly impose a price on emissions in the same way as a tax would but do so indirectly by requiring certain actions to be taken. Standards can be environmentally effective in some cases. If enforced, they can ensure that the desired emission levels are met. One of the key complaints about standards, however, is that they do not allow sufficient scope for differences between situations. This lack of variance can lead to both reduced environmental effectiveness and higher cost. The difficulty for the government is that it has to be able to pick the optimal level or product standard. The government may have less information in making these decisions than the producers. Further, the use of standards may dampen innovation and therefore decrease long-run emission reductions. If a producer meets the emission standards, there is no incentive for it to go beyond this, including by investing in research and development concerning new products or methods that further reduce GHG emissions. Standards can induce innovation by constantly changing but this again requires more information than government agencies usually possess.

Providing information
Instead of requiring producers to meet particular standards, government may also regulate the information that producers provide about their products, and in particular about their GHG emissions or energy efficiency. Such information requirements may take the form of mandatory labelling about the GHG emissions of the product (for example, of the type of car) or from the production of the product. Many countries have used general eco-labelling programmes such as Germany's Blue Angel programme and Canada's Environmental Choice programme. There may also be more specific programmes relating to the emissions from particular products or groups of products.

Such information programmes are intended to activate consumers' preferences for environmentally friendly products. The direct costs of such programmes can be low, depending on how they are created, but their environmental effectiveness may also be low. The effectiveness obviously depends in large part on the intensity of the preferences and knowledge of consumers. If consumers do not care about climate change or do not care enough to pay the price difference for more environmentally friendly products, information concerning GHG emissions will not make a difference. Further, if consumers do not understand the information or the potential harms from climate change, the information will be ineffective. For example, climate change gives rise to a small probability of catastrophic climate shifts and has effects in the future. To the extent that individuals have difficulty taking into account such small probability events or future harms, the information may not sufficiently change their behaviour even if they would otherwise want to make a different choice if they understood its implications.[1]

Trading emissions

Domestic cap-and-trade systems may also be used to reduce GHG emissions and/or costs of reducing emissions. Cap-and-trade systems involve setting a target level of emissions and then allocating permits to participants for emissions up to that level. These permits could be provided for free or auctioned to industry or to others. Companies must have sufficient permits for the amount of GHG they emit. Companies can buy and sell the permits. The emissions trading aspect of these systems is argued to reduce the costs of reducing emissions because those with higher costs of reducing emissions can purchase permits from those with lower costs. Whether or not the cap-and-trade system leads to greater emission reductions than traditional forms of regulation depends on the stringency of the cap. The system will only reduce emissions if the cap is set below the level of emissions that was previously allowed. These systems may also be environmentally effective if the caps are fixed and may be reduced over time.

These emissions trading systems generally cover a subset of industries such as large emitters. The most famous of such systems in the climate change context is the EU emissions trading system. There are a range of concerns in using emissions trading systems, making it difficult to determine the initial number and allocation of permits. For example, the EU system had difficulties when it began operating as too many permits were issued. In North America, such systems have sprung up on a regional basis, spreading across state borders. For example, REGGI (Regional Greenhouse Gas Initiative) is an emissions trading programme involving the electricity generation sector in the eastern US states. The federal government in both the US and Canada have discussed putting in place a

---

[1] Cass Sunstein, *The Laws of Fear* (Cambridge: Cambridge University Press, 2005); and Richard Posner, *Catastrophe: Risk and Response* (Oxford: Oxford University Press, 2004). Information campaigns may also not solve the collective action problem where individuals who may be inclined to respond to the information do not perceive other individuals as responding and therefore are unwilling to act.

joint emissions trading scheme, although as yet no such scheme has been implemented.

5.1.2 The Trade Impact of Regulations

Regulatory measures can have the same impact as tariffs in terms of influencing trade. They may raise the costs of imports relative to domestically produced goods. For example, a requirement for fuel efficiency in cars may be less costly for domestic producers to meet than foreign producers. If so, the regulation increases the cost of the import, allowing otherwise higher cost producers (but for the regulation) into the market at the expense of formerly lower cost producers. It also prices some consumers out of the market (because the price of the less efficient cars has increased).

Of course such regulatory measures are not necessarily bad. They may meet legitimate regulatory objectives including overcoming negative externalities. However, they may also be protectionist. Sykes describes protectionism as 'any cost disadvantage imposed on foreign firms by a regulatory policy that discriminates against them or that otherwise disadvantages them in a manner that is unnecessary to the attainment of some genuine, non-protectionist regulatory objective.'[2] He argues that protectionism through regulatory measures is more harmful than other forms of protectionism such as tariffs, quotas, or subsidies. All other forms of protectionism impose a loss on society but transfer some of the loss from the higher cost to others. Tariffs provide revenue for the government, quotas revenue for the quota holders, and subsidies benefit consumers. Regulations, on the other hand, do not transfer any of the loss to others if they are not necessary to a legitimate regulatory purpose. The increased cost is entirely wasted.

For example, a regulation requiring foreign producers of cars to adopt a form of emissions technology that does not work or is not necessary would merely raise the cost for the foreign producers. There is a dead-weight loss that is not related to climate change or any other objective. This loss can occur from any type of regulatory measure. It could be a standard that is not effective at reaching the environmental objective or is unnecessarily trade restrictive (where a weaker or more even-handed requirement would be sufficient to meet the policy objective). It could also be a requirement to provide information that raises the costs for importers but does not have any environmental impact. It could even be an emissions trading requirement that is unnecessarily costly to importers.

---

[2] Alan Sykes, 'Regulatory Protectionism and the Law of International Trade' (1999) 66 *University of Chicago Law Review* 1, at 3.

Public choice concerns are at the core of regulatory protectionism. Concentrated interests may be able to influence the government to put in place regulatory measures that purport to have a positive environmental impact but in reality protect those interests. This protection comes at a cost to domestic consumers (including producers who use the imported product). However, politicians may be willing to respond to the demands for a particular form of regulation if it provides benefits to interests that are more likely to provide benefits back to them (such as electoral support, campaign contributions or future job opportunities).

5.2   NATIONAL TREATMENT

The WTO attempts to address regulatory protectionism in part through the national treatment requirement. It is one branch of the non-discrimination principle that is a central principle of the WTO (like the GATT before it). The non-discrimination principle may be classed as a negative constraint. It limits the scope of what countries can do by ensuring that they treat others with a form of equal-handedness in applying policy decisions, but does not require them to actually make any particular policy decisions. The principle was in place in the initial GATT in the 1940s but has a longer history in trade agreements.[3] It has two elements: the most-favoured-nation (MFN) requirement and the national treatment requirement. This chapter will focus on the national treatment principle with particular focus on regulatory protectionism.

5.2.1   Two Approaches to National Treatment

The national treatment provision prohibits discrimination between imports and domestically produced goods. It is likely to be central to any disputes concerning climate change policies. The national treatment principle is found in a number of WTO agreements, but for the purposes of regulatory measures the main focus is Article III of GATT. Article III.1 sets the goal for the national treatment provisions[4] and Article III.1 prohibits the application of measures (including regulatory measures and taxes) to 'imported or domestic products so as to afford protection to domestic production'.

---

[3]   Michael Trebilcock and Shiva Giri, 'The National Treatment Principle in International Trade Law', in Choi and Hartigan (eds), *Handbook of International Trade*, Volume II (Oxford: Blackwell, 2005).

[4]   The other principal agreement relating to regulations is the TBT Agreement. As discussed below, it also has a national treatment provision.

The Appellate Body has stated that the purpose of the national treatment provisions is to avoid protectionist domestic measures:[5]

> Toward this end, Article III obliges Members of the WTO to provide equality of competitive conditions for imported products in relation to domestic products . . . Article III protects expectations not of any particular trade volume but rather of the equal competitive relationship between imported and domestic products.[6]

The Appellate Body has found that this general principle 'informs' how the principle relates to domestic regulatory measures.[7] In particular, it found that the principle informs Article III.4, which sets out the operative national treatment provision for regulations. Article III.4 states that imported products 'shall be accorded treatment no less favourable than that accorded to like products of national origin in respect of all laws, regulations and requirements affecting their internal sale, offering for sale, purchase, transportation, distribution or use'.

One could imagine two very different approaches to national treatment and its constraints on regulatory protectionism. First, the national treatment requirement could be a blanket rule – that is, no difference in treatment is allowed between domestic and imported products. They should be allowed to compete as openly as possible in the domestic market and no account should be taken of the purpose of the differences in treatment. This narrow approach would determine whether the domestic and imported products competed with each other and then prohibit any difference in treatment.[8] If the domestic government decides that there is a reason for different treatment (such as that imported cars are less fuel efficient), any regulatory requirements would have to be justified as an exception to the GATT rules under Article XX (discussed in Chapter 9) such as an exception for the conservation of exhaustible natural resources.

The alternate approach would be to attempt to develop a test for the legitimacy of the difference in treatment of two apparently similar products

---

[5] *European Communities – Measures Affecting Asbestos and Asbestos-Containing Products* (2000) WTO Doc. WT/DS135/AB/R (Appellate Body Report) at para. 97.

[6] *EC–Asbestos*, ibid., quoting the Appellate Body in *Japan – Taxes on Alcoholic Beverages* (1996) WTO Doc. WT/DS8/AB/R, WT/DS10/AB/R, WT/DS11/AB/R (Appellate Body Report).

[7] *EC–Asbestos, supra* note 5 at para. 98.

[8] See, for example, Trebilcock and Giri, *supra* note 3 (arguing for an economic conception of national treatment with tests drawn from economics and in particular competition law).

in the determination of whether the products are 'like'.[9] An early version of such an approach is the 'aims and effects' test, which attempts to determine whether the objective of the measure and/or the effect was to protect domestic industry. It would allow regulatory distinctions that are aimed at some legitimate regulatory objective. The idea behind such a test is that there should be no need to find an 'exception' on which to ground a demonstrably legitimate regulatory distinction. Any such regulatory measure should be within the permissible scope of domestic regulatory authority.

In part, the difference in the tests depends on the information available to the panels or the Appellate Body. If they can determine the actual intent behind a measure, then they are meeting the general concern about regulatory measures – that they can be inefficient, hidden protectionist measures. The argument for the economic tests is that they are relatively clear for panels to apply as it is difficult to obtain information on the aims and (non-economic) effects of any measure.

Another potential difficulty with the broader 'aims and effects' approach to national treatment is that it arguably provides too much discretion for panels to define legitimate regulatory purposes. The list of agreed-upon exceptions, the argument goes, is found in Article XX and if there are other legitimate purposes, the members should agree on them. Any attempt to examine the purpose of regulatory distinctions under the national treatment test provides too much power to the panels or Appellate Body. As we will see, however, there is a trade-off. Leaving the examination of regulatory ends to Article XX means that new issues, such as climate change, have to be shoehorned into provisions that arguably did not contemplate such concerns and cannot be easily changed.

5.2.2 How Does the WTO Approach National Treatment?

If there are these two basic divergent approaches to national treatment, how have panels and the Appellate Body approached this issue? To begin with, panels and the Appellate Body have established a very broad scope for the coverage of Article III.4. They have interpreted 'laws, regulations and requirements' to include traditional forms of legislation and regulations. Article III.4 would, for example, cover minimum fuel efficiency standards for cars whether such standards were set out explicitly in legislation or established in regulations under enabling legislation. However, panels and the Appellate Body have also interpreted this term to cover

---

[9] Michael Trebilcock and Robert Howse, *The Regulation of International Trade*, 3rd edn. (London: Routledge, 2005).

a broader range of government action including non-mandatory conditions that a private actor accepts in order to receive an advantage.[10] The interpretation is sufficiently broad to cover voluntary agreements between regulated parties and the government, such as a voluntary agreement by automobile companies to take steps to reduce GHG emissions from automobiles. Similarly, 'affecting' has been given a broad interpretation as encompassing any laws, regulations or requirements that might 'adversely modify the conditions of competition between domestic and imported products'.[11]

The national treatment provisions of Article III.4, however, require panels or the Appellate Body to make two difficult determinations. The first issue is whether the imported and domestic product are 'like'. If so, a second issue arises as to whether the imported product has been given 'less favourable treatment'. This sub-section will discuss each of these issues in turn.

Are they 'like' products?

Determining whether two products are 'like' has proven very controversial. To what extent, for example, are two cars 'like' if they are the same in all respects except that one is 50 per cent more fuel efficient than the other? What about US corn-based ethanol and Brazilian sugar-cane-based ethanol, which arguably have different GHG emissions over their life-cycles? What of two tonnes of steel, one made with electricity from a coal-fired generation plant and one with electricity generated from hydro-electricity or natural gas?

The term 'like' arises in a number of contexts under WTO agreements and the Appellate Body has found that the scope of the term depends on the context of the provision in which it is found. It stated that:

> [t]here can be no one precise and absolute definition of what is 'like'. The concept of 'likeness' is a relative one that evokes the image of an accordion.

---

[10] See, for example, *Canada – Certain Measures Affecting the Automobile Industry* (2000) WTO Doc. WT/DS139/R and WT/DS142/R (Panel Report). The issue was not appealed. Canada had exempted imported motor vehicles from a customs duty where the manufacturer's local production of motor vehicles reached a minimum amount of Canadian value added and a certain production to sales ratio in Canada. These conditions were set out in government orders and letters of undertaking to the government but were not deemed by the Canadian government to be legally enforceable. The Panel found these conditions to fit within the term 'requirements' under Article III.4.

[11] *Canada – Autos Panel Report, supra* note 10 at para. 10.80.

The accordion of 'likeness' stretches and squeezes in different places as different provisions of the WTO Agreement are applied.[12]

A key factor in determining whether products are 'like' is whether there is a competitive relationship between the domestic and imported products. An Appellate Body decision addressing a ban by France on asbestos fibres and cement containing asbestos found that 'like' in Article III.4 related to 'the nature and extent of a competitive relationship between and among products'.[13] To aid in this determination, the Appellate Body referred to a non-exhaustive list of four factors that have been central to 'likeness' in other cases. These factors are (i) the properties, nature and quality of the products; (ii) the end-uses of the products; (iii) consumers' tastes and habits; and (iv) the tariff classification of the products.[14]

The test is largely market-based, which makes it appear to be more in line with the economic approach to national treatment. In particular, panels and the Appellate Body have used economic tests at times to examine, for example, how consumers view particular products. In fact, at least in the tax context, the Appellate Body has specifically rejected the use of the 'aims and effect' test.[15] The difficulty is that the economic approach does not fully account for some legitimate regulatory measures that seek to change behaviour because individuals see a difference between certain products. For example, consumers may not fully understand the costs of their decisions (such as where they fail to take account of a small probability of catastrophic climate change) or do not act consistently in their choices over time (such as where they fail to take choices they would otherwise take because of impatience).[16] Regulatory measures may be designed

---

[12] *Japan – Alcoholic Beverages AB Report, supra* note 6 at p. 23.
[13] *EC – Asbestos AB Report, supra* note 5 at para. 99.
[14] These factors have been used in a large number of decisions which made the 'like' products determination. They are based in part on an early GATT Report of the Working Party on Border Tax Adjustments, BSID 18S/97, adopted on 2 December 1970, which set out the first three factors. These factors, along with the fourth relating to tariff classification, were used in an early GATT tax decision: *Japan – Customs Duties, Taxes and Labelling Practices on Imported Wines and Alcoholic Beverages* B.I.S.D. (34th Suppl.) 83 para. 5.8 (1988) (adopted 10 November 1987).
[15] *Japan – Alcoholic Beverages AB Report, supra* note 6.
[16] See Posner, *supra* note 1; Sunstein, *supra* note 1; and A. Green, 'Self-Control, Individual Choice and Climate Change' (2008) 26 (1) *Virginia Environmental Law Review* 77.

to aid individuals in reaching choices they would have otherwise taken if they were otherwise fully informed and rational.[17]

The Appellate Body has provided some scope for a broader view of this test. In *EC – Asbestos*, for example, examining bans on asbestos and asbestos-containing materials, the Appellate Body focused on the impact of the health effects of asbestos on the competitive relationship between the domestic and imported products. It noted the high degree of scientific consensus around the carcinogenicity of asbestos and found that, given the health effects of one of the products (imported asbestos), there was a heavy burden on Canada to show that asbestos and the domestic substitute for asbestos, PCG[18] fibres, were 'like'. It found asbestos fibres and PCG fibres were not like because, in part, the higher risk of cancer with asbestos fibres made them physically different. It found that these physical differences placed a burden on Canada to show a competitive relationship, which it failed to do as there were only a few similar end-uses, no evidence of consumer tastes and different tariff classification for the products.

Even more interestingly, the Appellate Body took a broader approach for cement containing these fibres. It found that consumers might view cement made with asbestos and with PCG fibres differently if they understood the different health risks. Canada, however, failed to provide any information on this issue. Howse and Tuerk argue that the Appellate Body in effect adopted a test of whether the products would have been competitive in an idealized market in which consumers had complete information (and tort liability was available).[19] As a result, consumer tastes are relevant to 'likeness', and perhaps even idealized consumer tastes, although these may be overcome with evidence that consumers understand the relevant environmental differences between products and do not care.

---

[17]   Gabrielle Marceau and Joel Trachtman, 'The Technical Barriers to Trade Agreement, the Sanitary and Phytosanitary Measures Agreement, and the General Agreement on Tariffs and Trade: A Map of the World Trade Organization Law of Domestic Regulation of Goods' (2002) 36 (5) *Journal of World Trade* 811; and Trebilcock and Giri, *supra* note 3 (arguing that an economic based national treatment test may be biased against such measures but noting that states may still invoke Article XX to save their measures).
[18]   The acronym PCG is used to refer collectively to polyvinyl alcohol fibres ('PVA'), cellulose and glass fibres.
[19]   Robert Howse and Elizabeth Tuerk, 'The WTO Impact on Internal Regulations – A Case Study of the Canada–EC Asbestos Dispute', in G. de Burca and J. Scott (eds), *The EU and the WTO: Legal and Constitutional Issues* (Oxford: Hart Publishing, 2001).

Is there 'less favourable treatment'?

If a panel determines that the products at issue are 'like', they still must decide whether the imports received 'less favourable treatment' than the domestic products. Again the focus is on the competitive relationship. According to the Appellate Body, 'whether or not imported products are treated "less favourably" than like domestic products should be assessed . . . by examining whether a measure modifies the *conditions of competition* in the relevant market to the detriment of imported products'.[20] However, as with many of these provisions, the actual test for modifying the conditions of competition is not clear. It appears that a mere regulatory distinction will not be sufficient. The Appellate Body has stated that:

> If there is 'less favourable treatment' of the group of 'like' imported products, there is, conversely, 'protection' of the group of 'like' domestic products. However, a Member may draw distinctions between products which have been found to be 'like', without, for this reason alone, according to the group of 'like' imported products 'less favourable treatment' than that accorded to the group of 'like' domestic products.[21]

There can therefore be some legitimate differences in the treatment of products, provided the group of imported 'like' products is not treated less favourably than domestic products.

There has been some debate about whether regulatory intent can be brought into this examination of 'less favourable treatment'. While there appears to be room for regulatory differences, Porges and Trachtman argue that it is unclear whether different treatment based on non-protectionist goals (such as environmental objectives) is permitted under Article III or whether any 'less favourable treatment' (protectionist or otherwise) would violate national treatment.[22] Regan, on the other hand, argues that regulatory intent is relevant in this determination and that 'less favourable treatment' only covers measures with an objective protectionist intent.[23]

A recent panel decision seems to comport with Regan's reasoning. The

---

[20] *Korea–Measures Affecting Imports of Fresh, Chilled and Frozen Beef* (2001) WTO Doc. WT/DS161. WT/DS169/AB/R (Appellate Body Report) at para. 137 (emphasis in original).

[21] *EC – Asbestos, supra* note 5 at para. 100.

[22] A. Porges and J. Trachtman, 'Robert Hudec and Domestic Regulation: The Resurrection of Aim and Effects' (2003) 37 (4) *Journal of World Trade* 783.

[23] Donald Regan, 'Further Thoughts on the Role of Regulatory Purpose Under Article III of the General Agreement on Tariffs and Trade' (2003) 37 (4) *Journal of World Trade* 737.

panel in the EC–GMOs decision noted that Argentina did not provide evidence that allegedly less favourable treatment of GMOs was based on the country of origin of the products. It stated that 'it is not self-evident that the alleged less favourable treatment of imported biotech products is explained by the foreign origin of these products rather than, for instance, a perceived difference between biotech products and non-products in terms of their safety, etc.' It appears that the complaining party will have to provide evidence that 'the alleged less favourable treatment is explained by the foreign origin of the relevant biotech products.'[24] This decision may open the door to examination of regulatory intent in the 'less favourable treatment' determination.

5.2.3 Climate Change, Product-related Distinctions and National Treatment

What do these articulations of the national treatment test mean for domestic regulation of products? It will in part depend on the type of difference that is the basis for the alleged different treatment of the imported and domestic products. Measures could be based on the characteristics of the product ('product-related measures') or on how products are made ('process and production methods' or 'PPMs'). Product-related measures are based on characteristics inherent in the product itself – the emissions level from the use of the car, the particular content of a fertilizer, or the carbon content of a particular fuel. Measures based on PPMs, on the other hand, relate to the manner in which the product is made – the GHG emissions resulting from the electricity needed to produce the car, the fuel needed to produce the fertilizer or the emissions from the processes for making the fuel. There may be an overlap in some cases such as where a chemical used in producing a good partially remains in that good when it is sold. In discussing PPMs, we will focus on the pure case of PPMs that do not result in differences in the products themselves (non-product-related PPMs) as they are the most contentious. This sub-section discusses product-related measures and the next sub-section examines PPMs.

The analysis of product-related measures will depend on whether there is a competitive relationship and this determination will be based principally on four factors: physical characteristics, end-uses, consumer tastes, and tariff classification. If, for example, two products have the same end

---

[24] *European Communities – Measures Affecting the Approval and Marketing of Biotech Products* (2006) WTO Doc. WT/DS291/R, WT/DS292/R and WT/ DS293/R (Panel Report) at para. 7.2505.

uses, then issues will arise as to the physical characteristics of the two products and whether consumers differentiate between them. A panel has considered an issue related to energy efficiency and emissions. The US had imposed a 'gas guzzler' tax on cars that had a fuel economy level of less than 22.5 miles per gallon. However, it was challenged as being discriminatory against imports, which tended to be less fuel efficient. The panel (in an unadopted report) found that cars that had a fuel economy level of less than 22.5 miles per gallon were not 'like' cars that were less fuel efficient. It found that the measure had a legitimate regulatory purpose and that any competitive effects did not result from a distinction that inherently arose between domestic and imported products as both had access to the same technology.

However, while this decision does seem to support measures aimed at fuel efficiency, and possibly emissions, there are a number of limitations on its use as a precedent. First, it relates to a tax and not a regulatory measure. As such it falls under the tax provisions of Article III.2 which, according to the Appellate Body, have a narrower interpretation of the term 'like' than Article III.4 (see discussion in Chapter 6). Further, the panel used the now disfavoured 'aims and effects' test as the basis for its likeness determination.

Imported and domestic products that are physically the same and have the same uses may still be found to be 'unlike' if there is evidence that consumers differentiate between them. There may be some evidence of differences in consumer tastes for products with differing GHG emissions or fuel efficiency. However, it will be a very fact-specific determination. Consumers may differentiate for some products but not for others, and it may be this very lack of differentiation that leads a government to regulate.[25] If there is no evidence that consumers actually differentiate, it is difficult to know the principled basis on which a panel could determine what choices a consumer would have made in an 'idealized' market with full information. Given the broad definition of 'like' used by the Appellate Body in cases such as *EC–Asbestos*, it would be difficult to find products unlike merely because of energy efficiency differences without solid evidence that consumers actually care about the differences.

As noted above, even if the products are found to be 'like', a panel would still have to find that there was less favourable treatment of the imports for there to be a violation of Article III. This will depend on whether the measure has modified the conditions of competition. *EC–Asbestos* seemed to open the door to permissible regulatory differences between domestic

---

[25]   Marceau and Trachtman, *supra* note 17.

and imported goods as long as imports as a group are not disfavoured. It may be that even if there is a legitimate basis for regulatory differentiation of imports as a whole (for example, differences in GHG emissions from automobiles), the measure will violate national treatment. For example, a panel examining EU regulations on automobile engine size would have to examine the structure of the provision to determine whether imported cars as a group are treated less favourably than cars produced in the EU. A panel may undertake this determination in isolation from consideration of the aims of the provisions. This approach would place considerable weight on Article XX for justification of the provisions if they do discriminate against imports as a group. The alternate approach of considering the purpose of the measures to determine whether there really is less favourable treatment, on the other hand, places considerable discretion in the hands of panels without apparent constraints, other than that they must believe that the true purpose of the measures was not protection of domestic industry.

5.2.4   PPMs and National Treatment

These issues are raised even more starkly by measures aimed at PPMs – that is, measures that relate to how the product was made (when this does not affect the product itself) as opposed to product-related measures. A panel would have to determine, for example, whether a regulation specifying how steel is produced based on the GHG emissions from the electricity used in production of the steel (which, by assumption, makes no difference to the quality of the steel) violated the tests for national treatment. Other examples could include restrictions on biofuels based on how the fuel was produced. The step back from a direct connection to the product itself makes the tests for national treatment more difficult.

   In terms of 'like', the products themselves are not physically different as a result of the PPMs nor are their end-uses different. Based on these factors alone, therefore, the products with different PPMs would be considered 'like'. The issue then largely becomes consumer preferences. If there is evidence that consumers care about the differences between the products based on PPMs, a panel could consider them not 'like'. If there is no direct evidence that consumers care, the test for likeness following *EC–Asbestos* would appear to involve determining whether consumers would care in a market with perfect information (and possibly tort liability for harm). In the case of asbestos, the panel was influenced by the evidence of the health effects. It is not clear what factors a panel would use to make such a determination in the context of climate change.

   The 'less favourable treatment' part of the test for national treatment is also difficult. As noted above, the Appellate Body in *EC–Asbestos* noted that measures can differentiate between products as long as imports as a whole are not provided less favourable treatment. It is unclear whether this actually provides an opening for differentiation between measures based on PPMs.[26] If it does, the case law has provided no clear guidance to panels on how to decide whether differentiations based on PPMs are legitimate and it may come down to what Hudec has called a 'smell test' – the panels make an intuitive judgment about whether the measure seems protectionist.[27]

5.3   INTERNATIONAL STANDARDS AND THE TBT AGREEMENT

The TBT Agreement, which came into force after the Uruguay Round, also sets requirements relating to regulatory measures. In part, it seems aimed at moving countries towards greater use of international standards and greater recognition of regulatory measures taken by other members. It also emphasizes the *process* by which regulations are created. As we will discuss, these provisions aim at reducing at least some avenues for using regulatory measures for protectionist purposes.

The TBT Agreement applies to a subset of regulatory measures called 'technical regulations'. It defines a technical regulation as 'a document which lays down product characteristics or their related processes and production methods, including the applicable administrative provisions, with which compliance is mandatory.' It therefore applies to a range of mandatory climate change regulations such as fuel efficiency or GHG emissions requirements for products or mandatory labelling.[28] It also, however, applies to certain voluntary 'standards' that are 'approved by a recognized body' and provide for 'common and repeated use, rules, guidelines or characteristics for products or related processes or production methods'. Climate change 'standards' would probably include voluntary eco-labelling where the standard is set by a recognized body such

---

[26]   See, for example, Howse and Tuerk, *supra* note 19 and Marceau and Trachtman *supra* note 17.

[27]   Robert Hudec, 'GATT/WTO Constraints on National Regulation: Requiem for an "Aim and Effects" Test' (1998) 32 *International Lawyer* 619.

[28]   The Appellate Body has given the term 'technical regulations' a very broad interpretation: *EC – Asbestos AB Report, supra* note 5, and *European Communities – Trade Description of Sardines* (*EC–Sardines*) (2002) WTO Doc. WT/DS231/ AB/R (Appellate Body Report).

as a government organization, but not if merely set by a private body.[29] Finally it also covers procedures used to determine whether technical regulations or standards have been followed, such as any testing or inspection procedures.

A key question that arises because of the language of the TBT Agreement is whether it extends to cover non-product-related PPMs such as GHG emissions from the production of a product. There has been no panel or Appellate Body decision specifically dealing with this question. It is not clear what is meant by 'related' processes or production methods and how broadly this would be interpreted. There is a stronger argument for the application of labelling to non-product-related PPMs as the definition of 'technical regulations' specifies that technical regulations include 'labelling requirements as they apply to a product, process or production method'.[30]

If the TBT Agreement covers a subset of regulations that are also covered by GATT Article III, which provision will be used? Unfortunately the relationship remains somewhat unclear. The WTO Agreement specifies that, in the event of a conflict, the provisions of agreements such as the TBT Agreement prevail over those of the GATT. However, there is no 'safe harbour' providing that a measure that complies with the TBT Agreement is presumed to comply with GATT.[31] So far, WTO decisions have not helped in understanding this relationship beyond noting that the TBT Agreement 'imposes obligations on members that seem to be *different* from, and *additional* to, the obligations under the GATT 1994' (emphasis in original). Any regulatory measure that falls under both Agreements will probably have to comply with both sets of provisions.[32]

So what does the TBT Agreement require? The TBT Agreement has a national treatment provision that is very similar to that under the GATT.[33] This provision would probably be interpreted similarly to the

---

[29] Mattias Buck and Roda Verheyen, 'International Trade Law and Climate Change – A Positive Way Forward' (FES-Analyse Okologische Marktwirtschaft, Bonn: Friedrich Ebert Stiftung, July 2001).

[30] TBT Agreement, Annex 1. Marceau and Trachtman, *supra* note 17.

[31] Article 2.4 of the SPS Agreement states that 'sanitary or phytosanitary measures which conform to the relevant provisions of this Agreement shall be presumed to be in accordance with the obligations of the Members under the provisions of GATT 1994 which relate to the use of sanitary and phytosanitary measures, in particular the provisions of Article XX(b).'

[32] Buck and Verheyen, *supra* note 29.

[33] TBT Agreement, Article 2.1 states, 'Members shall ensure that in respect of technical regulations, products imported from the territory of any Member shall

national treatment provisions of GATT.[34] However, the fact that the TBT Agreement does not have an equivalent exceptions provision to Article XX may make panels less willing to read 'like' products as broadly.[35] The TBT Agreement does have a requirement that members ensure that technical regulations are 'not prepared, adopted or applied with a view to or with the effect of creating unnecessary obstacles to international trade' and not 'more trade-restrictive than necessary to fulfil a legitimate objective, taking account of the risks non-fulfilment would create'.[36] The TBT Agreement specifically lists protection of the environment as a legitimate objective. It therefore does not have an exception provision like Article XX but provides some scope for states to argue that a trade restrictive measure is not more trade restrictive than necessary to protect the environment.

More interesting are the other requirements under the TBT Agreement. First, the TBT Agreement attempts to find common ground in the use of technical regulations and standards. One way it does this is by emphasizing the use of international standards. If 'relevant' international standards exist or are imminent, Members must use them as a basis for their technical regulations unless the international standards 'would be an ineffective or inappropriate means for the fulfilment of the legitimate objectives pursued, for instance because of fundamental climatic or geographical factors or fundamental technological problems'.[37] The TBT Agreement then establishes a presumption that any regulation which is in accordance with an international standard does not create an unnecessary obstacle to trade.

The Appellate Body has taken a broad view of international standards such as, for example, by not requiring that standards be adopted by consensus.[38] As a result, while the TBT Agreement does shift countries towards international standards, it provides room for particular countries to adopt a standard. In terms of our discussion in Chapter 2, a group of countries (such as developed countries) could adopt a technical standard that favours their producers. The Appellate Body has counterbalanced this

---

be accorded treatment no less favourable than that accorded to like products of national origin and to like products originating in any other country.'

[34] The term 'like' in Article 2.1 has not been interpreted yet so it is not clear how broadly panels or the Appellate Body will read this provision.

[35] Marceau and Trachtman, *supra* note 17.

[36] TBT Agreement, Article 2.2.

[37] TBT Agreement, Article 2.4. The Appellate Body has taken a broad view of what counts as a 'relevant' international standard (that is, 'relevant' encompasses a wide range of standards) but then appears to only require a 'contradiction' between the international standard and the technical regulation for the standard not to be the basis of the regulation: *EC–Sardines AB Report, supra* note 28.

[38] *EC–Sardines,* ibid.

possibility to a certain extent by requiring that the complaining country must prove that the international standard is effective and appropriate.[39] The TBT Agreement further has some provisions that require developed countries to provide technical assistance to developing countries in relation to regulations and international standards.[40]

The TBT Agreement also attempts to find common ground by weakly requiring mutual recognition of technical regulations. It requires that members 'shall give positive consideration to accepting as equivalent technical regulations of other Members, even if these regulations differ from their own'.[41] The requirement is weak as the regulating country only needs to give 'positive consideration', and even then only is required to accept the other regulations as equivalent if 'they are satisfied that these regulations adequately fulfil the objectives of their own regulations'.[42]

Second, the TBT Agreement contains a number of provisions aimed at transparency in decision-making, including notification to other Members of proposed technical regulations not in accordance with international standards, a duty to provide other Members with an explanation of the justification for technical regulations, reasonable time for comments by other Members, consideration of these comments, and publication of regulations.[43] These procedural requirements may reduce the probability of an inadvertent discriminatory regulation as other countries can review and comment on the regulations in advance.[44] However, the usefulness of such procedural requirements depends on the ability and resources of other countries to monitor new technical regulations, which may not be realistic for developing countries. Procedural requirements may have additional benefits such as increasing the quality of regulatory decisions. The requirements may induce regulators to obtain more and better information (such as from their own populations) to justify the regulations and may expose rent-seeking to public scrutiny.[45] As a result, panels or the Appellate Body may be more willing to give regulating members the benefit of the doubt for any regulation that has complied with these requirements.[46]

---

[39]   *EC– Sardines*, ibid.
[40]   TBT Agreement, Article 11.
[41]   TBT Agreement, Article 2.7.
[42]   TBT Agreement, Article 2.7.
[43]   TBT Agreement, Article 2.
[44]   Robert Howse, 'Democracy, Science and Free Trade: Risk Regulation on Trial at the World Trade Organization' (2000) *University of Michigan Law Review* 2329.
[45]   Howse, ibid.
[46]   Howse and Tuerk, *supra* note 19.

5.4   WHO DECIDES WHETHER REGULATORY MEASURES ARE APPROPRIATE?

The structure of the WTO agreements and their interpretation by panels and the Appellate Body raise issues about who determines which particular regulatory measures are legitimate and which constitute cheating on trade commitments. Article III, for example, only prohibits discriminatory measures. If the measure does not discriminate against imports, panels and the Appellate Body do not have a role in opining on its wisdom. It is in the regulating government's discretion to decide the nature of the regulatory measure (including its efficiency and general trade impacts). This scope for policy decisions accords with the desire both for flexibility with respect to local costs and benefits and for legitimacy in making choices based on values. The TBT Agreement, however, eliminates this area protected from scrutiny. All measures that fall under the TBT Agreement are required to be least trade restrictive, as that term is framed in the Agreement (it is in this sense 'post-discriminatory' as Hudec termed it[47]). A broader range of measures is therefore subject to some form of WTO scrutiny.

The interpretation of Article III also determines who gets to decide whether the measure is a violation. The 'aims and effects' test places greater emphasis on the motives of the regulating body, at least as seen by panels or the Appellate Body. This approach seems to have been rejected in favour of a more purely economic test under which the market determines at least the relationship between the products and whether they move to the second 'less favourable treatment' test. The Appellate Body in *EC–Asbestos* has, however, broadened out the economic test to look to how consumers do, and possibly with perfect information would, view the products. Further, it has signalled that some regulatory differences are permissible and do not constitute 'less favourable treatment', provided imports as a whole are not disfavoured.

These latter determinations tend to create a measure of discretion for panels or the Appellate Body. They determine, for example, whether an idealized consumer would care about a difference in products or whether there is a difference in treatment in imports as a whole against a backdrop of the panel's or Appellate Body's views of the legitimacy of the measure.[48] These discretionary determinations seem to lack the transparency

---

[47]   Robert Hudec, 'Science and "Post-Discriminatory" WTO Law' (2003) 26 *Boston College International and Comparative Law Review* 185.

[48]   Marceau and Trachtman, *supra* note 17 at 855, note, for example, that in determining whether there is less favourable treatment, panels 'presumably

of GATT Article XX, which contains a more explicit balancing of trade and other interests. Moreover they raise legitimacy concerns as it is a WTO panel or the Appellate Body that is determining the values that it believes should prevail.

The TBT Agreement in some sense tries to back away from these issues. It places emphasis on a few markers of legitimacy or, at least, ways to avoid having to directly address these questions. It looks to the legitimacy of the process of making decisions, which pushes oversight or policing of cheating back to domestic processes and, to some extent, international pressure. It also adopts a preference for international standards that, it could be argued, are less likely to be purely protectionist (or at least protectionist for a particular country although not necessarily for a group of countries).

There may be a different answer to the issue of what measures are legitimate depending on whose preferences and interests count: individuals as consumers or citizens, the market (as it exists rather than with full information), domestic regulators, international bodies, or the WTO Dispute Settlement Body. The tensions that arise from differences across these decision-makers run through most of the discussion in the subsequent chapters. How they play out in terms of Article XX will be discussed more fully in Chapter 9. First, however, we turn to a discussion of other types of domestic measures, starting with taxes in the next chapter.

---

examine, explicitly or implicitly, whether the less favourable treatment is justified by an appropriate regulatory goal'.

6. Taxes

6.1 INTRODUCTION

As noted in Chapter 2, global warming reflects a market failure, largely due to there being no price on emitting GHGs into the atmosphere in most countries.[1] Many economists therefore argue that pricing GHG emissions is one of the most effective and efficient mechanisms for mitigating climate change. The rationale is that pricing will deliver both short-term gains through efficiency and long-term gains from investments in research and switching to cleaner fuels.[2] Pricing GHG emissions may be done through a cap-and-trade system (as discussed in Chapter 5) or via taxation. Despite their potentially positive role in climate change mitigation, taxes may also be misused as a protectionist tool. International trade disciplines are thus critical to ensure that taxes are not abused, particularly at the expense of developing countries.

This chapter briefly outlines the case for using taxes to address climate change and surveys the extent of their current and proposed use. It then examines the WTO non-discrimination rules governing Members' use of internal taxes. Understanding the case for taxes is important when considering these rules and the most appropriate institutional framework for handling disputes between countries over their use and implementation.

6.2 TAXES TO ADDRESS CLIMATE CHANGE

Like a cap-and-trade system, a tax is a market-based mechanism that aims to affect market behaviour through setting a price on emissions.[3] There is an important distinction between energy taxes, and emissions,

---

[1] Kevin L. Doran and Alaine Ginnochio, *United States Climate Policy: Using Market-Based Strategies to Achieve Greenhouse Gas Emission Reductions* (University of Colorado Law School, 2008) at 3.

[2] Ibid.

[3] Joseph E. Aldy, Eduardo Ley and Ian W.H. Parry, *A Tax-Based Approach to Slowing Global Climate Change* (Washington, DC: Resources for the Future, 2008) at 2.

carbon dioxide or carbon taxes.[4] The term *energy tax* is generally used to refer to a tax imposed on both fossil fuels and carbon-free energy sources, according to their energy (or heat) content, with renewables usually being exempted.[5] In contrast, a *carbon dioxide* (or *carbon*) *tax* is imposed according to carbon content, and is usually charged on each ton of carbon emitted into the air.[6] It is different from an energy tax, which, because it is levied on energy not carbon, is not designed to set a uniform price for carbon across different types of energy.[7] Finally, the term *emissions tax* is often used in the same sense as a carbon tax to refer to taxes imposed on emissions of carbon dioxide. Here we will refer to carbon taxes, noting the possibility that taxes might also be imposed on other GHGs, including methane (CH_4), nitrous oxide (N_2O), sulphur hexafluoride (SF_6), perfluorocarbons (PFCs) and hydrofluorocarbons (HFCs).[8] Taxes on

---

[4]   Such taxes fall under the umbrella category of 'environmental taxes', which may be broadly defined as encompassing compulsory payments to governments on tax bases that are deemed to be of particular environmental relevance. Organisation for Economic Co-operation and Development (OECD), *Environmentally Related Taxes in OECD Countries: Issues and Strategies* (Paris: OECD, 2001) at 15.

[5]   Zhong Xiang Zhang and Andrea Baranzini, 'What do we Know about Carbon Taxes? An Inquiry into their Impacts on Competitiveness and Distribution of Income' (2004) 32 *Energy Policy* 507 at 508. See also David G. Duff, *Tax Policy and Global Warming* (University of Toronto, Faculty of Law, Public Law and Legal Theory Research Paper No. 03-03 and Law and Economics Research Paper No. 03-04, 2003) at 34. Duff finds that often the distinctions between energy and carbon taxes are blurred by the fact that many countries tax both energy and carbon, by the availability of energy tax exemptions and rebates for energy from clean and renewable sources, and by the existence of reductions or rebates for energy-intensive industries.

[6]   A carbon tax can be translated into a CO_2 tax, as a tonne of carbon corresponds to 3.67 tonnes of CO_2. Zhang and Baranzini, ibid. See also Kevin L. Doran and Alaine Ginnochio, *United States Climate Policy: Using Market-Based Strategies to Achieve Greenhouse Gas Emission Reductions* (University of Colorado Law School, 2008) at 5.

[7]   Gilbert Metcalf and David Weisbach, *The Design of a Carbon Tax* (John M. Olin Law and Economics Working Paper No. 447 (2nd series), Public Law and Legal Theory Working Paper No. 254, The Law School, The University of Chicago, 2009) at 9.

[8]   These are the GHGs in respect of which Annex I Parties to the Kyoto Protocol are expected to effect reductions in emissions and which are included in the UNFCCC's reporting guidelines. Taxes could also potentially be used to target indirect GHGs, including carbon monoxide (CO), nitrogen oxides (NO_x), non-methane volatile organic compounds (NMVOCs), and sulphur oxides (SO_x). Climate Change Secretariat, *United Nations Framework Convention on Climate Change: Handbook* (Bonn, Germany: United Nations Framework Convention on Climate Change, 2006) at 184.

these GHGs would probably use an equivalent carbon dioxide warming potential.[9]

The leading source of anthropogenic GHG emissions in OECD countries is the combustion of fossil fuels for energy.[10] Accordingly, fossil fuels and energy consumption are the main targets of carbon taxes.[11] Taxes may be imposed either *upstream* or *downstream*.[12] An upstream carbon tax would focus on fossil fuel production (oil, coal, and natural gas), while a downstream carbon tax would be imposed on emissions further down the production chain by focusing on major sources of carbon dioxide emissions, such as motor vehicle use.[13] An upstream carbon tax involves taxing the input (fossil fuel) rather than the output (the emission).[14] Economists argue that an upstream carbon tax is the most comprehensive and straightforward approach.[15] It would encompass all possible sources of emissions when fuels are later combusted and would minimize collection and monitoring costs due to the fact that there are far fewer upstream producers than there are downstream consumers.[16]

---

[9]   Duff, *supra* note 5 at 1.
[10]   Ibid. at 23.
[11]   Ibid.
[12]   Reuven S. Avi-Yonah and David M. Uhlmann, *Combating Global Climate Change: Why a Carbon Tax is a Better Response to Global Warming than Cap and Trade* (Ann Arbor: University of Michigan Law School, Public Law and Legal Theory Working Paper Series, 2008) at 32.
[13]   Ibid. See also Metcalf and Weisbach *supra* note 7 at 25.
[14]   Metcalf and Weisbach, ibid. at 23. It should be noted that taxing the input rather than the output does not necessarily affect who bears the burden of the tax. Ultimately, the burden of the tax will be borne by consumers if supply is elastic and demand inelastic. Taxes on inputs will result in lower prices received by fossil fuel producers and higher prices paid by consumers, depending on elasticities.
[15]   Ian W.H. Parry and William A. Pizer, 'Combating Global Warming' (2007) 30 (3) *Regulation* 18 at 19. See also Metcalf and Weisbach, ibid.
[16]   Avi-Yonah and Uhlmann, *supra* note 12 at 33. Metcalf and Weisbach, *supra* note 7 at 23. Metcalf and Weisbach outline various options for implementation of an upstream carbon tax in the US. For natural gas, they suggest that a convenient tax collection point would be the natural gas processor. Natural gas is wet when extracted and must be dried before it is put in the pipeline system. There are approximately 530 natural gas processors in the lower 48 states, which process almost 100% of natural gas used in the US. This compares with almost 450 000 natural gas wells in the US of which 100 000 would need to be taxed to get 90% coverage of US production. Thus taxing at the processing point is more convenient. Metcalf and Weisbach would add to this tax base the 55 locations where natural gas is imported from Canada (five liquefied natural gas facilities and 50 pipelines). For coal, they suggest taxing at the mine as this would encompass 1 438 operating mines and capture nearly all US coal production. Finally, for petroleum, they suggest taxing at the refinery, given that in 2007 there were only 149 operating

A carbon tax is widely considered by economists to be one of the most cost-effective ways to stabilize and reduce GHG emissions.[17] This is because carbon is a good proxy for carbon dioxide emissions, and taxes on carbon encourage both energy efficiency and the substitution of low-carbon fuels for high-carbon fuels.[18] The idea is that taxes result in higher energy prices, which encourage adoption of fuel- and energy-saving technologies across the economy and promote switching from carbon-intensive fuels like coal to less carbon-intensive fuels.[19] A key aspect of any carbon tax is that it covers as much of the total emission inventory as possible, hence the attraction of an upstream approach.[20]

In particular, economists widely consider a carbon tax to be a superior method when compared with non-market-based mechanisms such as regulatory and voluntary approaches.[21] Market-based mechanisms allow the costs of carbon dioxide emission reductions to be distributed more evenly across the economy.[22] They also have the ability to realize static and dynamic efficiencies. Dynamic efficiency is achieved through the tax providing an incentive to emitters to undertake ongoing emissions-reducing innovation. Static efficiency is delivered through the cost-effectiveness of the tax, which is achieved primarily through emitters seeking out cheap methods of abatement.[23] Cost-effectiveness may also be achieved through administration and compliance costs that are generally lower than under most alternative instruments, at least where the tax is applied upstream to

---

refineries in the US compared with 247 million drivers as well as millions of users of other petroleum distillates. They suggest that refineries could pay a separate tax on each distillate depending on the carbon content. Imports of crude and refined products would be subject to the tax at the refinery.

[17] Duff, *supra* note 5 at 34.

[18] Ibid.

[19] Parry and Pizer, *supra* note 15 at 20.

[20] Kevin L. Doran and Alaine Ginnochio, *United States Climate Policy: Using Market-Based Strategies to Achieve Greenhouse Gas Emission Reductions* (University of Colorado Law School, 2008) at 3.

[21] Duff, *supra* note 5 at 11. Referring to, *inter alia*, OECD, *Environmentally Related Taxes in OECD Countries: Issues and Strategies* (Paris: OECD, 2001) at 14 and 22. See also Joseph E. Aldy, Eduardo Ley and Ian W.H. Parry, *A Tax-Based Approach to Slowing Global Climate Change* (Washington, DC: Resources for the Future, 2008) at 2.

[22] Avi-Yonah and Uhlmann, *supra* note 12 at 32.

[23] Romain Duval, *A Taxonomy of Instruments to Reduce Greenhouse Gas Emissions and Their Interactions* (Paris: Organization for Economic Co-operation and Development, Economics Department Working Paper No. 636, ECO/WKP(2008)44, 2008) at 9.

the wholesale use of fossil fuels.[24] Regulations, on the other hand, tend to impose a single set of standards on different economic actors and create little or no incentive to achieve further improvements beyond stipulated requirements.[25]

There is some debate as to the merits of a carbon tax versus a cap-and-trade system, with economists citing several advantages for a tax. Most significantly, a carbon tax ensures cost certainty and therefore provides a stable price signal to investors. However, this comes at the price of uncertainty about total emissions as emitters have flexibility to choose to pay the tax or to reduce their emissions.[26] While a tax may lead to reductions beyond the target, in order to be sure of reaching any given mitigation target, a tax would need to be revised on a regular basis in view of environmental outcomes; if the tax 'overcorrected' and produced greater than anticipated reductions, it could be decreased, and vice versa. In order, however, to maintain the certainty of the tax, revisions should be infrequent and subject to rules and constraints. Thus, a key challenge for countries designing a tax is to do so in such a way that its future changes in response to environmental outcomes and mitigation costs remain sufficiently predictable to limit possible detrimental effects on research and development and technology adoption incentives.[27] Given that a carbon tax will not guarantee emission levels at or below a desired target in all cases, Doran and Ginnochio argue that its appropriateness is limited to situations where it is acceptable to allow the stock of GHGs to grow in the interim, where there is some room to rearrange emissions over time, and where a short-term quantity control on emissions is unnecessary.[28] Arguably, however, climate change is the ideal context for a tax because

---

[24] Ibid. at 10. Duval notes, however, that cost-effectiveness may be undermined by several factors, including high costs of monitoring certain emission sources, failure to address information failures, other policies that distort the tax's substitution incentives (including fiscal incentives to energy production/use and agricultural subsidies), and the fact that public or quasi-public enterprises may not face strong incentives to respond adequately to the tax, partly due to objectives other than profit maximization and softer budget constraints than in the private sector.

[25] Duff, *supra* note 5 at 10.

[26] Duval, *supra* note 23 at 12. See also National Round Table on the Economy and the Environment (NRTEE), *Getting to 2050: Canada's Transition to a Low-emission Future* (Ottawa: NRTEE, 2007) at 22.

[27] Avi-Yonah and Uhlmann, *supra* note 12 at 33.

[28] Kevin L. Doran and Alaine Ginnochio, *United States Climate Policy: Using Market-Based Strategies to Achieve Greenhouse Gas Emission Reductions* (University of Colorado Law School, 2008) at 6.

the only concern is to reduce the stock of carbon in the atmosphere, rather than being to control where it is discharged (as opposed to a traditional air pollutant where the desire is to control the amount of the pollutant in populated areas). Each country is responsible for only a portion of the global stock of carbon and so it does not matter when or how it is emitted; the only concern is to reduce the total contribution over time.

Second, a carbon tax has the potential to be simpler, particularly if imposed upstream. A cap-and-trade system, on the other hand, has various complexities, including how allowances will be created and distributed (whether for free or by auction), the design of a system to manage and supervise trading, prevention of cost uncertainty through banking and borrowing allowances, and offsets for projects such as carbon sequestration.[29]

Third, a carbon tax generates revenue that may be used to assist in mitigating GHG reductions, for example, by supporting carbon sequestration projects and other projects that reduce GHG emissions, such as development of public transit.[30] Using revenue in this manner may help reduce uncertainty about emission reductions.[31] It may also be used to finance income or other tax reductions to ensure a revenue-neutral tax.[32] A cap-and-trade system may also be used to generate revenue if all the allowances are auctioned rather than being distributed for free. However, in reality, schemes adopted or proposed to date give out at least some allowances for free.[33]

The optimal tax rate for a carbon tax is a matter of debate among economists. Estimates of the optimal tax per tonne of carbon have ranged from $3 to $95 per tonne.[34] It is difficult to calculate the rate because it involves combining uncertain science, such as predicting the local effects of climate change, with predictions of economics and technological developments far in the future, and discounting those values to the present.[35]

Proposals for the introduction of carbon taxes are vulnerable to domestic political opposition.[36] The loudest objection comes from industries

---

[29] Avi-Yonah and Uhlmann, *supra* note 12 at 40.
[30] Ibid. at 42.
[31] Ibid.
[32] Parry and Pizer, *supra* note 15 at 20. See also Gilbert E. Metcalf, *A Green Employment Tax Swap: Using a Carbon Tax to Finance Payroll Tax Relief* (Washington, DC: The Brookings Institution, The World Resources Institute, 2007).
[33] Avi-Yonah and Uhlmann, *supra* note 12 at 42.
[34] Metcalf and Weisbach, *supra* note 7 at 12.
[35] Ibid.
[36] Taxes attract opposition given that the costs they impose are highly

who fear negative implications for their international competitiveness.[37] One possible outcome of such opposition is that governments implementing a carbon tax will be pressured to enact exemptions for affected industries, which will weaken the effectiveness of the tax and increase its complexity.[38] Exemptions also raise the spectre of protectionism, as do other efforts to appease domestic interests such as applying taxes unevenly across domestic and foreign products. However, tax regimes tend to be more transparent in nature than cap-and-trade schemes, which can be overly complex, and it may be easier to detect inconsistencies in the application of exemptions and to ascertain where this amounts to protectionism.

Despite political opposition, carbon taxes have – in combination with energy taxes – been implemented in various countries. Finland, Denmark, Norway and Sweden introduced carbon taxes in the 1990s.[39] These countries' taxes tend to have very narrow bases, and do not impose a uniform rate on emissions from covered sources. Further, the impact of the taxes has reportedly been weakened by exemptions granted to energy-intensive industries.[40] For example, in Sweden, industry only pays about 50 per cent of the tax, while the commercial horticulture, mining, manufacturing, and pulp and paper sectors are all exempt from the tax.[41] The UK implemented the Climate Change Levy (CCL) in 2001.[42] It is a

---

transparent, occur immediately, and are concentrated on relatively well-organized groups. However, the benefits accrue to no clearly identifiable agent, are widely dispersed, and are reaped only in the future. Political economy literature suggests that, in the absence of any political constituency with a strong interest in maintaining the tax, affected groups will be in a position to lobby successfully against the tax. Such opposition may be mitigated through partial redistribution of the tax revenues to affected industries. Duval, *supra* note 23 at 12.

[37] These potential implications are discussed in detail in Chapter 8 which deals with border tax adjustments.

[38] Avi-Yonah and Uhlmann, *supra* note 12 at 50, noting that an upstream carbon tax would minimize the opportunity for pressure to be placed on governments to receive exemptions, seeing as only three industries (coal, oil, and natural gas) would be affected.

[39] Metcalf and Weisbach, *supra* note 7 at 10.

[40] Simonetta Zarrilli, 'Domestic Taxation of Energy Products and Multilateral Trade Rules: Is This a Case of Unlawful Discrimination?' (2003) 37 (2) *Journal of World Trade* 359 at 365. Citing IEA, 'An Overview of Green Tax Reform and Environmentally Related Taxes in OECD Countries' (IAE, First Quarter 2002).

[41] T. Tietenberg, 'Can Eco-taxation be Effective in Reducing Carbon Emissions?' Online at: www.colby.edu/personal/t/thtieten/eco-taxation.htm (date accessed: 6 November 2009).

[42] Finance Act 2000, section 30 and Schedules 6 and 7.

revenue-neutral tax on the use of energy in industry, commerce, and the public sector. There are various exemptions, including for use in the domestic, transport, charitable and small business sectors. As well, energy-intensive sectors were able to negotiate an 80 per cent discount by agreeing to targets for improving energy efficiency or reducing carbon dioxide emissions.[43] In France, a carbon tax of $US25 per tonne applies to the consumption of petrol, gas and coal (but not electricity) and is designed to be fiscally neutral. Exemptions apply to heavy industry (on the grounds that it is covered by Europe's cap-and-trade scheme), and the fishing and agriculture sectors. Energy taxes in Europe include those on vehicles that exceed certain threshold levels of carbon dioxide emissions. In France, for example, consumers pay a tax on the purchase of a car when its emissions exceed 160gms of carbon dioxide per kilometre, while in Ireland the registration tax is based on carbon dioxide emission levels.[44]

In Canada, the province of British Columbia introduced a carbon tax in July 2008 that imposes a uniform rate on carbon across different fossil fuels.[45] The tax is broad-based, meaning that it applies to nearly all fossil fuels, including gasoline, diesel, natural gas, coal, propane, and home-heating fuel.[46] There is an exemption for emissions that will be 'dealt with under other climate action policies in the future and for efficient administration'.[47] This appears to include emissions from large industrial emitters, who would be captured under a planned emissions trading scheme. Quebec also introduced a carbon tax in 2007. It applies to all oil and gas companies on all non-renewable fuels sold in bulk to retailers.[48]

While OECD countries have not widely applied taxes to GHGs other than carbon, Duff identifies two types of taxes that have been used in

[43]   See details at Department of Energy and Climate Change, online at: http://www.decc.gov.uk/en/content/cms/what_we_do/change_energy/tackling_clima/ccas/ccas.aspx (date accessed: 6 November 2009).

[44]   See European Automobile Manufacturers' Association, 'Overview of CO_2 Based Motor Vehicle Taxes in the EU', 22 February 2008, available online at: www.acea.be (date accessed: 6 November 2009).

[45]   Government of British Columbia, *Balanced Budget 2008, Backgrounder: BC's Revenue-Neutral Carbon Tax* (Victoria, 2008). Available online at: http://www.bcbudget.gov.bc.ca/2008/backgrounders/backgrounder_carbon_tax.htm (date accessed: 6 November 2009).

[46]   Ibid.

[47]   British Columbia Ministry of Finance, *Budget and Fiscal Plan 2008/09–2010/11* (19 February 2008), available at: http://www.bcbudget.gov.bc.ca/2008/bfp/2008_Budget_Fiscal_Plan.pdf (date accessed: 16 June 2008), at p. 12.

[48]   *Regulation Respecting the Annual Duty Payable to the Green Fund*, R.Q. c. R-6.01, available online at: http://canlii.org/qc/laws/sta/r-6.01/20080515/whole.html (date accessed: 16 June 2008).

Europe, namely taxes on synthetic fertilizers (the production and application of which release nitrous oxides) and taxes on packaging and solid
wastes deposited at landfills (the most significant anthropogenic sources
of methane).[49]

There appears to be broad consensus among economists that a carbon
tax would be most effective either where it was imposed on a global basis
or where domestic taxes were fully harmonized. Such a tax would 'be
expected to induce all emitters to equalize marginal abatement costs to
the level of the tax, thereby ensuring that the cheaper abatement options
are fully exhausted'.[50] However, the political barriers to achieving such
consensus are formidable. In the absence of a global or fully harmonized
tax, WTO rules will come into play to protect against protectionist use of
tax measures. We examine the key provisions and their application in the
next section.

6.3   TAXES AND NON-DISCRIMINATION

The WTO framework for taxes is similar to that for regulatory measures
as discussed in Chapter 5, but differs in important respects. As with regulatory measures, the key constraint on the imposition of carbon taxes is
GATT Article III (national treatment). Article III.1 sets out the broad
purpose of the provision, recording the contracting parties' recognition
that measures (including internal taxes and other charges) affecting the
internal sale, offering for sale, purchase, transportation, distribution or
use of products should not be applied to imported products 'so as to afford
protection' to domestic production. Article III.2 makes specific provision
for the application of the national treatment principle to taxes. It does
so by creating two separate tests, one stated in the first sentence, and the
other stated in the second sentence. Article III.2 reads:

> The products of the territory of any contracting party imported into the terri-
> tory of any other contracting party shall not be subject, directly or indirectly, to
> internal taxes or other internal charges of any kind in excess of those applied,
> directly or indirectly, to like domestic products. Moreover, no contracting

---

[49]   Duff, *supra* note 5 at 38. The WTO/UNEP Report also notes that Norway
taxes the import and production of hydrofluorocarbons (HFCs) and perfluorocarbons (PFCs), while Denmark taxes HFCs, PFCs, and sulphur hexafluoride (SF_6).
Ludivine Tamiotti et al., *Trade and Climate Change*: A Report by the United
Nations Environment Programme and the World Trade Organization, (Geneva:
WTO, 2009) at 91.
[50]   Duval, *supra* note 23 at 9.

party shall otherwise apply internal taxes or other internal charges to imported or domestic products in a manner contrary to the principles set forth in paragraph 1.

Article III.2 is accompanied by a supplementary provision, Interpretative Note, Ad Article III. Paragraph 2 of Ad Article III states that

> a tax conforming to the requirements of the first sentence of paragraph 2 would be considered inconsistent with the provisions of the second sentence only in cases where competition was involved between, on the one hand, the taxed product and, on the other hand, a directly competitive or substitutable product which was not similarly taxed.

There are thus two crucial differences between the first and second sentences of Article III.2. The first difference is that, pursuant to the first sentence, there can only be a violation of the national treatment rule where the taxes in question are applied to *like* imported and domestic products. Under the second sentence, however, there may be a violation where the imported and domestic products are merely *directly competitive or substitutable.*

The second difference is that with respect to the first sentence there is no *de minimis* requirement, meaning that even a negligible difference between the taxes imposed on like imported and domestic products is too high and will result in a finding of a violation. However, the second sentence, which applies to directly competitive or substitutable products, provides that a violation of national treatment may only be found where the products in question are 'not similarly taxed'. Accordingly, some limited differences in taxation may be acceptable where the products are found to be directly competitive or substitutable under Article III.2, second sentence.[51]

6.3.1   Article III.2, First Sentence

The two issues to be addressed under Article III.2 first sentence are, first, whether the imported and domestic products subject to the tax are 'like' and, second, whether the imported product is taxed 'in excess' of the domestic product.

'Like' products

The GATT does not define the term 'like products' in the context of Article III.2 and, as with regulatory measures, its meaning has given rise

---

[51]   *Japan – Taxes on Alcoholic Beverages* (1996) WTO Doc. WT/DS8/AB/R, WT/DS10/AB/R, WT/DS11/AB/R (Appellate Body Report) section H(2)(b) at p. 28.

to considerable dispute. There has been general agreement in the cases, however, that likeness should be determined on a case-by-case basis using four criteria: the products' end-uses in a given market; the products' properties, nature, and quality (including a requirement that the products should share the same physical characteristics); consumers' tastes and habits in a particular country; and tariff classification.[52] Further, the Appellate Body has accepted that interpretation of 'like' involves 'an unavoidable element of individual discretionary judgment'.[53]

While these criteria are the same as those laid out for regulatory measures pursuant to Article III.4, the word 'like' has been interpreted in a less permissive manner in the context of taxes under Article III.2, first sentence than it has for regulatory measures under Article III.4. In *Japan – Taxes on Alcoholic Beverages*, the Appellate Body found that in interpreting Article III.2 the two separate obligations in the first and second sentences must be interpreted in a harmonious manner that gives meaning to both sentences. It noted that 'the second sentence of Article III.2 provides for a separate and distinctive consideration of the protective aspect of a measure in examining its application to a broader category of products that are not "like products" as contemplated by the first sentence'.[54] Thus, it considered that likeness in Article III.2, first sentence should be construed narrowly.[55] This ensures that scope is left for application of the second sentence (products that are 'directly competitive or substitutable').

Given that a determination of likeness must be made on a case-by-case basis and that every set of products to be compared will have different characteristics, it is impossible to draw any generalized conclusions about the likeness test in the context of carbon taxes. We will, however, comment on two stylized examples: first, an *upstream* carbon tax imposed

---

[52] Ibid. at section H(1)(a). The first three of these criteria were articulated by the 1970 GATT Working Party Report on Border Tax Adjustments: BSID 18S/97, adopted on 2 December 1970, para. 18. The Appellate Body in *Japan – Alcoholic Beverages* noted that the final criterion, tariff classification, had been referred to in: *EEC – Measures on Animal Feed Proteins* B.I.S.D. (25th Supp.) 49 (1979) (adopted 14 March 1978) at para. 4.2; *Japan – Customs Duties, Taxes and Labelling Practices on Imported Wines and Alcoholic Beverages* B.I.S.D. (34th Suppl.) 83 (1988) (adopted 10 November 1987) at para. 5.6; and *United States – Standards for Reformulated and Conventional Gasoline* (1996) WTO Doc. WT/DS2/R (Panel Report) at para. 6.8.

[53] *Japan – Alcoholic Beverages AB Report*, *supra* note 51 at section H(1)(a).

[54] Ibid. The Appellate Body affirmed this interpretation in *European Communities – Measures Affecting Asbestos and Asbestos-Containing Products* (2000), WTO Doc. WT/DS135/AB/R (Appellate Body Report) at para. 95.

[55] Ibid.

by country A on petroleum at the refinery and at the border upon importation; second, a *downstream* carbon tax on cars based on their levels of
carbon dioxide emissions (gms of carbon dioxide emitted per km).

Regarding country A's upstream carbon tax, let us assume that country
B complains that its gasoline exports to country A are being subjected
to a carbon tax, while algae biofuel produced in country A is free of any
taxes, thus giving it a competitive advantage in country A's transportation market.[56] Any complaint by country B would require determination
as to whether gasoline is 'like' algae biofuel. The physical characteristics
of the two are quite distinct; one is petroleum-based, while the other is
algae- (or plant-) based. Gasoline consists of a mixture of hydrocarbons
and its use causes carbon dioxide emissions. Algae biofuel, on the other
hand, consists of chemically modified natural oil and, rather than emitting carbon dioxide, algae actually pulls carbon dioxide from the air
during its growth process.[57] On the other hand, the products' end-uses are
very similar, in particular their use as transportation fuels. Tariff classification would depend on the particular countries in question. Consumer
tastes and habits would depend on the particular facts; however, it is
quite possible that – given the publicity and concern surrounding climate
change – consumers would view the two products as distinct due to their
different carbon profiles. In the light of the extremely different physical
characteristics and probably consumer preferences, it is likely that gasoline and algae biofuel would be considered unlike under Article III.2, first
sentence.

Regarding country A's downstream carbon tax on cars based on levels
of carbon dioxide emissions, slightly different considerations would arise.
Let us assume a complaint by country B that its cars are being burdened
with a higher tax rate on importation into country A than similar models
of cars made domestically in country A. Let us assume further that the
cars in question have similar engine sizes, fit within the same category
(hatchback), share the same basic properties and quality, but, differ on
their carbon dioxide emission levels. Country A's cars average emissions
of 95gm/km, while country B's cars average emissions of over 150gm/
km. The question facing a panel in this scenario would be whether the
differing emission levels would be sufficient to render the cars 'unlike'.

---

[56] Algae biofuel is still in the early phases of development; however, this
example assumes commercial exploitation.

[57] For general information on algae biofuel, see John Sheehan et al., *A Look
Back at the U.S. Department of Energy's Aquatic Species Program: Biodiesel from
Algae, Close-Out Report* (Golden, CO: National Renewable Energy Laboratory,
1998).

Even if emission levels were not considered to form part of the physical characteristics of the cars, consumers' preferences would come into play as discussed in relation to the 'upstream' tax example. Given the narrow construction of likeness adopted by the Appellate Body to date, it is quite possible that consumers' preferences may not be sufficient to render otherwise 'like' cars 'unlike' unless they were quite clearly evidenced in some manner. Clearly the nuances of the facts in any given case will be critical to the outcome.

These are highly simplified cases that illustrate the key tenets of Article III.2. In any case where a determination of likeness is required, panels will be asked to make difficult judgments and there will inevitably be uncertainty regarding outcomes. However, given that there is an almost infinite range of goods that may come under scrutiny, it would be virtually impossible to identify any kind of predetermined set of like goods. Nevertheless, the goals of the trade and climate change regimes demand that panels and the Appellate Body be effective in sifting out genuine environmental taxes from attempts at protectionism. This will require them to take into account criteria that reflect the relative environmental impact of the products in question. Information problems may occur in this regard where the environmental impact of products is not fully known. Further, problems may occur in comparing products – what difference in emissions between two products is sufficient to render them unlike? How much consumer recognition of environmental concerns is required to distinguish between products? In addition, as with the determination of a violation of Article III.4, one of the more intractable problems will be that of process and production methods (PPMs). As discussed in Chapter 5, some recognition of PPMs in the likeness determination will be necessary to enable countries to fully take into account the environmental impact of products when imposing taxes. However, the scope for protectionism will increase the less information is known about the relative impact. The discussion of PPMs in the regulation context in Chapter 5 is therefore equally relevant and important to the case of taxes.

Taxes 'in excess of' those applied to like domestic products

If imported and domestic products are found to be like, the second element of the first test – that imports cannot be taxed 'in excess of' domestic products – is relatively easy to determine. The Appellate Body has held that 'even the smallest amount in excess is too much', including where the trade effects of the tax, such as trade volumes, are non-existent.[58] Thus, it is

---

advantageous for a complaining party to argue that products are like since once this hurdle is crossed the remainder of the test is so easy to satisfy. This highlights the importance of the task facing panels in determining likeness. If they afford a narrow interpretation to the term, they give more flexibility to importing countries in their climate change taxation policies. A broad interpretation lessens that flexibility.

6.3.2 Article III.2, Second Sentence

Article III.2, second sentence may provide relief for a complaining Member where it is unable to show that the domestic and imported products in question are like. Three elements must be present for a Member to prove a violation of the second sentence: (i) the two products must be 'directly competitive or substitutable'; (ii) the two products must not be 'similarly taxed'; and (iii) the dissimilar tax must operate 'so as to afford protection' to the domestic product.

'Directly competitive or substitutable' products
As with the term 'like' products, the GATT contains no precise definition of the phrase 'directly competitive or substitutable', meaning a case-by-case analysis is necessary. It will encompass a broader category of products than 'like' products. As the Appellate Body has observed, while all goods that are 'like' are *a fortiori* directly competitive or substitutable, the converse is not true, that is, directly competitive or substitutable products are not necessarily 'like' each other.[59]

Decisions concerning Article III.2 to date have adopted a much more explicitly economic approach than in the test for 'like' goods. In *Japan – Taxes on Alcoholic Beverages* the Appellate Body agreed with the Panel, which had emphasized the need to look not only at physical characteristics, common end-uses, and tariff classifications but also at the 'marketplace'. Further, it endorsed the Panel's legal analysis, which included the approach of examining elasticity of substitution as one means of examining competition in the relevant markets.[60] That is, the more sensitive demand for one product is to changes in the price of the other product, all other things being equal, the more directly competitive they are.[61] The Panel also suggested that factors like marketing strategies could also be

[59] *Korea – Taxes on Alcoholic Beverages* (1999), WTO Doc. WT/DS75/AB/R, WT/DS84/AB/R (Appellate Body Report) at para. 118.
[60] *Japan – Alcoholic Beverages, supra* note 51 at section H(1)(b).
[61] *Japan – Taxes on Alcoholic Beverages* (1996), WTO Doc. WT/DS8/R, WT/DS10/R, WT/DS11/R (Panel Report) at para. 6.31.

relevant, since what is at issue is the responsiveness of consumers to the various products offered in the market.[62]

In *Korea – Taxes on Alcoholic Products* the Appellate Body accepted the relevance of cross-price elasticity of demand but noted that it is not exclusive or even decisive in nature.[63] The Panel had noted that end-use was particularly relevant to assessing competition or substitutability but also added pricing and channels of distribution to the list of factors that may be examined in making a determination of 'directly competitive or substitutable'.[64] The Appellate Body was not asked to review these criteria, but did consider Korea's argument that the Panel erred in holding that the competitive relationship does not need to be analysed exclusively in the light of current consumer preferences. The Appellate Body rejected this static view of the term 'competitive or substitutable'. It held that evidence of trends and changes in consumption patterns were relevant and, further, that the requisite competitive relationship '*may* exist between products that are not, at a given moment, considered by consumers to be substitutes but which are, nonetheless, *capable* of being substituted for one another.'[65]

The Appellate Body held in *Korea – Taxes on Alcoholic Beverages* that there may well be latent demand for a product and that this must be examined in assessing whether products are directly competitive or substitutable.[66] Latent demand may exist for various reasons including where there are regulatory barriers to trade or to competition, such as a discriminatory taxation system that has had the consequence of creating and even freezing preferences for domestic goods.[67] The Appellate Body held further that products are competitive or substitutable when they are interchangeable or, less demandingly, if they offer 'alternative ways of satisfying a particular need or taste'.[68] The Appellate Body did, however, stress the requirement that the word 'directly' infers a degree of proximity in the competitive relationship between the domestic and imported products.[69]

---

[62]   Ibid. at para. 6.28.
[63]   *Korea – Alcoholic Beverages, supra* note 59 at 109.
[64]   *Korea – Taxes on Alcoholic Beverages* (1999), WTO Doc. WT/DS75/R, WT/DS84/R (Panel Report), at 10.43 and 10.78.
[65]   *Korea – Alcoholic Beverages, supra* note 59 at 114 (emphasis in original).
[66]   Ibid. at 115.
[67]   *Japan – Alcoholic Beverages, supra* note 61 at para. 6.28.
[68]   *Korea – Alcoholic Beverages, supra* note 59 at para. 115. On the interpretation of 'alternative ways' cf. 'interchangeability', see Raj Bhala, *Modern GATT Law: A Treatise on the General Agreement on Tariffs and Trade* (London: Sweet & Maxwell, 2005) at 41.
[69]   *Korea – Alcoholic Beverages, supra* note 59 at para. 116.

In another case several months after the Appellate Body report was adopted in *Korea – Taxes on Alcoholic Beverages*, a panel was called upon to rule in a similar dispute between Chile and the EC. In this case, the Panel stated that products do not have to be substitutable for all purposes at all times to be considered competitive. Rather, 'it is sufficient that there is a pattern that they may be substituted for some purposes at some times by some consumers'.[70]

In *Chile – Taxes on Alcoholic Beverages*, the Panel introduced the notion advanced by consumer theory that, from a consumer's perspective, goods are not really perceived as commodities that are in themselves direct objects of utility. Rather, it is the properties or characteristics of the goods from which utility is derived, and these are the relevant considerations. The Panel noted that goods 'may share a common characteristic but have other characteristics that are qualitatively different, or may have the same characteristics but in quantitatively different combinations. Substitution possibilities arise because of these shared characteristics.'[71] The Panel used the textbook example of butter and milk being dairy products that share important characteristics that margarine does not have. However, butter and margarine each have combinations of characteristics that make them good substitutes as complements for bread, which is not the case with milk. These characteristics are physical properties such as spreadability, taste, colour, and consistency.

Taking our stylized examples provided above, let us assume that a finding has been made that the products in question are not like; that is, algae biofuel is not like gasoline, and a car with a carbon dioxide emission level of over 200gm/km is not like a car with a level of only 95gm/km. The question now arises as to whether these products are 'directly competitive or substitutable'. First, regarding the upstream tax on fuels, having established that algae biofuel and gasoline are physically quite distinct but have similar end-uses, the attention would turn under an Article III.2, second sentence investigation to elasticity of substitution, and, pursuant to *Korea – Taxes on Alcoholic Beverages*, whether the products are capable of being substituted for one another. Assuming that our scenario arises once algae biofuel has been developed for the commercial market and is capable of fuelling the same private cars as gasoline (that is, consumers can choose at the pump which to purchase), then it may well be found competitive or directly substitutable for gasoline. That is, the products

---

[70]   *Chile – Taxes on Alcoholic Beverages* (1999) WTO Doc. WT/DS87/R, WT/DS110/R (Panel Report), at para. 7.43.
[71]   Ibid. at para. 7.82.

share characteristics that make them substitutable, namely, their combustibility. If, however, some kind of converter would be required to utilize the algae biofuel, or only certain cars could run on it, then the products may not be found capable of substitution. Thus, much will depend on the factual evidence available.

Second, regarding the downstream tax on cars, again much will turn on evidence of consumers' preferences and elasticity of substitution. From a practical standpoint, any two hatchback cars can serve the same function and therefore be practically substitutable for each other. However, whether or not consumers regard the cars in this manner is another question to be determined. In both scenarios, panels will have discretion in determining the extent of substitutability – the more willing they are to find that products are substitutable, the less room for importing countries to experiment with climate change taxes on different products. The inevitable discretion of panels in making judgment calls will thus have significant practical effects on domestic regulatory decision-making.

'Not similarly taxed'
The second element to prove a violation of Article III.2, second sentence is that the products must be shown to be 'not similarly taxed'. Unlike Article III.2, first sentence, where even a small difference is sufficient to form the basis of a violation, here the tax differential must be more than trivial to be 'not similar'. The rationale for this interpretation appears to be that a complainant's burden ought to be easier if the complainant has already passed the more difficult test of proving products are like, whereas their burden ought to be harder if all they can do is show products are competitive or substitutable.[72]

Panels will act on a case-by-case basis to determine whether taxes meet the test of being 'not similarly taxed'.[73] This case-by-case approach leaves some uncertainty around when a tax is too much, yet it would be difficult to draw a bright line and set a certain percentage value of what that level would be. In assessing whether domestic and imported products are similarly taxed, reference is made not only to the tax rates themselves but also to other aspects of the tax, such as the methods of calculation. Thus, an imported product with a different taxation level from the domestic product may be considered 'similarly taxed' where it results from the same method of calculation (for example, by carbon content). In *Japan – Taxes*

---

[72] Raj Bhala, *Modern GATT Law: A Treatise on the General Agreement on Tariffs and Trade* (London: Sweet & Maxwell, 2005) at 119.
[73] *Japan – Alcoholic Beverages, supra* note 51 at section H(2)(c).

on Alcoholic Beverages, the Panel used a number of indicators to help determine whether the products in dispute were similarly taxed, including tax per litre of product, tax per degree of alcohol, *ad valorem* taxation, and the tax/price ratio.[74]

'So as to afford protection'

The final element required to prove a violation of Article III.2, second sentence is that the tax measure must have been applied 'so as to afford protection'. The critical issue in making such a determination is how the tax measure is actually applied and what are its effects. That is, does it actually afford protection to domestic producers? It does not matter what the intended objective of the measure was and so the decision does not involve examining the aims or actual intent of the regulating body.[75] Also, the Appellate Body has confirmed that the objective of Article III is to protect competitive relationships between products, and not to protect expectations of trade volumes.[76] In other words, the mere exposure of a product to a risk of discrimination is itself a form of discrimination; it is not necessary to show a decrease in the quantity of exports. This approach gives countries imposing taxes some degree of certainty in their decision-making as they should be capable in most cases of determining at the time of imposing the tax whether or not the competitive relationship between imported and domestic products is likely to be affected to the detriment of the imports.

In *Japan – Taxes on Alcoholic Beverages*, the Appellate Body stated the need for a 'comprehensive and objective analysis of the structure and application of the measure in question on domestic as compared to imported products'. It further required an objective examination of 'the underlying criteria used in a particular tax measure, its structure and its overall application to ascertain whether it is applied in a way that affords protection to domestic products'.[77] Noting that the aim of a measure may not be easily ascertained, the Appellate Body suggested that, nonetheless, 'its protective application can most often be discerned from the design, the architecture, and the revealing structure of a measure'.[78]

In *Korea – Taxes on Alcoholic Beverages*, the Appellate Body emphasized that even though the tax differential may prove that a tax is applied 'so as to afford protection', other factors may also be relevant

---

[74]   *Japan – Alcoholic Beverages, supra* note 61 at para. 6.33.
[75]   *Japan – Alcoholic Beverages, supra* note 51 at section H(2)(c).
[76]   Ibid. *Korea – Alcoholic Beverages, supra* note 59 at para. 119.
[77]   *Japan – Alcoholic Beverages, supra* note 51 at section H(2)(c).
[78]   Ibid.

to the determination, including the structure and design of the tax.[79] For instance, if in our hypothetical example the upstream carbon tax on gasoline was designed in such a way as to shield country A's algae biofuel producers from taxes, yet at the same time taxes were imposed not only on gasoline but also on imported biofuel made from jatropha,[80] this may be an indication that the tax is really aimed at affording protection to domestic products, altering the competitive relationship between imported and domestic products in the market place. A similar conclusion may be reached if taxes on cars are structured in such a way that higher taxes are only imposed on imported cars, and lower taxes on domestic cars.

6.4   INSTITUTIONAL FRAMEWORK

In the absence of a global or harmonized carbon tax, the WTO dispute settlement system is likely to be called upon to adjudicate on the consistency of countries' taxes with international trade rules. This chapter has highlighted a number of uncertainties surrounding interpretation of GATT Article III.2. When will products be found 'like' (Article III.2, first sentence) and when will they be 'directly competitive or substitutable' (Article III.2, second sentence)? Also unclear is when a tax will be found to have been applied 'so as to afford protection'. Determination of these issues will play a significant role in delineating a country's ability to unilaterally make distinctions between products based on their contribution to climate change. Given the uncertainty of the interpretation and application of the current rules, clarification is desirable. Particularly important is the PPM question as it is critical in drawing the boundaries between what is acceptable taxation policy and what is not.

Unfortunately, clarification through the dispute settlement process will inevitably be a lengthy affair, requiring disputes to be heard by panels or the Appellate Body in order for new interpretations to be made. Chapter 10 will consider alternative options that might bring more certainty to the process. Arguably, the status quo affords countries a certain amount of flexibility in designing taxation policy – measures can be designed and amended from time to time so as to meet national values (for example,

---

[79]   *Korea – Alcoholic Beverages, supra* note 59 at paras 148 and 150.

[80]   Jatropha is a tree native to Central America that is considered to be a promising candidate for biodiesel production. This hypothetical is based on the assumption that biofuel based on jatropha does not have a high carbon dioxide emissions profile. This assumption is made purely for the purposes of the hypothetical.

how to allocate the burden of taxes) and to respond to the information available at the time (for example, information as to the environmental benefits of a given product). However, this conclusion is dependent on the outcome of future disputes and any flexibility afforded is thus counterbalanced by a lack of certainty as to the consistency of a given taxation measure with GATT rules.

While questions as to the validity of PPM-based distinctions may not have been resolved, the positive aspect of this from a climate change perspective is that WTO Members are in a position to advocate for interpretations that support mitigation through the use of taxes. The vagueness of the rules provides a certain flexibility in determining what types of taxes and on what products will be most environmentally effective. Again, however, there is a lack of certainty as to whether or not a particular policy will attract a WTO challenge. Further, this situation could present problems from an equity standpoint. Developed countries might take advantage of the uncertainty inherent in the rules to take protectionist action under the cover of climate change motivations and can reasonably expect that not all Members will have the capacity to bring a claim should protectionism be suspected. This possibility supports an argument for greater clarification of the rules, as will be discussed in Chapter 10.

7. Subsidies

7.1 WHY SUBSIDIZE?

Instead of imposing costs on individuals to force them to address climate change, many countries provide subsidies. There are subsidies for wind power, for biofuels, for research and development, for individuals to insulate their homes or to purchase energy efficient appliances and for carbon sinks. Some of these subsidies may be useful elements of a country's climate change plan. Yet, as with tariffs, regulations and taxes, subsidies have trade impacts. They can hinder access of exports from non-subsidizing countries to the markets of the subsidizing country or third countries. They can also lead to displacement of domestic products in home markets of non-subsidizing countries.

This chapter examines the WTO rules relating to subsidies and what they mean for domestic climate change policies. As it turns out, WTO rules on subsidies are quite strict, particularly for export subsidies. We first look at why countries may want to use subsidies and the potential advantages and disadvantages of this approach to climate change. We then turn to the specific WTO rules and examine what constitutes a subsidy under WTO agreements and the basic rules around both domestic and export subsidies. Finally, we draw together some of the lessons from the chapter to return to our central questions about whether WTO rules can address climate change effectively, and the implications of the rules for who determines what policy choices are permissible.

7.1.1 Subsidies and Externalities

Many countries have turned to subsidies as a primary means of addressing climate change. While economists tend to dislike subsidies, they can help to address market failures.[1] To the extent that climate change is a problem

---

[1] Alan O. Sykes, 'The Economics of WTO Rules on Subsidies and Countervailing Measures', in A. Appleton, P. Macrory and M. Plummer (eds), *The World Trade Organization: Legal, Economic and Political Analysis*, vol. II (New York: Springer Verlag, 2005).

of the commons, subsidy policies can change the incentives that individuals or companies face in undertaking activities that emit greenhouse gases (GHGs). In this sense, they are in effect the flip-side of taxes – creating an opportunity cost for taking the non-subsidized (higher emitting) activity.

Subsidies policies can encompass a range of objectives. First, in some ways least controversially but most politically difficult, governments can reduce subsidies that currently exist for activities that create GHGs. The most obvious form of these subsidies is for fossil fuels used to generate energy such as coal. One recent estimate found that reducing coal production subsidies could reduce global emissions of carbon dioxide by up to 8 per cent relative to business as usual.[2] Further, some developed countries have used subsidies to keep electricity prices artificially low to foster economic growth. To the extent that generation of this electricity creates GHGs, the greater demand for electricity is harmful in terms of climate change. However, reducing existing subsidies generally meets strong political resistance and has proven difficult.

Second, governments may subsidize industry for reducing GHG emissions. For example, governments may subsidize the reduction in production, such as by subsidizing lower levels of logging. Alternatively, the subsidies may be provided for reducing the level of emissions associated with a given level of production. Such subsidies may be provided for adopting emission control technology or more energy efficient equipment.

Third, subsidies could be used to foster new forms of production that have lower emissions. The primary example of such subsidies has been for renewable forms of energy. Many countries provide various forms of subsidies for wind, solar or other forms of 'clean' energy. The subsidies, often in the form of minimum prices, tax exemptions or direct production subsidies, look to reduce the cost advantage of fossil fuels such as coal or natural gas.[3] Depending on opinions on the waste generated, subsidies for nuclear energy may also be included in this category since they lead to reduced levels of GHG emissions.

---

[2] Kym Anderson and Warwick McKibbon, 'Reducing Coal Subsidies and Trade Barriers: Their Contribution to Greenhouse Gas Abatement' (2000) 5 *Environment and Development Economics* 457, and Anthony Owen, 'Environmental Externalities, Market Distortions and the Economics of Renewable Energy Technologies' (2004) 25 (3) *The Energy Journal* 127.

[3] Owen, *supra* note 2, and A. Green and D. Duff, 'Market-Based Policies for Renewable Energy: A Comparative Evaluation', in N. Chalifour, J. Milne, H. Ashiabor, K. Deketelaere and L. Kreiser (eds), *Critical Issues in Environmental Taxation: International and Comparative Perspectives*, vol. V (Oxford: Oxford University Press, 2008).

Fourth, a related form of subsidy is for carbon sinks. Carbon sinks such as forests or agricultural land take carbon out of the atmosphere. A price for such services may arise under a carbon trading regime. However, without such a regime, if there is no market for these services, there is no incentive to create sinks and subsidies may be used to foster them.

Finally, governments have expended significant resources subsidizing research and development. The subsidies have been provided for research both into climate change itself and into new technologies for reducing GHG emissions or adaptation. Basic research and development has public goods characteristics. To the extent that the party undertaking it cannot appropriate the benefits (for example, because the country's intellectual property laws are weak), it will tend to be underproduced in the absence of subsidies. Note that these last two types of subsidies (for carbon sinks and for research and development) are different because they do not cause concerns about lowering the price of carbon emissions like the other types of subsidies. For example, subsidies to encourage wind power alone may leave the price of electricity too low as the price of electricity will not reflect the true cost of coal power to the environment or of wind power. The result is that there is no incentive for the consumer to conserve. Subsidies for carbon sinks and for research and development do not cause a similar concern.

Individuals may also be subsidized to undertake activities that lead to lower levels of GHG emissions. For example, governments may provide incentives for individuals to purchase more energy efficient cars and appliances, to take public transit, or retrofit their homes. As with industry, a beneficial but hard to implement subsidies policy would be to reduce subsidies to activities that emit significant GHGs, including indirect or hidden subsidies such as for parking or use of electricity. Changing individuals' behaviour will be important for addressing climate change and subsidies may be a politically feasible means of doing so, even if not the most efficient.

7.1.2 Subsidizing Values?

Subsidies may then be used to overcome a market failure including a commons problem like climate change. Another possible use for subsidies is not to directly address a market failure but to protect or create particular values within a society. Sykes, for example, posits 'a society in which the electorate has a taste for rural, agrarian life and wishes it preserved' and supports subsidies to preserve farming.[4] He points out that it is difficult in

---

[4] Sykes, *supra* note 1 at 8.

such a case to determine whether the subsidy is legitimate and may in part turn on whether the program is a legitimate reflection of preferences rather than of pressure from agricultural interest groups.

However, subsidies may be used not only to vindicate certain preferences but to create preferences. Some environmentalists argue that climate change cannot be adequately addressed through technical means, such as pricing carbon, but that it will require a fundamental shift in how individuals view the environment.[5] Changing norms about climate is, in a sense, a means of addressing a market failure. A shift in individuals' values towards the environment may make them reduce their emissions, not because they experience an increase in the price of their action in monetary terms but because they bear other costs of non-environmental action. These costs may, for example, come in the form of a feeling of guilt or in loss of esteem from fellow citizens.[6] Behaviour may also change if the individuals no longer view certain GHG emitting activities as legitimate choices; it may not, for example, be an option for an individual to drive an SUV given her values. Subsidies could change preferences in a number of ways such as by changing habits of consumers or by indicating the preferences of the other members of society.

A difficult question in terms of subsidies is whether governments can use them to create such norms or values in their citizens. Subsidies that reflect the existing preferences of citizens may be seen as a legitimate expression of political choice depending on the process for arriving at the decision to subsidize. The answer may be the same for subsidies that attempt to create preferences. However, it may be much more difficult to determine whether the subsidies are the result of a fair, deliberative process or of political pressure from organized interest groups.

---

[5] See, for example, James Gustave Speth, *Red Sky at Morning* (New Haven: Yale University Press, 2004) and D. Boyd, *Unnatural Law: Rethinking Canadian Environmental Law and Policy* (Vancouver: UBC Press, 2003).

[6] The literature on law and social norms and values is voluminous. For discussions of how norms or values are created, internalized and enforced, see for example C. Sunstein, 'Social Norms and Social Roles' (1996) *Columbia Law Review* 903 at 905, 918 and 958–9; R. McAdams, 'The Origin, Development and Regulation of Norms' (1997) 96 (2) *Michigan Law Review* 338 at 353–4; A. Sen, *Rationality and Freedom* (Cambridge, MA: Harvard University Press, 2002); Richard McAdams and Eric Rasmusen, 'Norms in Law and Economics' in A. Mitchell Polinsky and Steven Shavell (eds), *Handbook of Law and Economics* (Amsterdam: Elsevier Science, 2007) and A. Green, 'You Can't Pay Them Enough: Subsidies, Environmental Law and Social Norms' (2006) 30 *Harvard Environmental Law Review* 407.

7.1.3 The Downside of Subsidies

While subsidies may be capable of reducing GHG emissions or possibly protecting or creating values, they also have a downside. Economists in general do not like subsidies because they are often not the most efficient instrument to solve a problem. Even if legitimately aimed at resolving a market failure, subsidies may cause a welfare loss because of the distortions caused by needing to raise taxes to pay for the subsidies. Moreover, a concern with subsidies is that they will not be used in an efficient manner because of collective action problems. The benefits tend to be visible and often concentrated, while the costs are hidden and diffuse, often imposed through a non-transparent tax increase.

If the use of subsidies was merely inefficient from the perspective of the society providing them, the WTO should not have rules concerning them. Any such rules would be merely paternalistic. However, subsidies may have impacts similar to those of tariffs in terms of their trade effects. Some subsidies for domestic producers of a good may lower their costs and therefore increase the amount produced domestically relative to imports.[7] For example, a subsidy for the production of wind turbines may reduce the cost for the domestic producers relative to imports, thereby reducing the number of imports. Interestingly, subsidies do not harm consumers in the subsidizing country in the same manner as tariffs, regulations or taxes. For a small country, the amount consumed of the product would remain the same because it continues to import products at the world price. Unlike for tariffs, taxes or regulations, the consumer does not face an increased price and no consumers are priced out of the market. The amount of imports would, however, decrease where the subsidy lowers the domestic cost of production. As discussed in Chapter 5, the social costs for the country subsidizing production may be greater than for taxes or tariffs that actually increase government revenues, although less than for regulatory measures.[8]

In addition, subsidies may impact trade in other countries.[9] They may, for example, lower the costs (and the price) of exports from the subsidizing country. These cheaper exports may then harm industries in other countries that cannot compete with the subsidized imports. Further, the cheaper exports may harm the exports from other countries to third

---

[7] Alan Sykes, 'Regulatory Protectionism and the Law of International Trade' (1999) 66 *University of Chicago Law Review* 1, at 3.

[8] Ibid.

[9] Sykes, *supra* note 1; Michael J. Trebilcock and Robert Howse, *The Regulation of International Trade, 3rd Edn* (London: Routledge, 2005).

countries – that is, reduce the exports from some countries into a market to which industry in the subsidizing country also exports.

It is clear that some subsidies may have negative impacts on imports and on domestic industries in other countries. However, not all subsidies will have these trade impacts or at least have negative impacts about which we should be concerned.[10] The negative impact of subsidies comes from the impact on the relative cost of production. If the subsidy does not impact these costs, it will not have these trade impacts. Moreover, subsidies may be merely offsetting some other advantage or disadvantage provided by governments and therefore normatively it is not clear subsidies are problematic. For example, is a subsidy to solar power that is designed to offset subsidies to coal a concern? Issues about the actual impact and normative understanding of subsidies underlie a concern about the over-inclusiveness of WTO subsidies rules, which we discuss in the next section.

Subsidies may harm trade incidentally but the greater fear is that they do so as a result of rent-seeking by powerful domestic interest groups. The government may have a legitimate environmental objective in subsidizing a particular industry or activity but use the subsidy in a manner that discriminates against foreign producers. Alternatively, the subsidy may only appear to have the objective of addressing climate change and in reality may be aimed solely at protecting a domestic industry. Subsidies may be particularly pernicious in this regard if it is more difficult to identify whether a subsidy is the result of rent-seeking than with other instruments such as taxes or tariffs. Concerns about transparency and information concerning subsidies are also important to our discussion of the WTO rules. These arise in the discussion of what constitutes a subsidy, to which we turn next, as well as how various subsidies are characterized and their effects identified.

7.2   WHAT IS A SUBSIDY?

WTO rules regarding subsidies have changed considerably since the inception of the GATT. The initial GATT had few restrictions on the use of subsidies, particularly on domestic subsidy policies. The principal direct restriction on domestic subsidies was a provision permitting countervailing duties if one contracting party was injured by subsidies in another.[11]

---

[10]   Sykes, *supra* note 1.
[11]   The GATT 1947 provisions relating to subsidies permitted a country to impose countervailing duties against a subsidizing contracting party where the

There was also a possible challenge under Article XXIII, which permits a contracting party to complain if a benefit it has under the GATT (such as a tariff concession) 'is being nullified or impaired . . . as a result of . . . the application by another contracting party of any measure, whether or not it conflicts with' the provisions of the GATT. If the measure is found to nullify or impair the benefit of the complaining party, the party taking the measure must restore the competitive relationship between the parties as the purpose of the provision is to ensure that competitive opportunities are not frustrated.[12] The complaining party must prove that the measure could not have been 'reasonably anticipated' when the concession was made. The Panel in *Japan–Film and Paper* found there is a presumption that the measure could not have been reasonably anticipated if it was not in place at the time of negotiations.[13] However, the complaining party faces a heavier burden in proving the measure could not have been anticipated if the measure relates to a matter under Article XX (such as health or the environment) due to the importance accorded to such matters under the GATT.[14]

The main restrictions on subsidies are found in the Subsidies and Countervailing Measures (SCM) Agreement.[15] Under the SCM Agreement, a 'subsidy' is defined as 'a financial contribution by a government or any public body within the territory of a Member' that confers a 'benefit'.[16]

---

industry in the non-subsidizing country was injured. Its national treatment provisions created an exception for domestic subsidies. Sykes, *supra* note 1.

[12] *Japan – Measures Affecting Consumer Photographic Film and Paper* (1998) WTO Doc. WT/DS44/R (Panel Report).

[13] Ibid.

[14] *EC – Measures Affecting Asbestos and Asbestos-Containing Products* (2000) WTO Doc. WT/DS135/ R (Panel Report) at para. 8.282 (Article XXIII upheld by Appellate Body, *EC – Measures Affecting Asbestos and Asbestos-Containing Products* (2001) WTO Doc. WT/DS135/B/R (Appellate Body Report).

[15] The Agreement on Agriculture is also relevant to some measures addressing climate change. In particular, the Agreement on Agriculture is relevant as there are a range of subsidies which relate to biofuels. Subsidies for ethanol are likely to fall under the Agreement on Agriculture while subsidies for biodiesel appear more likely to fall under the SCM Agreement (see Doaa Abdel Motaal, 'The Biofuels Landscape: Is There a Role for the WTO?' (2008) 42 (1) *Journal of World Trade* 61). This chapter discusses principally the SCM Agreement, although it does discuss the approach of the Agreement on Agriculture in the final section.

[16] SCM Agreement, Article 1.1. The Appellate Body has interpreted government provision of goods and services broadly to include a right to harvest standing timber. *US – Final Countervailing Duty Determination Softwood Lumber with Respect to Certain Softwood Lumber from Canada* (2004) WTO Doc. WT/DS257/ AB/R (Appellate Body Report).

The term 'financial contribution' covers most measures that would be typically thought of as subsidies including direct grants, loans, and government provision of goods or services. It also includes government revenue 'otherwise due' that is forgone or not collected. The Appellate Body has found that 'otherwise due' must be based on the tax rules of the member taking the measure as each member has the right to set its own tax levels.[17] For example, where all pollution control devices are taxed but there is an exemption for devices that control emissions of GHG, a panel would be likely to find the exemption to be a subsidy. The definition of 'financial contribution' therefore covers most measures in the climate change area that would be thought of as subsidies.[18]

The definition of 'benefit', however, is more controversial. The comparison for whether a measure has conferred a benefit is the marketplace – is the measure or the terms of the measure more favourable than the receiving party could obtain on its own in the market?[19] Is a loan provided at less than market rates? Are goods and services sold more cheaply than they could be bought from private vendors? Such a determination is not always easy. For example, Howse argues that the definition of subsidy under the SCM Agreement covers governments providing emission permits for free or less than the market price under an emissions trading regime.[20] According to Howse, the distribution of permits can be seen as a provision of goods and services in the form of providing access to an exhaustible natural resource (the atmosphere). However, a difficulty arises in determining whether there is a benefit and, if so, what is its size. Howse argues that there is a benefit to the extent that the government does not charge the market price for the permit. He points to WTO case law holding that the market price can be

---

[17] *United States – Tax Treatment for 'Foreign Sales Corporations'*, (2002) WTO Doc. WT/DS108/AB/R (Appellate Body Report).

[18] Economist Joseph Stiglitz has argued that lack of climate change regulation could be an actionable subsidy (see J. Stiglitz, 'A New Agenda for Global Warming' (2006) 7 (3) *The Economists' Voice* (available at: http://www.bepress.com/ev/vol3/iss7/art3). However, such a lack of regulation probably does not satisfy the definition of a subsidy under the SCM Agreement (J. Bhagwati and P. Mavroidis, 'Is Action Against US Exports for Failure to Sign the Kyoto Protocol WTO-legal?' (2007) 6 (2) *World Trade Review* 299).

[19] *Canada – Measures Affecting the Export of Civilian Aircraft* (1999) WTO Doc. WT/DS70/AB/R (Appellate Body Report). The benefit must be examined with reference to the prevailing market conditions in the subsidizing country and not the exporting country (*United States – Preliminary Determinations with Respect to Certain Softwood Lumber from Canada* (2002) WTO Doc. WT/DS222/R (Panel Report).

[20] R. Howse, 'Subsidies to Address Climate Change: Legal Issues' (Winnipeg, Canada: International Institute for Sustainable Development, 2009).

determined from the domestic market, or, if there is no domestic market, from another functioning market. For example, where the US has in place an emissions trading programme but it is not fully functioning, a panel may be able to look to the market price in the EC market.

While there may be difficulties in some cases in determining the market price, the use of the market as the basis for assessing whether there has been a benefit has the advantage of administrative simplicity. Unfortunately, this market-based determination is problematic for measures in the climate change area as it is overly broad in two ways. First, even though the terms of the financial contribution are better than the market, it may not confer a 'benefit' once all other costs and benefits from the government are taken into account.[21] The government may, for example, have imposed costs on the industry in terms of pollution control devices and provided a grant to offset the costs. Alternatively, the government may use a grant or tax exemption to level the playing field where it has provided benefits to other industries such as grants to coal. As Sykes notes, there is no pure market equilibrium from which to judge whether a benefit has been conferred. The Appellate Body has decided, however, that subsidies are to be determined by examining the market as it exists, rather than attempting to take into account the various regulatory and tax programmes. This approach has the benefit of simplicity and relative ease of application but it is over-inclusive.

Second, the current test does not require any form of impact on production.[22] The subsidy must merely be in one of the forms of financial benefit set out by the SCM Agreement and provide a benefit relative to the market. Yet it might not lead the company or industry to increase output, such as in the case of some lump sum grants. If a subsidy does not change output or impact the market in relation to foreign goods, it should not be subject to international trade disciplines. Again not including a test for impact on production has the benefit of administrative ease of application but sweeps in more measures than would a more tailored test.

In the definition of what is caught by the SCM Agreement, then, the Appellate Body has chosen administrative simplicity over a more tailored test that provides more policy space for domestic governments. The breadth of measures caught by this simpler initial screen may be beneficial in one sense. It may allow the WTO to assess a broader range of potentially trade-impacting measures to determine which ones truly are barriers.

---

[21] A. Sykes, 'The Questionable Case for Subsidies Regulation: A Comparative Perspective' (Stanford University School of Law, Law and Economics Research Paper Series, No. 380, 2009).
[22] Ibid.

This approach, however, depends on how well the other tests under the SCM Agreement operate to separate permissible from impermissible subsidies.[23] We turn to these provisions now.

7.3   PROHIBITED SUBSIDIES

The SCM Agreement establishes three broad types of subsidies: prohibited subsidies, actionable subsidies, and non-actionable subsidies. There are two types of prohibited subsidies.[24] First, the SCM Agreement prohibits export subsidies, which it defines as subsidies that are de jure or de facto contingent on export performance. There is a debate in the literature about whether export subsidies may be welfare enhancing in some circumstances. As the subsidized goods are, by definition, to be exported, export subsidies may be seen to be beneficial to the extent that they increase trade.[25] However, like other subsidies, export subsidies distort the market away from more efficient producers towards the subsidized producers.[26] For our purposes, the important point is that export subsidies are not likely to be designed to address a market failure.[27] There does not appear to be a reason why a subsidy to address climate change, for example, needs to be contingent on export of the good. The prohibition on export subsidies is therefore not as such problematic in terms of addressing climate change.

The second form of prohibited subsidy is a subsidy contingent on the use of domestic goods over imports. This prohibition may be more relevant to climate measures. A government may, for example, provide grants for the purchase of electricity from domestic renewable energy sources in order to foster the domestic industry.[28] There is, however, an inconsistency in how the SCM Agreement treats subsidies. Subsidies to consumers

---

[23]   N. Chalifour, 'Encouraging the Transition to Sustainable Forestry in Canada with Ecological Fiscal Reform – Potential and Pitfalls' (2004) 14 *Journal of Environmental Law and Practice* 254.

[24]   SCM Agreement, Article 3.

[25]   K. Bagwell, 'Remedies in the WTO: An Economic Perspective', in Merit E. Janow, Victoria J. Donaldson and Alan Yanovich (eds), *The WTO: Governance, Dispute Settlement & Developing Countries* (Huntington, NY: Juris Publishing, 2008).

[26]   A. Green and M. Trebilcock, 'Enforcing WTO Obligations: What Can We Learn from Export Subsidies?' (2007) 10 (3) *Journal of International Economic Law* 653, and Sykes, *supra* note 1.

[27]   Sykes, *supra* note 1.

[28]   Z. Zhang and L. Assunçao, 'Domestic Climate Change Policies and the WTO' (2004) 27 *The World Economy* 360.

are prohibited yet subsidies to producers, which have essentially the same effect, are only actionable (that is, as discussed in the next section, must only be removed if they cause certain forms of harm).[29] Again the WTO rules may be leaning towards ease of application – it may be easier to identify subsidies to producers than those to consumers, although this is not necessarily true.

However, again there is a loss from this simplicity. First, subsidies to consumers may be more transparent to domestic constituencies than subsidies to producers. Consumers know they are being subsidized (with their own money) to purchase the domestic goods. Such transparency may make the subsidizing government more accountable for its policies and increase the likelihood that the subsidies actually address a market failure. Subsidies to producers may be more hidden from the general public and therefore more easily made for non-welfare-enhancing (protectionist) purposes.

Second, subsidies may have an expressive function. Action on climate change is likely to require a change in social norms. Individuals need to understand the consequences of their actions and appreciate the harm they are causing to other countries, later generations, and the environment itself. Providing subsidies to consumers and to producers may in one sense have the same effect – for example, the price of renewable energy is lower and output increased. In addition, providing a subsidy to consumers expresses to the individuals directly, and most clearly, societal approval and recognition of the importance and the value of such actions.[30] This expressive function still exists with subsidies to producers but is less evident and therefore possibly less effective.

However, in the case of both export subsidies and subsidies contingent on the purchase of domestic goods, the objective could probably be met equally with subsidies that do not overtly favour domestic producers. The subsidies could, for example, be provided for the production of a climate friendly product whether or not it is exported or whether or not it is produced at home or abroad. Prohibiting these types of subsidies therefore may achieve an efficient result by removing subsidies that appear to be barriers to trade. The loss may take the form of reduced action on climate change because of the relatively greater political ease with which either export subsidies or subsidies contingent on domestic production are put in place. There may, therefore, be a trade-off in this case between having climate action of some form (including potentially protectionist measures) and reducing the inefficiencies from trade barriers.

---

[29] Sykes, *supra* note 1.
[30] Green, *supra* note 6.

7.4 ACTIONABLE SUBSIDIES

While some subsidies are prohibited, others are merely 'actionable' – that is, they may be impermissible if certain conditions hold but otherwise are not. Non-prohibited subsidies are actionable if they are 'specific' and if they cause certain forms of harm. Both conditions have been controversial, in part because it is difficult to formulate an easily administered test that clearly identifies permissible uses of subsidies. As with the definition of subsidy, ease of administration has tended to trump countries' domestic autonomy to regulate.

The 'specificity' requirement arises because the Members wished to ensure that the Agreement did not cover broad programmes that might be considered subsidies such as general education and health care. Such broadly applicable subsidies are argued not to distort trade.[31] The SCM Agreement requires that to be actionable a subsidy must be 'specific' to 'certain enterprises' but does not define 'certain enterprises' other than as 'an enterprise or industry or group of enterprises or industries'.[32] It does, however, set out certain principles for determining whether a subsidy is specific, including whether:[33]

- the granting authority explicitly limits the subsidy to certain enterprises;[34]
- the subsidy is distributed according to objective criteria or conditions governing eligibility or amount where the criteria do not favour some enterprises over others and are 'economic in nature and horizontal in application, such as number of employees or size of enterprise';
- the subsidy is de facto specific even though based on objective criteria and not explicitly limited to certain enterprises where de facto specificity is determined by such factors as whether it is wholly or predominately used by a small number of enterprises;
- the subsidy is limited to enterprises in a designated region.

The key then is determining how narrowly a subsidy must be tailored to be considered specific. Many subsidies that are used in the climate change area would probably be considered specific because they may in

---

[31] Sykes, *supra* note 1; Trebilcock and Howse, *supra* note 9.
[32] SCM Agreement, Article 2.
[33] SCM Agreement, Article 2.
[34] The tailoring need not be deliberate: *United States – Final Countervailing Duty Determination with Respect to Certain Softwood Lumber from Canada* (2003) WTO Doc. WT/DS257/R (Panel Report) at para. 7.116.

fact be disproportionately provided to certain industries. Subsidies that are aimed at promoting energy efficiency or emission reduction payments across all sectors appear to be non-specific. However, if there are a few industries (large emitters) that 'disproportionately' use these subsidies, such subsidies could be seen as de facto specific. The level of use that is 'disproportionate' is not clear. For example, the oil and gas industries and fossil-fuel-based electricity generation account for a significant proportion of GHG emissions in some countries and therefore may make considerable use of a subsidy based on emission reductions. This subsidy may then be seen as 'specific' to these industries. However, there are a number of other sectors (such as the chemical and smelting and refining industries) that account for a significant share of emissions but are not as large as the oil and gas industries or electricity generation.[35] The same broad-based subsidy may not be seen as specific to these other sectors.

Subsidies for the development of renewable energy also raise concerns. They could be seen as specific as they are provided not to the energy sector as a whole but to a sub-sector. The subsidy could be argued to be spread across many different types of renewable energy and therefore be not specific. However, panel decisions have found that the term 'certain enterprises' refers to a 'type of product' (such as 'wood products') rather than specific end-products ('the wooden kitchen cabinet' industry).[36] However, a panel has, in obiter, noted that not all government provision of natural resources would be specific as some natural resources could be widely used (such as oil, gas, or water).[37] If governments can provide oil without it being held to be specific because oil benefits many industries, certain subsidies to renewable energy (such as for research and development) could possibly be viewed as non-specific.

The difficulty with the specificity test is that, as Sykes argues, 'where a principled justification for a subsidy exists, it will likely arise narrowly and case-by-case, so that the policy response will often appear specific'.[38] Subsidies addressing climate change, whether based on market failures or

---

[35] C. Forcese, 'The Kyoto Rift: Trade Law Implications of Canada's Kyoto Implementation Strategy in an Era of Canadian–US Environmental Divergence', in Kevin Kennedy (ed.), *The First Decade of NAFTA; The Future of Free Trade in North America* (Ardsley, NY: Transnational Publishers, 2004).

[36] *US – Final Determination Softwood, supra* note 34. See also *US–Subsidies on Upland Cotton* (2005) WTO Doc. WT/DS267/R (Panel Report). The Panel used the same test to find that subsidies that went solely to upland cotton were specific, as were subsidies that went to other subsets of agricultural products in addition to cotton.

[37] *US – Final Determination Softwood, supra* note 34 at para. 7.116.

[38] Sykes, *supra* note 1 at 20.

value choices, may be broadly based (such as widely distributed energy efficiency subsidies). However, they may be beneficially limited to specific subsidies of an industry – such as is the case for subsidies for renewable energy sources or for particular energy-efficient products (such as cars). Limiting countries' use of such subsidies may have a significant impact on their ability to address climate change efficiently. As such, it is over-inclusive in the sense of capturing more subsidies than desirable. It is not even, as the case law shows, easy to administer as panels have difficulty drawing the line between specific and non-specific subsidies.

Under the SCM Agreement, for a subsidy to be 'actionable', it must not only be specific but must also cause one of three forms of harms or 'adverse effects': injury to the domestic industry of another member; impairment of the benefits of a tariff concession for another member; or serious prejudice to the interests of another member.[39] The harms essentially relate to ensuring that the subsidy does not injure producers in other countries, through export of subsidized products into their market, reducing exports to the subsidizing country, or impacting exports to third country markets. Given the breadth of the other tests under the SCM Agreement, the harm requirement could act as a filter to separate out those subsidies that actually have a negative effect on trade.

Unfortunately, the tests for adverse effects are also not well specified. There are two concerns with the current tests. First, the evidence for a finding that a subsidy is actionable is difficult to obtain. It requires, for example, evidence of prices in the domestic market, or that the subsidy displaces or impedes imports of like products into the subsidizing country or into a third country or that the subsidy significantly undercuts the product price.[40] Moreover, there should be evidence of the amount of the subsidy. However, while panels do gather significant evidence concerning price and impacts, in a recent decision, the Appellate Body found no error where the panel did not quantify the amount of the subsidy and relied solely on the finding that the subsidy was 'very large' in its analysis of serious prejudice. It only found that the quantification could be important in some cases and that 'in the present case, the Panel could have been more explicit and specified what it meant by "very large amounts"'.[41]

Second, in order for a subsidy to be impermissible, the subsidy should cause whatever harm occurs to the producers in other countries. It is only

---

[39]   SCM Agreement, Article 5.
[40]   SCM Agreement, Articles 15 and 6.
[41]   *US–Subsidies on Upland Cotton* (2005) WTO Doc. WT/DS267/AB/R (Appellate Body Report) at para. 468.

those subsidies that actually harm international trade that should concern the WTO. However, the tests developed by the WTO panels and the Appellate Body have tended to rely more on correlation than causation – that is, there is evidence of a subsidy and evidence of harm at the same time and that is largely sufficient for a finding that the subsidy caused the harm.[42] In the recent *US–Cotton* case, the Appellate Body appeared to place greater emphasis on showing causation.[43] It noted that 'mere correlation between the payment of subsidies and significantly suppressed prices would be insufficient, without more, to prove that the effect of the subsidies is significant price suppression.'[44] Unfortunately, the Appellate Body established a low threshold for reasons for the panel, stating merely that 'the Panel could have provided a more detailed explanation of its analysis of the complex facts and economics arising in this dispute . . . to demonstrate precisely how it evaluated the different factors bearing on the relationship between the price-contingent subsidies and significant price suppression.'[45] Even then, as Howse notes, it will be difficult in many cases to determine causation given the large variety of factors that influence various markets such as that for fossil fuels.[46]

These findings place a low threshold on evidence and causality. Panels need not necessarily provide detailed explanations of how they reached their conclusions and need not even have particularly precise estimates of the amounts of the subsidies. A strong causality requirement is important to the ability of panels to distinguish subsidies that harm producers in other countries and those that do not and therefore to allow space for countries to use subsidies that do not have a negative impact on trade. Again administrative simplicity appears to have prevailed over the ability of countries to use subsidies as a policy tool.

7.5 NON-ACTIONABLE SUBSIDIES

The SCM Agreement therefore has an overbroad definition of subsidies and an insufficiently targeted set of tests for when a subsidy is actionable. However, these constraints might not be of great concern if countries had the ability to argue that, despite the harms to international trade, the subsidy is legitimate as it addresses a market failure or has some other

---

42   Sykes, *supra* note 21.
43   *US–Cotton AB Report*, *supra* note 41.
44   Ibid. at para. 451.
45   Ibid. at para. 458.
46   Howse, *supra* note 20; Sykes, *supra* note 21.

appropriate objective. Initially the SCM Agreement did in fact have a category of non-actionable subsidies, which included subsidies that were specific but fell within three exceptions: research and development, regional development, and environmental compliance costs.[47]

Unfortunately, these exceptions were very narrowly circumscribed. To qualify for the environmental compliance cost exception, for example, the subsidy must provide assistance to 'promote adaptation of existing facilities to new environmental requirements imposed by law and/or regulations which result in greater constraints and financial burden on firms'. It must be a one-time subsidy, must be limited to 20 per cent of the adaptation costs, must not cover the cost of replacing and operating the assisted investment, must be 'directly linked to and proportionate to a firm's planned reduction of nuisances and pollution', must not cover any manufacturing cost savings and must be available to all companies which can adopt the new technology.[48]

More importantly, perhaps, these provisions expired in 2000 and have not been renewed.[49] There is therefore no general exception for subsidies with a legitimate public purpose such as addressing climate change. As will be discussed in Chapter 9, this lack of a public interest exception is in stark contrast to exceptions to requirements of other WTO Agreements such as under Article XX of the GATT.

7.6   WHY ARE SUBSIDIES SO RESTRICTED?

Subsidies are therefore significantly restricted by WTO rules.[50] The rules as they exist are both under-inclusive and over-inclusive. The difficulty from the perspective of climate change is that the rules are over-inclusive.

---

[47]   SCM Agreement, Article 8.2.

[48]   SCM Agreement, Article 8.2(c). See Howse, *supra* note 20 and Sykes, *supra* note 21 for discussions of the difficulties with this Article due to its narrowness and arbitrariness.

[49]   SCM Agreement, Article 31.

[50]   Members have two options for addressing non-compliant subsidies of other Members. They can bring a challenge under the SCM Agreement and seek to have a panel declare the measure non-compliant. The responding Member must then withdraw the measure without delay or the complaining Member can request the option of imposing countermeasures. The second option is for the Member to impose countervailing duties against the subsidizing Member. Neither option has been used extensively, with the possible exception of challenges to export subsidies (see A. Sykes, 'The Questionable Case for Subsidies Regulation: A Comparative Perspective' (Stanford University School of Law, Law and Economics Research

They take away a tool from governments wishing to address the market failure underlying climate change. The loss comes in the form of reduced benefits from complexity. The rules make no allowance for differences in costs of action across countries, most specifically of political costs of action when subsidies are the only (or most) politically feasible means of addressing climate change. They make no allowance for variations in values across countries. The rules prohibit subsidies causing adverse effects even where they are a legitimate expression of the underlying preferences of the society. Moreover, they stifle innovation in means for reducing emissions since the rules do not permit targeted subsidies for research and development. Nor do they permit innovation in the form of tools that governments may use to address climate change – they cut off attempts to use subsidies to address climate change where they have trade impacts.

Why do the WTO rules take such a hard line on subsidies? Sykes points to three reasons why the WTO Members may have wanted disciplines on subsidies.[51] First, as noted above, subsidies can have similar effects to tariffs in the sense of restricting market access and the rules were meant to address such effects. The risk of simply replacing the trade impacts of a relatively transparent tariff with a potentially much less transparent subsidy may have been felt to be too great. Second, governments may face pressure from industry to subsidize leading to 'subsidies wars'. The rules may be aimed at reducing the risk of harmful forms of competitive subsidization. Finally, governments may seek multilateral rules as a form of commitment to forestall pressure to subsidize. In each of these cases, however, there is a loss – a loss of flexibility in the sense of governments being able to use subsidies where efficient to address a market failure or, possibly, to vindicate domestic values.

If the benefits of flexibility could not come from domestic governments making their own completely independent choices on the use of subsidies and the current rules seem inadequate to provide this flexibility, what are possible options for reform? One possibility is that flexibility could be improved through better standards or better interpretation and application of existing standards. There could, for example, be an improved definition of what counts as a subsidy such that the definition takes into account other costs or benefits imposed by the government or the impact of the measure on trade. There could also be an improved definition of specificity that explicitly takes into account the need to tailor certain

---

Paper Series, No. 380, 2009) and Green and Trebilcock, *supra* note 26). Remedies are discussed further in Chapter 10.

[51] Sykes, *supra* note 21.

measures to market failures (such as potentially climate change). It would
be difficult, however, to design a rule that took these factors into account
and even more difficult (and costly) to obtain the information necessary to
engage in such a tailored examination.[52] These would probably be blunt
methods of addressing climate subsidies. Moreover, refining the notion
of harm is not self-evidently relevant to the climate change context. It is
not clear that a domestic subsidy that effectively addresses an aspect of
the climate change problem should be prohibited solely because it injures
industry in another country. A more refined notion of impermissibility
seems to be required. However, as Sykes notes, '[d]ue to the complexity
of the modern economy and the wide panoply of government activity that
both encourages and discourages the activities of business enterprise, it is
arguably impossible to fashion general principles for the identification, let
alone measurement, of undesirable subsidies.'[53]

If the rules cannot be reformed, it could be possible to control subsidies through bargaining.[54] The bargaining could come in the form of a
detailed list of permissible types or levels of subsidies. Howse argues that
such bargaining could include both the levels at which countries agree to
bind their subsidy levels and reduction commitments on harmful subsidies
(such as for fossil fuels) and agreements on WTO-consistent subsidies.[55]
The hope would be to follow the pattern of the Agreement on Agriculture
and develop an agreement over specific climate subsidies.[56]

The difficulty with this approach is that the transaction costs of bargaining would be very high. There would be many groups involved or
interested in the negotiations and too much information required about
the forms or types of subsidies that might be used in the climate change
area. The cost to reach agreement on a sufficiently detailed set of rules
might be very high. Moreover, as Howse notes, there are concerns about

---

[52]   R. Howse, 'From Politics to Technocracy – And Back Again: The Fate of
the Multilateral Trading Regime' (2002) *American Journal of International Law* 94;
Sykes, *supra* note 1; and Trebilcock and Howse, *supra* note 9. For example, Sykes,
supra note 1 argues 'it is by no means clear that general principles to sort unacceptable from acceptable domestic subsidy programs can be devised and administered
successfully' (at 26).

[53]   Sykes, *supra* note 21 at 2.

[54]   Ibid.

[55]   Howse, *supra* note 20.

[56]   See, for example, M. Buck and R. Verheyen, 'International Trade Law
and Climate Change – A Positive Way Forward' (FES-Analyse Okologische
Marktwirtschaft, Bonn: Friedrich Ebert Stiftung 2001) arguing for negotiations
over energy subsidies following the approach of the Agreement on Agriculture.

whether the WTO is the appropriate place for such negotiations over climate action.[57]

One form of assessing permissibility is not currently available for subsidies – an environmental exception.[58] There is no equivalent to GATT Article XX in the SCM Agreement. As noted above, the non-actionable category was very narrow and in any event has now expired. Allowing subsidies under a broader exception such as that found in Article XX may be an answer, but first we must discuss how Article XX is structured and has been interpreted. We turn to this discussion in Chapter 9, following a discussion in the next chapter of measures that have aspects of both taxes and subsidies: border tax adjustments.

---

[57] Howse, *supra* note 20 and see Chapter 16 discussing the institutional choice issues.

[58] There has been some discussion of the possibility that a panel could allow a Member to rely on Article XX in the face of non-compliance with the SCM Agreement. However, such an interpretation of the agreements seems unlikely (Howse, ibid.)

8. Border tax adjustments

Border tax adjustments (BTAs) are a controversial area of overlap between international trade rules and climate policy. Governments in (mostly developed) countries proposing to price carbon through regulations or taxes have faced significant opposition from industries concerned that they will suffer a loss of competitiveness vis-à-vis industries in other (mostly developing) countries that do not face the costs associated with such measures.[1] A related concern is that of 'leakage', whereby increased production costs lead industries to shift their operations from developed to developing countries with less stringent emission practices. Such leakage, it is argued, will have a negative impact on the competitiveness of developed country economies and will undermine the environmental integrity of a country's environmental policy due to the resulting increase in emissions outside the country.[2]

One possible response to these concerns is to impose border tax adjustments (BTAs) on imports from countries that have not comparably offset the GHG emissions associated with a good's production.[3] Alternatively, taxes may be remitted or exempted on exports. BTAs targeted in this manner will help to secure the international competitiveness of local industry and prevent leakage. In principle, BTAs may be designed so as to be compatible with WTO rules. The potential benefit of BTAs lies in the hope that, if competitiveness can be secured and leakage minimized, the path to implementing regulations or taxes will be much smoother. However, the very significant downside is that their use may undermine climate change

---

[1] In Australia, for example, climate change legislation was rejected in the Senate after the opposition Liberal-National coalition spoke out about the impact of the bill on trade-exposed industries and the agricultural and mining sectors: 'Climate Defeat', *The Economist*, 14 August 2009.

[2] John Stephenson and Simon Upton, *Competitiveness, Leakage, and Border Adjustment: Climate Policy Distractions?* (Paris: Organisation for Economic Co-operation and Development (OECD), Round Table on Sustainable Development SG/SD/RT(2009)3, 2009) at 11.

[3] International Centre for Trade and Sustainable Development (ICTSD), Trade and Climate Change Briefing, Issue 3, Border Carbon Adjustment, UNFCCC COP 15, Copenhagen 2009, 5 December 2009.

objectives as the industry or industries that are protected by the BTA no longer have an incentive to reduce GHG emissions. Further, their use is likely to lead to trade and political friction.[4]

This chapter explores the legal issues surrounding the use of BTAs as a means to neutralize domestic opposition to climate change action. It begins with a brief background on the competitiveness concerns that have led to calls for their use as well as concerns about leakage. It then moves on to an overview of how BTAs work, and their likely consistency or otherwise with WTO rules. We consider firstly the use of BTAs to adjust taxes, and secondly, the scenario where BTAs are used as a means of neutralizing potential competitiveness losses caused by a 'cap-and-trade' or emissions trading scheme. Finally, we draw some conclusions regarding the most appropriate institutional framework to deal with the inevitable trade-related issues that will arise from the use of BTAs.

8.1   COMPETITIVENESS

As discussed in Chapter 6, environmental taxes may play a role in countries' climate change mitigation strategies. In considering the impact of such taxes, it is important to draw a distinction between impacts at a national level and those at a sectoral level. Economists have not established a direct causal link between environmental taxes and competitiveness at the national level.[5] At the sectoral level, however, studies show that the use of environmental taxes will have negative impacts on the international competitiveness of certain emission-intensive and trade-exposed industrial sectors.[6]

Studies have found that only 0.5 to 2 per cent of post-industrial

---

[4]   See for example Angel Gurría, 'Carbon has no Place in Global Trade Rules', *Financial Times*, 4 November 2009 (reporting on a statement by the Secretary General of the OECD). See also Jagdish Bhagwati and Petros C. Mavroidis, 'Is Action against US Exports for Failure to Ratify Kyoto Protocol WTO-legal?' (2007) 6 (2) *World Trade Review* 299.

[5]   Organisation for Economic Co-operation and Development (OECD), *The Political Economy of Environmentally Related Taxes* (Paris: OECD, 2006) at 91.

[6]   The OECD notes three key determinants of the impacts of environmental taxes, finding that the effects on competitiveness will be stronger: (1) the lower the ability to pass on cost increases in prices; (2) the lower the feasibility of substitution possibilities; and (3) the higher the energy intensity of the sector (ibid., 71). Affected sectors include lime and cement, basic iron and steel, refined petroleum, aluminum, inorganic basic chemicals, and pulp and paper. Stephenson and Upton, *supra* note 2 at 8.

countries' national GDP will be exposed to significant increases in production costs from the imposition of a carbon tax.[7] While this may not seem large, the reality for governments remains that they will face opposition to climate change policies from domestic industries in negatively affected sectors.[8] The concern for such industries is that taxes will diminish their international competitiveness by raising their costs relative to competitors in countries that do not have similar taxes, leading to a loss of market share and profits.

Several recent studies have looked at the actual competitiveness impacts of climate change related taxes. In 2006, the OECD found that the use of economic instruments to reduce GHGs is likely to have negative impacts on the international competitiveness position of some industrial sectors, especially when the instruments are not imposed globally.[9] It simulated imposition of a carbon tax on the steel and cement industries in OECD countries and found significant contractions in each following imposition of the tax.[10] Total steel production was predicted to fall by 9 per cent in the short to medium term, while production outside the OECD would rise by almost 5 per cent, resulting in a fall in world steel production of approximately 2 per cent. The projected decline in cement production was smaller than for steel, which the study explained by the ability of the sector to increase operating profits by passing more of their marginal cost increases on to customers.[11]

Despite the OECD's findings, the Stern Review emphasized that it is only likely to be a relatively small number of carbon-intensive industries that will suffer significant impacts as a result of pricing carbon. Using the UK as a case study, the authors found that only six out of 123 industries (gas supply and distribution, refined petroleum, electricity production and distribution, cement, fertilizers, and fishing) would face an increase in vari-

---

[7]   Ibid.

[8]   According to the OECD, international competitiveness concerns have been responsible for the scrapping of proposals to introduce the 1993 BTU Tax legislation in the US (a tax on each unit of energy consumed, measured in BTUs, or British Thermal Units), the 'Greenhouse Levy' in Australia in 1994, and the EU Council's Directive to establish a common EU framework on energy taxation in 2003. They were also at issue in the EU debate over its emissions trading scheme, which eventually included concessions to reduce adverse impacts on energy-intensive and trade-exposed industries. OECD, *Linkages Between Environmental Policy and Competitiveness* (Paris: Organisation for Economic Co-operation and Development ENV/EPOC/GSP(2008)14/FINAL,OECD, 2009).

[9]   OECD, *supra* note 5 at 17.

[10]   Ibid. at 79.

[11]   Ibid.

able costs of 5 per cent or more based on an illustrative carbon price of $30 per tonne of carbon dioxide. Typically, these kinds of industries tend not to be significantly trade exposed, with competition coming from regional blocs. Further, the authors identified a number of country-specific factors that are a more important determinant of location and trade than environmental policies, including capital intensity, availability of technology and skilled labour, access to markets and technology, and efficiency of the tax and regulation system.[12]

Additional factors that indicate whether or not measures to address competitiveness losses are warranted include the fact that some firms will be able to pass increases to consumers while maintaining profitability (although it is difficult to ascertain the extent to which they are able to do so), and the reality that, at the core of climate policy, is the goal of driving a change in resource allocation (demand for emission-intensive goods will decline) such that some firms and sectors will see reduced profits. To what extent should firms therefore be compensated for losses from reduced competitiveness?[13]

The World Bank found in a 2008 study that, while carbon taxes have a statistically negative effect on competitiveness through their impacts on bilateral trade, in many cases countries act to prevent such a loss of competitiveness by providing either a full or partial tax exemption for energy-intensive industries and export industries. In some cases, the subsidies and exemptions are likely to be so generous that trade actually increases as a result. The OECD report found more than 1 150 exemptions in approximately 375 taxes applied by OECD countries.[14] These included a large number of exemptions for taxes on various fossil fuels, motor vehicles, and fuel linked to sea and air transport, as well as refund mechanisms designed to reduce the tax burden of industry facing a loss of competitiveness.[15] While such exemptions may provide comfort to industry, they have the significantly negative effect of undermining the environmental effectiveness of the policy. A climate change policy that exempts the most GHG-intensive sectors will not achieve much in terms of emission reduction.

---

[12] Nicholas Stern, *The Economics of Climate Change: The Stern Review* (Cambridge: Cambridge University Press, 2007) at Part III The Economics of Stabilisation. See also Stephenson and Upton, *supra* note 2 at 8.

[13] Stephenson and Upton, ibid.

[14] OECD, *supra* note 5 at 43.

[15] Ibid. It should be noted that in some cases reductions are only applied on condition of improved environmental performance. The OECD cites the example of an 80% rate reduction for energy-intensive firms in the UK that reach targets set in negotiated Climate Change Agreements.

Regardless of the actual competitiveness effects of taxes or regulations on industry, or the broader effects on the economy as a whole, many governments contemplating climate change measures will nevertheless come under pressure from domestic interests to protect their position. As Stephenson and Upton note, this is inevitable given that research to date is not definitive as to the existence or magnitude of competitiveness risks; policy debate must admit, and 'cannot categorically refute', a wide range of claims including extreme impacts.[16]

8.2 LEAKAGE

Leakage occurs where industries relocate to countries with lower environmental costs. The channel of leakage considered here is movement of energy-intensive industries to countries without commitments. But more important is that if participating countries succeed in reducing consumption of high-carbon fossil fuels, coal and oil, demand will fall and prices of these fuels will fall on world markets (all else being equal). Non-participating countries would respond to declines in world prices by increasing consumption.[17]

Where leakage occurs, the home country faces loss of the benefits of the domestic industry with little or no ultimate reduction in GHG emissions. Leakage is thus considered a problem for the economy as a whole, as well as reducing the effectiveness of climate policies.[18] Unlike competitiveness, which is primarily a concern at the firm level, leakage is a broader problem for a country.[19] It is 'the extent to which economy-wide emissions have migrated after sector-specific increases and decreases have been taken into account'.[20]

A problem with addressing leakage is determining the extent of the problem. There are wide-ranging estimates with studies at both the sectoral level and the economy-wide level showing leakage rates ranging from 0.5 to 75 per cent of emission reductions.[21] It has been noted that while

---

[16]   Stephenson and Upton, *supra* note 2 at 10.

[17]   Peter Wooders, Julia Reinaud and Aaron Cosbey, *Options for Policy-Makers: Addressing Competitiveness, Leakage and Climate Change* (Winnipeg, Canada: International Institute for Sustainable Development, October 2009) at 9–10.

[18]   OECD, *supra* note 5.

[19]   Stephenson and Upton, *supra* note 2 at 10.

[20]   Ibid. at 12.

[21]   Ibid. at 11. Interestingly, Stephenson and Upton suggest that the most

identifying leakage is mathematically possible for any given sector, identifying systemic leakage that would undermine overall global objectives to stabilize climate change is not.[22] Even if leakage is substantial, should it be addressed? While the environmental objectives behind preventing leakage are justifiable, the problem is that the principle of common but undifferentiated responsibilities will be undermined if, through imposition of BTAs, products from developing countries are subjected to the same costs as industries in developed countries.[23]

As with the competitiveness issue, regardless of the merits or otherwise of adjusting for leakage, governments will come under pressure to do so. The following section outlines how BTAs might operate to protect domestic competitiveness and prevent leakage.

8.3   TAXES AND BTAS

It has long been recognized by domestic taxation authorities that the movement of goods across international borders requires countries to adjust their taxation systems, in order not only to avoid double taxation but also to ensure continuation of the desired tax base and to equalize the conditions of competition between domestic and foreign producers with respect to taxation so as to allow comparative cost to govern trade patterns.[24] Adjustment using the destination principle requires that: (i) the same taxes be imposed on imported goods as on domestically produced goods destined for consumption by domestic consumers; and (ii) domestically produced goods destined for consumption by foreigners receive a rebate of the tax.[25] The effect of the destination principle is that imports are brought into the domestic system, while exports are taken out of it.[26]

---

important form of leakage is that which takes place through the so-called fossil fuel price channel. Reduced demand for fossil fuels in countries taking action on climate change lowers world prices and increases demand and carbon dioxide emissions elsewhere in the world.

[22]   Stephenson and Upton, *supra* note 2 at 13.

[23]   Ibid. at 20.

[24]   Harry Johnson and Mel Krauss, 'Border Taxes, Border Tax Adjustments, Comparative Advantage, and the Balance of Payments' (1970) 3 (4) *The Canadian Journal of Economics* 595 at 596.

[25]   Ibid.

[26]   Michael Keen and Sajal Lahiri, 'The Comparison between Destination and Origin Principles under Imperfect Competition' (1998) 45 *Journal of International Economics* 323 at 324. See also Gene M. Grossman, 'Border Tax Adjustments: Do they Distort Trade?' (1980) 10 *Journal of International Economics* 117 at 127.

Where a country brings imported goods into the domestic system by imposing taxes on them, we refer in this chapter to 'BTAs on imports'; where it removes goods from the domestic system by exempting or refunding taxes on exports, we refer to 'BTAs on exports'.

BTAs are distinct from *border taxes*, which are taxes on goods as they cross borders, for example, a tariff. Border taxes restrict trade flows below what would be considered desirable if trade were to be governed by comparative advantage.[27] Under the GATT, countries have committed not to impose tariffs above negotiated (bound) levels on certain products. BTAs based on the destination principle, on the other hand, are in general trade neutral. The 2006 OECD report examined the effects of BTAs in response to falls in production and suggested that in the case of steel, they could – depending on their design – reduce the decline in total OECD production from 9 per cent to as little as 1 per cent. Further, the reduction in global emissions would be larger because BTAs would keep a higher share of world steel production within the OECD area, thus making more steel producers subject to the OECD-wide carbon tax assumed in the simulations.[28]

Border adjustment may either be origin-specific (targeting certain countries) or it may be implemented in a manner that does not depend on the origin of products.[29] The latter is commonly used in respect of consumption and excise taxes on a variety of goods, including fossil fuels and alcohol.[30] In the climate change context where BTAs are being used to neutralize any competitiveness loss, they will be origin-specific. This clearly implicates WTO rules that prohibit discrimination between countries.

BTAs may be ineffective from an environmental perspective if they eliminate or reduce the intended tax incentive of developing more carbon-efficient production processes or shifting to carbon-neutral energy sources, such as renewable energy.[31] Importantly, they are likely to be deficient from a fairness standpoint as they aim to neutralize the competitive advantage otherwise held by (mostly developing) countries without a carbon pricing mechanism in place. Given the UNFCCC's principle of common

---

[27]   Johnson and Krauss, *supra* note 24 at 596.
[28]   OECD, *supra* note 5 at 78.
[29]   Stephenson and Upton, *supra* note 2 at 15.
[30]   The OECD reports, for example, that they are used by all countries that levy domestic taxes on fossil fuels for fiscal purposes. OECD, *supra* note 5.
[31]   See Frank Biermann and Rainer Brohm, 'Implementing the Kyoto Protocol without the USA: the Strategic Role of Energy Tax Adjustments at the Border' (2005) 4 *Climate Policy* 289.

but differentiated responsibilities, such countries are currently under no international obligation to reduce emissions. In the following section, we explain the relevant WTO rules, and then consider the legal complications that ensue when BTAs are used to address competitiveness concerns in the climate change context. We take up the policy objections to the use of BTAs in the final section and again in Chapter 12.

8.4   BTAS AND WTO RULES

BTAs were first considered under GATT rules in the late 1960s following attempts by some countries to harmonize indirect taxes. Indirect taxes are those levied on products (such as specific excise duties, sales taxes, and value added taxes). In 1968, the GATT set up a Working Party on Border Tax Adjustments (the 'Working Party') to examine various issues relating to the use of BTAs. In its final report, the Working Party adopted the following definition of BTAs:[32]

> any fiscal measures which put into effect, in whole or in part, the *destination principle* (i.e., which enable exported products to be relieved of some or all of the tax charged in the exporting country in respect of similar domestic products sold to consumers on the home market and which enable imported products sold to consumers to be charged with some or all of the tax charged in the importing country in respect of similar domestic products.

WTO rules applicable to BTAs differ according to whether the BTAs are on imports or exports. They are both permitted; however, BTAs on imports must not constitute illegal discrimination under the GATT's most-favoured-nation and national treatment provisions, while BTAs on exports must not constitute an illegal subsidy pursuant to either the GATT or the SCM Agreement.

8.4.1   BTAs on Imports

BTAs on imports are permitted pursuant to Article II.2(a) of the GATT, which allows countries to impose internal taxes on imported products.[33] Ordinarily, Article II requires contracting parties to accord to other contracting parties treatment 'no less favourable' than that provided for in

---

[32]   GATT, *GATT Working Party on Border Tax Adjustments*, BSID 18S/97, GATT, 1970 (emphasis added).
[33]   Ibid.

its Schedule of tariff concessions. However, Article II.2(a) states that the aforesaid commitment does not prevent parties from imposing on the importation of any product

> a charge equivalent to an internal tax imposed consistently with the provisions of paragraph 2 of Article III in respect of the like domestic product or in respect of an article from which the imported product has been manufactured in whole or in part.

BTAs may only be applied to indirect taxes. Direct taxes – those imposed on producers, such as payroll taxes, income taxes, and taxes on profits – may not be adjusted.[34]

Further, Ad Article III confirms that any internal tax or charge collected at the time or point of importation which applies to both the imported product and the like domestic product is to be regarded as an internal tax or other charge. This brings BTAs within the scope of the Article I (most-favoured-nation) and Article III (national treatment) obligations.

The most contentious requirement for BTAs on imports is that they must not constitute illegal discrimination under the Article III.2 national treatment obligation. As described in Chapter 6, Article III.2 contains two sentences, each creating a separate test depending upon whether the domestic and foreign products in question are 'like' or 'directly competitive or substitutable'. The first sentence provides that imported products 'shall not be subject, directly or indirectly, to internal taxes or other internal charges of any kind in excess of those applied, directly or indirectly, to like domestic products'. Only the first sentence will be applicable in the case of BTAs given that, pursuant to Article II.2(a), BTAs are only permitted in respect of 'like' products. For a BTA to violate Article III.2 then, it must be found, first, that the domestic product which is being compared is 'like'; and second, that the amount of tax imposed on imports 'exceeds' the amount levied on the 'like' domestic product.

The meaning of likeness is explored in Chapter 6 and will not be repeated here, save to note a possible caveat to the conclusion reached there that 'like' in the first sentence is afforded a narrow interpretation in order to leave room for application of the second sentence (products that are 'directly competitive or substitutable').[35] As BTAs are only allowed

---

[34] Ibid. at para. 14. Article II.2(a) refers to an 'internal tax imposed consistently with the provisions of paragraph 2 of Article III'. Article III.2 refers to 'internal taxes or other charges . . . applied, directly or indirectly, to like domestic products'. The tax or charge is thus one applied to *products.*

[35] *Japan – Taxes on Alcoholic Beverages*, WTO Doc. WT/DS8/R, WT/

on 'like' products, it is possible that a panel may construe the meaning of 'like' more broadly; however, this issue has not yet arisen in a case. The issue of process and production methods (PPMs) discussed in Chapter 6 is also relevant here. That is, are products rendered 'unlike' by their different PPMs? Where a country imposing a BTA faces a complaint that a tax imposed on imports exceeds that on domestic products, and the tax is indeed higher, it may want to argue that the products are rendered unlike by their different PPMs in order to avoid violation of the national treatment rule.

The prohibition of taxes 'in excess of' those applied to like domestic products means that, if imported and domestic products are found to be like, even the smallest amount in excess will be too much, including where the trade effects of the tax, such as trade volumes, are non-existent.[36]

8.4.2 BTAs on Exports

Traditionally, BTAs on exports have been used in accordance with the destination principle, which assumes that products will be taxed on reaching their destination. Thus the exemption or remission prevents a product from being taxed twice. In the climate change context, however, the assumption is slightly different, namely that neither the product nor its competitors will be taxed in the country of destination and therefore the BTA is needed to ensure a level playing field between the product and its non-taxed competitors. This very rationale for BTAs calls into question their efficacy for a country wishing to introduce climate change measures. There is a risk that BTAs on exports will undercut environmental benefits as domestic producers will not have the same incentive to reduce carbon emissions as they would if they had to incorporate the price of carbon into their decisions. Any carbon tax imposed may therefore become impotent if adjusted to level the international playing field.

BTAs on exports must not constitute an illegal subsidy under either Article XVI of the GATT or Article I.1(ii) of the SCM Agreement. Both Agreements prohibit subsidies (including tax credits) for exports, but provide that BTAs will *not* constitute subsidies where they: (i) exempt an exported product from duties or taxes borne by the 'like' product when destined for domestic consumption; or (ii) remit duties or taxes borne by the 'like' product when destined for domestic consumption in amounts *not in*

DS10/R, WT/DS11/ /R, 1996 (Panel Report) at para. 6.21.

[36] *Japan – Taxes on Alcoholic Beverages* (1996), WTO Doc. WT/DS8/AB/R, WT/DS10/AB/R, WT/DS11/AB/R (Appellate Body Report), at p. 23.

excess of those which have accrued.[37] As with BTAs on imports, only indirect taxes may be exempted or remitted at the border under WTO rules.[38]

The meaning of 'like' has not been considered by a panel or the Appellate Body in the context of either Article XVI.4 of the GATT or Article I.1(ii) of the SCM Agreement. It is likely that a dispute settlement panel would apply similar tests to those developed in the context of Article III.2.[39] As to whether or not the amount 'exceeds' that levied on domestic like products, as with BTAs on imports, there is no *de minimis* requirement and, where the products are 'like', even the smallest difference would appear to support a finding that a BTA is an illegal subsidy.

8.4.3 BTAs on Inputs Incorporated or Exhausted in the Production Process

A critical issue is whether BTAs are permitted where the tax in question is imposed not on the final product but on an input incorporated or exhausted in the production process. This question needs to be addressed separately depending upon whether the BTA is on imports or exports. In both cases the law is in a state of uncertainty.

BTAs on imports
A GATT panel has interpreted Article II.2(a) to allow BTAs with respect to taxes on inputs which are physically incorporated into the final product.[40] However, the situation is not so clear with respect to taxes on inputs consumed or exhausted during production or on emissions caused by production. First, if BTAs are only allowed on indirect taxes (taxes imposed on products), the question arises as to whether taxes on inputs exhausted during production or emissions would qualify as being 'indirect', with some commentators suggesting that they would not qualify.[41] However, a tax on inputs or emissions is arguably more akin to a tax on products

---

[37]   GATT Article Ad XVI.4; footnote to SCM Agreement Article 1.1(a)(1)(ii).

[38]   Paragraph (c) of Annex I of the SCM Agreement includes exemptions of direct taxes paid or payable by industrial or commercial enterprises in its illustrative list of illegal subsidies. A 1976 GATT panel in the United States Tax Legislation (DISC) case confirmed the ineligibility of direct taxes for adjustment: *United States Tax Legislation (DISC)*, BSID 23S/98, 1976.

[39]   Although, as noted above, it may interpret the meaning of 'like' more broadly, given that there is no equivalent to Article III.2's second sentence.

[40]   *United States – Taxes on Petroleum and Certain Imported Substances ('Superfund')*, BSID 34S/136/154, 1987.

[41]   Zhong Xiang Zhang and Lucas Assunção, 'Domestic Climate Policies and the WTO' (2003) 27 (3) *The World Economy* 359.

than it is to a direct tax on income or the like. It is thus arguable that it is an indirect tax. Further, as Pauwelyn argues, the very reason for the tax is to make carbon-intensive products more expensive; therefore, the tax is (like other indirect taxes) shifted forward to consumers and should be adjustable at the border.[42]

Second, it might be argued that the ordinary meaning of the words 'in respect of the like domestic product' and 'an article from which the imported product has been manufactured or produced', as used in Article II.2(a), does not suggest prima facie that they refer to anything other than the final product. There is nothing to suggest that WTO Members intended them to do so. On the other hand, there is nothing precluding the contrary result. Exhausted inputs or emissions are arguably integral to the product – especially in the light of environmental concerns about production processes – and a tax on them might legitimately be considered to be a tax 'in respect of the product'.

In 1970, the GATT Working Party on BTAs decided to leave this issue unanswered. The Working Party felt that the importance of this area of taxation was not such as to justify further examination.[43] Since then, two cases have touched on the matter, but only in a peripheral manner. In the first, *Argentina – Hides and Leather*, the EC complained, among other things, about an additional value added tax (VAT) on imports of leather products into Argentina.[44] The Panel found that, in assessing whether or not there is discrimination under Article III, account must be taken not only of the rate of the applicable internal tax but also 'of the taxation methods (e.g., different kinds of internal taxes, direct taxation of the finished product or indirect taxation by *taxing the raw materials used in the product during the various stages of its production*) and of the rules for the tax collection (e.g., the basis of assessment)' (emphasis added).[45] The reference to raw materials might arguably be seen as analogous to energy inputs used in the production process. However, it was far from

---

[42] Joost Pauwelyn, *US Federal Climate Policy and Competitiveness Concerns: The Limits and Options of International Trade Law* (Nicholas Institute for Environmental Policy Solutions, Duke University, 2007).

[43] *GATT Working Party on Border Tax Adjustments, supra* note 32 at para. 15.

[44] *Argentina – Measures on the Export of Bovine Hides and the Import of Finished Leather* (2001), WTO Doc. WT/DS155/R (Panel Report); *United States – Taxes on Petroleum and Certain Imported Substances* (1987), WTO Doc. BISD 34S/136/154 (Panel Report).

[45] Ibid. at 101. *Japan – Taxes on Alcoholic Beverages* (1996), WTO Doc. WT/DS8/AB/R, WT/DS10/AB/R, WT/DS11/AB/R (Appellate Body Report), at para. 5.8.

a declaration that BTAs on inputs or emissions would be permitted, and even if it was, later panels would not be bound to follow.

A dispute settlement panel touched more directly on the issue in *US – Taxes on Petroleum and Certain Imported Substances* (the *Superfund* case).[46] This involved US legislation designed to raise revenue for a trust fund devoted to the clean-up of contaminated toxic waste sites. In order to raise revenue, taxes were imposed on various chemicals and substances listed in a Schedule to the Act and sold in the US. It also applied to certain untaxed chemicals that had been manufactured using the taxed chemicals as feedstock.

The tax was adjusted for both imports and exports. Imported chemicals were subject to a tax equivalent to that imposed on US manufacturers, while any tax previously collected on exports was rebated. The significance of the BTA for our present discussion is that the tax was calculated by reference to the amount of chemicals used in the manufacturing process. It was not necessary for all of the atoms contained in the taxable chemical to be physically incorporated into the final substance, and the tax rate was not adjusted if only a portion of the original chemicals were actually present at the end. As the OECD notes, it was thus a true process-based BTA.[47]

Canada, the EC and Mexico challenged the US tax, arguing that it violated the GATT's national treatment provision. The Panel ruled that the tax on chemical substances in imported products was a tax directly imposed on products and was therefore eligible for adjustment. The tax on imported substances was equal to the tax borne by similar domestic products according to their inputs. It was therefore consistent with the national treatment obligation. The Panel accepted the US argument that the GATT contemplated the possibility of BTAs in respect of imported products that contained substances subject to an internal tax. Unfortunately for our analysis, the Panel did not indicate whether or not the chemicals had to be physically incorporated in the final product, or whether they could be consumed in the production process. This limits the usefulness of the ruling in the case of taxes on inputs consumed (or emissions generated) in production processes where the inputs/emissions are not apparent in the final product.

There is a precedent in practice, however, for such an adjustment. In the late 1990s, the US introduced an excise tax on certain ozone-depleting chemicals (ODCs) in order to implement the Montreal Protocol on Substances that Deplete the Ozone Layer.[48] Imports of ODCs were charged

---

[46] *Supra* note 40.
[47] OECD, *supra* note 5 at 101.
[48] Pursuant to the Omnibus Budget Reconciliation Act of 1989.

with a tax equal to the domestic tax; for exports, the tax was rebated. The tax was adjusted on imports of either the substances themselves or products containing or produced with them.[49] Hoerner notes that the tax was a substantial one without which the US domestic industry would have been quickly 'extinguished' by foreign imports, with no resulting benefit to the environment and that, given this market reality, the political reality was that the US Congress would never have enacted the tax without BTAs.[50] This tax was never challenged under WTO rules.

BTAs on exports
Regarding BTAs on exports, the situation is rather different. Annex I(h) of the SCM Agreement allows a Member to exempt or remit prior-stage indirect cumulative taxes on inputs that are consumed in the production of the exported product, making allowance for waste. There will be a violation of the Agreement if the remission is in excess of the taxes actually levied on inputs that are consumed in the production of the exported product.

'Inputs consumed' are defined in Annex II (footnote 61) to include not only those inputs physically incorporated but also *energy*, fuels and oils used in the production process. On its face, therefore, the SCM Agreement appears to provide significant flexibility for BTAs on exports in relation to inputs consumed during the production process.

However, there is a complicating factor relating to the definition of 'prior-stage indirect cumulative taxes'. 'Prior-stage indirect taxes' are defined in the SCM Agreement as 'those levied on goods or services used directly or indirectly in making the product', while 'cumulative' taxes are defined as 'multi-staged taxes levied where there is no mechanism for subsequent crediting of the tax if the goods or services subject to tax at one stage of production are used in a succeeding stage of production'.[51]

It appears from this wording that while BTAs on energy are allowed in countries that have a cumulative tax system, they may not be allowed in countries with a non-cumulative (that is, value added) tax system.[52] The

---

[49]   Duncan Brack, *International Trade and Climate Change Policies* (London: Earthscan, 2000).
[50]   J.A. Hoerner and F. Muller, 'Compatibility of Offsets with International Trade Rules', in E. Staehelin-Witt and H. Blöchliger (eds), *Okologish orientierte Steuerreformen: Die fiskal- und außenwirtschaftspolitishen Aspekte* (Bern: Haupt 1997) 235.
[51]   In footnote 58 to Annex I.
[52]   Javier de Cendra, 'Can Emissions Trading Schemes be Coupled with Border Tax Adjustments? An Analysis vis-à-vis WTO Law' (2006) 15 (2) *RECIEL* 131 at 140.

provision in the SCM Agreement that allows BTAs on energy for cumulative taxes was put in at the request of India and other countries that utilize such a system.[53] However, many countries do not have prior-stage cumulative taxes and hence cannot benefit from the provision. It is not clear from the SCM Agreement whether these countries may use BTAs on energy. The US has suggested that they may not. When the provision was inserted into the SCM Agreement during the Uruguay Round negotiations, a US trade official claimed in a letter that the provision allowing BTAs on energy where the taxes were of a cumulative type was not intended to be read widely. The letter indicated that the language in paragraph (h) of the SCM Agreement[54] resulted from an informal agreement that was 'never intended to fundamentally expand the right of countries to apply border adjustment for a broad range of taxes on energy, especially in the developed world'.[55]

Various commentators have argued that this letter would have limited influence in interpreting the SCM Agreement. Further, Pitschas,[56] Hoerner and Muller[57] and Biermann and Brohm[58] argue that taxes on inputs that have not been physically incorporated into exported products are eligible for adjustment. However, in the absence of guidance in the SCM Agreement, this outcome is not certain. Technicalities will arise as to interpretation of the particular country's taxation system and whether or not the taxes in question are cumulative.

8.5   BTAS AND EMISSIONS TRADING

Emissions trading (or cap-and-trade) is an administrative system being adopted by a growing number of jurisdictions. It involves setting a cap on the amount of carbon that may be emitted, together with the issuance

---

[53]   Ibid.

[54]   This language did not exist in the 1979 Code on Subsidies and Countervailing Measures (Subsidies Code). The Subsidies Code prohibited the adjustment of prior-stage cumulative indirect taxes unless levied on products physically incorporated into the product.

[55]   Letter written by USCIB President Abraham Katz to the Clinton administration seeking clarification regarding the permissibility of BTAs on exports vis-à-vis inputs.

[56]   C. Pitschas, 'GATT/WTO Rules for Border Tax Adjustment and the Proposed European Directive Introducing a Tax on Carbon Dioxide Emissions and Energy' (1995) 24 (3) *Georgia Journal of International and Comparative Law* 479.

[57]   J. Andrew Hoerner and Frank Muller, *Carbon Taxes for Climate Protection in a Competitive World* (Swiss Federal Office for Foreign Economic Affairs, 1996).

[58]   See Biermann and Brohm, *supra* note 31.

of emission permits which give companies the right to emit a set amount. Producers that need to increase their emissions beyond this amount must buy credits from those who pollute less. Such producers may have competitiveness concerns vis-à-vis foreign producers who are not required to hold emission permits. Where they face competition from imports, they may ask their government to impose a tax by way of adjustment for the emission permit which they are required to purchase.[59]

Where it is desired to tax importers, the question arises as to whether the domestic obligation to hold an emission permit qualifies as an 'internal charge equivalent to an internal tax' such that a tax can also be imposed on imports under GATT Article II.2(a). The WTO has not addressed this question, introducing another area of uncertainty into the broader question of the WTO-compatibility of using trade measures to address competitiveness concerns. The wording of Article II.2(a) suggests that there is a distinction to be made between 'internal taxes' and 'internal charges'. These phrases are used in Article III (the national treatment provision), but Article II.2(a) only refers to 'internal taxes', thus suggesting that BTAs are only permitted on 'internal taxes'. Pauwelyn, however, suggests that while Article II:2(a) only refers to an 'internal tax', it cross-refers to Article III:2 so that it can be argued that the broader reference to 'internal taxes or other internal charges of any kind' is controlling.[60] This argument is plausible in the sense that the terms 'tax' and 'charge' are found together in Article III.2. However, on an ordinary meaning of the words, it would be more convincing to argue that only taxes can be adjusted. If the negotiators intended charges other than taxes to be adjustable, they could have said so explicitly by using the same set of adjectives in Article II.2(a) as in Article III.2. The decision not to do so suggests that only taxes are covered by Article II.2(a). Despite this uncertainty, it should be considered whether the obligation to hold an emissions permit can be considered a tax.

A standard definition of a tax is 'a compulsory contribution imposed by the government for which taxpayers receive nothing identifiable in return'.[61] It is 'unrequited' in that the benefits provided by government to

---

[59] Stephenson and Upton note that the amount imposed or rebated would in the case of an emissions trading scheme be linked to prevailing market permit prices. This contrasts with BTAs based on a tax scheme where the rate would be fixed by government. Stephenson and Upton, *supra* note 2 at 16.

[60] Pauwelyn, *supra* note 42 at 21.

[61] Roland Ismer and Karsten Neuhoff, 'Border Tax Adjustment: a Feasible Way to Support Stringent emission trading' (2007) 24 *European Journal of Law and Economics* 137.

taxpayers are not usually in proportion to their payments.[62] Based on this definition, Ismer and Neuhoff[63] and de Cendra[64] argue that, in principle, the cost of having to possess an emission permit can qualify as a tax. De Cendra suggests that, in some cases, the amount charged for an emission permit could be regarded as 'unrequited'.[65] Similarly, Pauwelyn argues that the need to hold a permit for emitting carbon dioxide almost exclusively serves the interest of the wider community; 'companies subject to the obligation do not receive anything specific or identifiable in return'. Carbon emissions are an externality that affects the whole community and their reduction in turn provides a benefit to the community (both national and global). Thus, Pauwelyn finds that, in principle, the cost of having to present an emission credit can qualify as a tax.[66]

An opposing argument might be made that an emission permit is *not* a tax. One could argue that companies are in fact receiving a benefit from having to hold an emission permit. The regulatory scheme creating the emissions trading system has made it a requirement to hold an emission permit in order to emit carbon dioxide. The ability to emit carbon dioxide is therefore the benefit gained. The amount able to be emitted is directly proportional to the amount paid.

In the end, the answer to this dilemma can only be found on a case-by-case basis that considers the specifics of the emissions trading system in question. De Cendra suggests that emission permits would constitute taxes in cases where a government auctions emission permits, and thereby converts permit trading to a taxation/levy during the period of the auction. 'During that period, the government takes all the revenues from the auction for itself, and then has to decide whether and how to recycle them into the economy'.[67] However, emissions trading systems will take many forms and this argument may not always hold.

If an emission permit was defined as a tax, then countries with an emissions trading system would be able to impose a BTA on imports and, in doing so, would have to comply with the GATT's MFN and national treatment provisions. If the requirement to hold an emission permit is not considered to be a tax for the purposes of the GATT, an attempt to impose a tax on imports based on the cost of holding an emission permit would still be subject to the disciplines of Article II.2. The legality of a tax based

---

[62]   de Cendra, *supra* note 51 at 135.
[63]   Ismer and Neuhoff, *supra* note 60. See also Pauwelyn, *supra* note 42.
[64]   de Cendra, *supra* note 51 at 135.
[65]   Ibid.
[66]   Pauwelyn, *supra* note 42 at 21.
[67]   de Cendra, *supra* note 51 at 136.

on the cost of holding an emission permit would be subject to greater uncertainty than that of a BTA based on a carbon tax as there would be no equivalent internal tax with which to compare it.

Pauwelyn argues that if a domestic requirement to hold emission permits could qualify as an internal tax, then so could a regulatory requirement to hold a permit for imports at the border. The border requirement to hold a permit is arguably a charge which is equivalent to the internal requirement to hold a permit, which is in turn a kind of internal tax.[68] If Pauwelyn is wrong on this count, a requirement for importing countries to hold permits would nevertheless be a regulation subject to the disciplines of Article III.4 and thus would violate the rules if it treated the foreign products less favourably than like domestic products.

8.6   JUDGING BTAS

The question raised in this chapter is whether WTO rules allow countries to impose BTAs as a means of quashing domestic opposition to climate change policy. As the discussion has shown, there are significant legal uncertainties. These point to an important role for the WTO in determining the legitimacy of BTAs should disputes arise over their use. Key threshold issues are, first, whether BTAs on either imports or exports ought to be permitted in the case of production inputs and/or emissions (energy) and, second, whether a requirement to hold an emission permit constitutes a 'tax' or 'internal charge' under Article II.2(a) of the GATT.

Legal complexities and uncertainties aside, governments will face domestic political pressure to use border taxes. This was evident through 2009 and is discussed in more detail in Chapter 12. Most notably, in the US, Democrats insisted that they will not support climate change legislation that does not include border adjustments (in the form of a tariff on imported goods) to level the playing field for US manufacturers.[69]

The outcome of these legal determinations in any given case will have important implications for developed countries as they assess available domestic policies. It will also have important implications for developing countries who stand to lose the benefit of competitive advantages gained through having less stringent environmental measures. It is plausible that BTAs may be useful as between developed countries in allowing countries

---

[68]   Pauwelyn, *supra* note 42.
[69]   *The Wall Street Journal*, Environmental Capital, 'Cap and Trade: Will the Senate Go for Carbon Tariffs, Too?' 1 October 2009.

to quell political opposition to climate change measures. Of course, it remains possible that the exporting countries will be antagonized and may, in retaliation, impose sanctions that impact sectors other than that which applied the original pressure. The use of BTAs by developed countries on products from developing countries will undermine the principle of common but differentiated responsibilities. There will also be implications for international relations, with the potential for political and trade friction evident, particularly given that BTAs have the potential to be discriminatory and a disguise for protectionism.

These political implications (which we address further in Chapter 12) transform the legal questions into important policy ones – are WTO rules and dispute resolution capable of addressing such questions? WTO panels and the Appellate Body have increasingly taken on the role of adjudicating questions of broad societal importance and have demonstrated their capacity to look for a balance between environmental and trade goals. The most effective institutional framework for disciplining the use of BTAs, so as to achieve the dual goals of mitigating climate change while deterring protectionism, is one that is most capable of detecting protectionist measures. WTO dispute panels have developed expertise in this regard across a wide variety of cases. There is no obvious alternative to this framework.

At the implementation level, there are numerous questions around the practicality of using BTAs, particularly around how to calculate appropriate adjustment levels. Problems include determining the origin of emissions embodied in a product. As Stephenson and Upton note, calculating the origin of emissions would add a complex and expensive layer to trade administration. They report that existing documentary costs for proving origin are estimated to be between 2 and 3 per cent of the value of trade. Many businesses may choose to face increased costs regardless of the origin of their products rather than the cost of proving origin.[70] Countries will inevitably adopt different methods for determining the appropriate amount of adjustment, for example, by using a legislated baseline.[71] The potential complexity involved in setting adjustment levels for imports from different countries may provide possibilities for disguising protectionist measures. WTO dispute panels called upon to review BTAs will face difficulties in judging the appropriateness of adjustment levels and in sifting out cases of protectionism. There will always be a risk that BTAs

---

[70]   Stephenson and Upton, *supra* note 2 at 16.
[71]   There is also a potentially large margin for error in measuring emissions given variable production methods even amongst similar products. One suggested approach is to establish emissions caused by the 'best available technology' and apply this to all producers. Stephenson and Upton, ibid. at 17–19.

could become a focal point for vested interests and a means of protectionism.[72] However, such difficulties would not be any more severe than in other cases and do not bring into question the ability of panels to decide such cases.

Nevertheless, such difficulties do raise the question of the desirability of some kind of international agreement around BTAs, given the significance of the issues in question and the potential for adverse impacts on developing countries. An international agreement would have greater potential than dispute panels to look beyond legal technicalities to take into consideration broader questions of fairness and equity. However, the administrative costs involved in negotiating the details of such an agreement and of enforcing it would arguably be prohibitive. The current rules are uncertain (as discussed in Chapter 6) but uncertainty provides a degree of flexibility which may help countries address climate change. Flexibility is not unlimited, however, and provided that panels are able to police protectionism, the status quo provides some in-built deterrents to stop countries from using BTAs in an antagonistic or protectionist manner. However, as we will discuss in Chapter 10, such deterrents are not likely to be sufficient to deter all countries and the status quo thus carries with it the risk of generating trade and political friction, particularly where BTAs are seen as undermining the principle of common but differentiated responsibility. To this end, political agreement would be desirable to set boundaries as to when it would be unacceptable to impose BTAs.

As Stephenson and Upton argue, recognition of the widely different capacities of the Parties to the UNFCCC and their differing levels of historical responsibility for GHG emissions means that domestic policies in developed economies will impose costs that are not imposed elsewhere. As they argue, competitiveness pressures 'flow from the very nature of the global compact that has been entered into'.[73] BTAs should not be used to try to prevent exposure to these costs.

---

[72] Ibid.
[73] Stephenson and Upton, *supra* note 2 at 7.

9. The role of environmental exceptions

9.1 ENVIRONMENTAL EXCEPTIONS IN THE WTO

The previous chapters have discussed a number of agreements and associated rules setting limits on the permissible form of domestic measures that impact trade. However, the WTO agreements also contain exceptions setting out circumstances in which measures that do not comply with these limits may be saved. These exceptions provide some space for countries to take action affecting trade in certain circumstances where the goal is to protect the environment. The difficulty, of course, is in determining whether a measure is actually aimed at protecting the environment (such as by reducing GHG emissions) or is really focused on protecting domestic industry.

For example, suppose a country puts in place a regulatory measure imposing fuel efficiency requirements on new cars, which a panel finds violates a substantive provision of the GATT, such as the national treatment requirement discussed in Chapter 5. The country may argue that the provision is nonetheless saved under GATT Article XX, which lists various measures that a country can take even though they violate other rules in the Agreement. As we discuss, environmental protection measures are among those that may be saved. However, the measure may (i) not have any environmental protective effect but instead only provide an advantage to domestic industry; (ii) have a lesser environmental effect than would otherwise be the case because it is in part protecting domestic industry; or (iii) have the same effect on the environment as it would if it were not protecting domestic industry but could have been done with less impact on foreign producers. Panels must determine whether the measure falls within any of these cases in order to ensure that international trade is not unnecessarily burdened.

There are a range of different types of exceptions relating directly or indirectly to the environment under WTO agreements. These include:

- GATT Article XX: Article XX contains a list of exceptions to the substantive provisions of the GATT and a 'chapeau' (the opening words of Article XX). The two exceptions most relevant for climate change are XX(b) (measures 'necessary to protect human, animal or plant life or health') and Article XX(g) (measures 'relating to the conservation of exhaustible natural resources if such measures are made effective in conjunction with restrictions on domestic production and consumption'). The chapeau then requires that, even if the measure fits within a listed category, it not 'be applied in a manner which would constitute a means of arbitrary discrimination between countries where the same conditions prevail or a disguised restriction on international trade'.

- SCM Agreement, Article 8(2): As discussed in Chapter 7, the SCM Agreement, as originally drafted, specified certain 'permissible' subsidies. These permissible subsidies included a narrow class of subsidies covering environmental compliance costs. However, this provision expired in 2000 and so far has not been revived.
- TBT Agreement, Article 2.2: The TBT Agreement requires that technical regulations 'not be more trade-restrictive than necessary to fulfil a legitimate objective, taking account of the risks non-fulfilment would create. Such legitimate objectives are, *inter alia*: . . . protection of human health or safety, animal or plant life or health, or the environment.'
- SPS Agreement: The SPS Agreement as a whole in a sense provides an exception for certain types of measures. The structure of the Agreement is to allow measures addressing certain risks to plants, animals or humans. It allows such measures if they are based on internationally accepted standards. If a measure adopts requirements that are more stringent than international standards, it must be 'based on scientific principles and . . . not maintained without sufficient scientific evidence.'[1]

Much of the debate around trade rules and climate change has focused on GATT Article XX since it potentially applies to taxes and regulations as well as to border tax adjustments. We will focus primarily on its requirements in this chapter.

9.2 ARTICLE XX

If a panel finds that a measure violates a substantive provision of the GATT (such as the Article III requirements relating to national treatment), the

---

[1] SPS Agreement, Articles 2.2 and 5.1.

regulating country may nonetheless try to save the measure under Article XX if it is primarily aimed at addressing climate change. Article XX has two exceptions that are relevant to climate change measures, set out in paragraphs XX(b) and XX(g). It also has a 'chapeau' (the opening words of Article XX), which prescribes how the measure must be applied. The Appellate Body has required that, in examining whether a measure fits within Article XX, it is first necessary to determine whether it falls under one of the exceptions and, if so, to assess whether it has been applied in a manner consistent with the chapeau.[2] The defending country has the burden of justifying its measure under Article XX.

In order to examine the Appellate Body's approach to assessing whether a measure is likely to be saved under Article XX, we will examine four issues:

1. To what extent will the Appellate Body scrutinize the Member's regulatory goal?
2. How does the Appellate Body determine whether the measure is legitimately connected to this goal?
3. Does the Appellate Body examine alternatives that the Member could have taken and whether the measure is consistent with the Member's other policy decisions?
4. How does the Appellate Body determine whether the Member's measure, while purportedly aimed at an environmental goal, is nonetheless applied in a protectionist fashion?

These issues will be discussed in turn.

9.2.1 Scrutinizing the Goal

An important line of demarcation of regulatory authority is the extent to which panels or the Appellate Body will examine a Member's stated regulatory goal. If they seek to evaluate the goal in order to determine whether it is legitimate or is a sufficient reason to restrict trade, panels or the Appellate Body will increase their powers to police for protectionist measures, but at the expense of limiting the Members' policy flexibility. On the other hand, to the extent they do not evaluate these goals, panels reduce their ability to police for protectionism or must place more weight

---

[2] *United States – Standards for Reformulated and Conventional Gasoline (US – Reformulated Gasoline)* (1996) WTO Doc. WT/DS2/AB/R (Appellate Body Report) at p. 22.

on other indicators of protectionism. The WTO, through the rules set out in the agreements, and the Appellate Body, through its interpretation of those rules, have in general tended to attempt to limit review of policy objectives.

Under Article XX(b), the measure must be 'necessary to protect human, animal or plant life or health'. The test for 'necessary' is central to this exception. In *Korea – Beef*, the Appellate Body made two famous and controversial statements about what necessary means and how to determine whether a measure is necessary.[3] First, in terms of the meaning of necessary, the Appellate Body stated that,

> As used in Article XX(d), the term 'necessary' refers, in our view, to a range of degrees of necessity. At one end of this continuum lies 'necessary' understood as 'indispensible'; at the other end, is 'necessary' taken to mean as 'making a contribution to.' We consider that a 'necessary' measure is, in this continuum, located significantly closer to the pole of 'indispensible' than to the opposite pole of simply 'making a contribution to.'[4]

Measures therefore do not have to be 'indispensible' to be necessary. The second statement of the Appellate Body explains how to determine where on the continuum the measure lies. It stated that determining whether a measure is necessary

> involves in every case a process of weighing and balancing a series of factors which prominently include the contribution made by the compliance measure to the enforcement of the law or regulation at issue, the importance of the common interests or values protected by that law or regulation, and the accompanying impact of the law or regulation on imports or exports.[5]

The determination therefore depends on at least three factors: the importance of the objective; the measure's contribution to the objective; and the trade impact of the measure. However, as Regan notes, there is a contradiction that lies beneath this analysis.[6] At the same time as the Appellate Body has put in place this apparent balancing test, which includes the

---

3 *Korea – Measures Affecting Imports of Fresh, Chilled and Frozen Beef* (2001) WTO Doc. WT/DS161. WT/DS169/AB/R (Appellate Body Report). These statements were made by the Appellate Body in the context of Article XX(d) but in general have been applied to Article XX(b). Article XX(d) allows countries to take measures that are 'necessary to secure compliance with laws or regulations that are not inconsistent with the provisions of this Agreement'.

4 Ibid. at para. 161.

5 Ibid. at para. 164.

6 Donald Regan, 'The Meaning of "Necessary" in GATT Article XX and

importance of the objective, it has held that each country has the right
to set its own public health or environmental objectives and the level of
protection related to those objectives.[7] How then does the Appellate Body
undertake a 'weighing and balancing' exercise if a country is allowed to set
its own level of protection? Does the Appellate Body actually examine the
importance of the common interests or goals in determining necessity?

In assessing necessity under Article XX(b), the Appellate Body has
generally found that the goals of the measure are important, especially in
the health and safety area. For example, the Appellate Body has found
that measures relating to protecting life and health from the risks of asbestos, dengue fever and malaria and measures relating to protection of the
environment are important.[8] However, inclusion of the importance of the
objective in the weighing and balancing exercise seems to provide scope
for the Appellate Body to permit the Member greater scope to take action
if the goal is more important. In fact, in the context of Article XX(d) the
Appellate Body has stated that 'the more vital or important those common
interests or values are, the easier it would be to accept as "necessary" a
measure designed as an enforcement measure.'[9] This role for objectives
may be taken as providing, as Regan has put it, a 'margin of appreciation'
for the balancing between the contribution and the trade effects.[10] Sykes
puts it slightly differently, as creating a 'crude cost–benefit analysis' with
the importance of the interests standing in for the cost of error – that is, the
more important the goal, the more the Appellate Body will defer to the
Member in the analysis because the cost of improperly finding that a
measure does not fall within Article XX(b) is so high.[11]

However, Regan argues that even if there is a 'margin of appreciation',
there is no cost–benefit balancing, despite the Appellate Body's language.
The right of the Member to set its own level of protection is inconsistent

---

GATS Article XIV: The Myth of Cost-Benefit Balancing' (2007) 6 (3) *World Trade
Review* 347.

[7]   *US – Reformulated Gasoline AB Report, supra* note 2; *European Communities
– Measures Affecting Asbestos and Asbestos-Containing Products* (2001) WTO
Doc. WT/DS135/AB/R (Appellate Body Report) at para. 168.

[8]   *EC – Asbestos AB Report,* ibid. *Brazil – Measures Affecting Imports of
Retreaded Tyres* (2007) WTO Doc. WT/DS332/AB/R (Appellate Body Report).

[9]   *Korea – Beef AB Report, supra* note 3 at para. 162.

[10]   Regan, *supra* note 6 at 356 (arguing though that the Appellate Body did
not write the *Korea – Beef* judgment in terms of the importance of the goal providing a margin of error but instead as a cost–benefit test which they never actually
applied).

[11]   A. Sykes, 'The Least Restrictive Means' (2003) 70 (1) *University of Chicago
Law Review* 403.

with full cost–benefit analysis. He further argues that the Appellate Body stated that a measure that was indispensible was automatically 'necessary', which seems to negate a role for considering the importance of the goals at stake in at least that category of cases. According to Regan, 'there is no logical space left for cost–benefit balancing with the underlying goal.'[12] An indispensible measure would pass the test even if the objective was insignificant.

In its most recent decision in this area, *Brazil – Tyres*, the Appellate Body appears to agree that the test is not a strict cost–benefit analysis. It stated that in determining 'necessity', 'a panel must assess all the relevant factors, particularly the extent of the contribution to the achievement of a measure's objective and its trade restrictiveness, in the light of the importance of the interests or values at stake.'[13] This test then seems to be a weak (rather than strict) form of proportionality test, as the importance of the interests or values at stake is not directly part of the analysis but informs the balancing of the contribution of the measure and its trade effects.

The other exception relevant to climate change measures is Article XX(g), which has a seemingly more specifically defined goal. The measure has to relate to 'the conservation of exhaustible natural resources'. While this provision may appear to relate to natural resources such as coal, the Appellate Body has taken a much broader view of legitimate goals under Article XX(g). For example, in *US – Reformulated Gasoline* the panel found that clean air was an exhaustible natural resource as it was a resource, was natural, and could be depleted.[14] Perhaps more importantly, the Appellate Body in *US – Shrimp I* held that Article XX(g) must be interpreted in accordance with evolving global concerns and that international agreements could be used in interpretation of the provision. It found that Article XX(g) covered not only mineral resources but also living resources such as turtles.[15] As a result, the Appellate Body has set a broad scope for permissible measures under Article XX(g) but has attempted to constrain its scope somewhat through the connection to international agreements.

---

12 Regan, *supra* note 6 at 352.
13 *Brazil – Tyres AB Report*, *supra* note 8 at para. 156.
14 *US – Standards for Reformulated and Conventional Gasoline* (1996) WTO Doc. WT/DS2/R (Panel Report) at para. 6.37. This aspect of the ruling was not appealed.
15 *United States – Import Prohibition of Certain Shrimp and Shrimp Products (US – Shrimp I)* (1998) WTO Doc. WT/DS58/AB/R (Appellate Body Report) at para. 129ff.

9.2.2 Connecting the Measure to the Goal

Another important factor in assessing whether a measure is legitimate is the connection of the measure to the goal. If the measure is closely connected to a legitimate objective, then (depending on how the objective is specified) it seems less likely to be protectionist in nature. The nature of this connection, however, raises concerns about what evidence Members need to provide on whether the measure will be effective in achieving the desired end. This concern about evidence of effectiveness is particularly acute in the context of climate change, where there is considerable uncertainty and debate about which measures will actually work.

In terms of Article XX(b), if the measure is 'indispensible' to achieving the end, it will be considered 'necessary'.[16] However, if the measure is not indispensible, then the Appellate Body requires the balancing of the three factors discussed in the last section. In addition to the importance of the objective and the trade effects, the Appellate Body in *Brazil – Tyres* held that a 'necessity' determination requires consideration of the contribution of the measure to the objective. It found that this entails a 'genuine relationship of ends and means between the objective pursued and the measure at issue'.[17]

However, the Appellate Body also noted that the greater the trade effects, the greater the contribution that would be required for a finding of necessity. For example, in *Brazil – Tyres*, Brazil had put in place a trade ban on retreaded tyres. The Appellate Body stated that 'when a measure produces restrictive effects on international trade as severe as those resulting from an import ban, it appears to us that it would be difficult for a panel to find that measure necessary unless it is satisfied that the measure is apt to make a material contribution to the achievement of its objective.'[18] It found that, even if the measure aims at reducing a health risk, when the Member bans imports the contribution must be more than marginal or insignificant.

This emphasis on the contribution of the measure raises two issues relevant to climate change policies. First, the framing of the objective will be important. If the objective is framed very narrowly (for example, to reduce GHG emissions by increasing the use of ethanol in cars), the measure may more readily be found to be indispensible or to make a material contribution. However, with such a narrowly defined objective, the ability to police

---

[16] *Korea – Beef AB Report, supra* note 3 at para. 161.
[17] *Brazil – Tyres AB Report, supra* note 8 at para. 145.
[18] *Brazil – Tyres AB Report, supra* note 8 at para. 150.

for protectionist policies is correspondingly weakened. On the other hand, if the objective is very broadly framed (for example, to reduce GHG emissions by 80 per cent by 2050), no measure will be indispensible. Moreover, even the requirement of a 'material' contribution could be problematic. This aspect could be problematic in the climate change area if a panel looked to not only domestic actions but international actions and found a measure not 'material' given actions by other countries.[19]

This reduced likelihood of being found to be 'indispensible' or to making a material contribution may also arise where the measure is part of an overall climate change action plan. For example, it is harder for a tax credit on equipment for alternative energy to be viewed as providing a material contribution if its effects are combined with other measures in an alternative energy plan. However, the Appellate Body has recently stated that the relationship of the measure to a plan must be taken into account. In *Brazil – Tyres*, it recognized that 'certain complex public health or environmental problems may be tackled only with a comprehensive policy comprising a multiplicity of interacting measures. In the short term, it may prove difficult to isolate the contribution to public health or environmental objectives of one specific measure from those attributable to the other measures that are part of the same comprehensive policy.'[20] The Appellate Body went on to find that the import ban at issue was central to Brazil's overall goal of reducing risk from used tyres and therefore likely to bring about a material contribution.[21]

Second, the nature of the evidence required to show effectiveness will also be important. The effectiveness of many of the measures used to increase the use of alternative energy is uncertain. If quantitative evidence of effectiveness were required, it would reduce the policy flexibility and ability of regulating states to innovate. However, the Appellate Body has taken a liberal approach to such evidence. In the recent *Brazil – Tyres* decision, the Appellate Body went out of its way to be flexible in these evidentiary requirements. It found that the analysis did not have to be quantitative but could be qualitative,[22] and the selection of the method for determining the contribution depends on the 'nature, quantity, and

---

[19] For example, the ineffectiveness of a particular policy (controls on emissions of new cars) was argued (unsuccessfully) as part of a challenge to the US Environmental Protection Agency's failure to regulate GHG emissions from new cars under the Clean Air Act: *Massachusetts v. EPA*, 127 S.Ct. 1438 (2007).

[20] Appellate Body, *Brazil – Tyres AB Report, supra* note 8 at para. 151.

[21] Ibid. at paras 154 and 155.

[22] *Brazil – Tyres AB Report*, ibid. at para. 146; *EC – Asbestos AB Report, supra* note 7 at para. 167.

quality of evidence existing at the time the analysis is made'.[23] Further, it stated that 'the results obtained from certain actions – for instance, measures adopted in order to attenuate global warming and climate change, or certain preventive actions to reduce the incidence of diseases that may manifest themselves only after a certain period of time – can only be evaluated with the benefit of time'.[24] These statements provide room for regulating states to argue that the measures at issue may make a contribution.

The Appellate Body therefore seems to have set a high bar under Article XX(b) in terms of the contribution of the measure, particularly where there are severe trade effects. However, it has provided greater scope for actions relating to climate change by reducing the proof requirements and specifying that panels should take into account that some measures may be important parts of an overall package.

The test for the connection between the measure and the objective is in general less strict in the context of Article XX(g). Article XX(g) requires that the measure be 'related to' the conservation of exhaustible natural resources. While the Appellate Body initially interpreted 'related to' to mean 'primarily aimed at'[25], it broadened the interpretation in *US – Shrimp I* to mean 'reasonably related to the ends'.[26] This latter test appears to be less strict than 'primarily aimed at' and involves an examination of the 'general design and structure' of the measure and its relationship to the objective.[27]

There is, however, an interesting additional element to the Article XX(g) test. The Appellate Body in *US – Shrimp I* noted that, given the design of the measure in question, it was 'not disproportionately wide in its scope and reach in relation to the policy objective . . . The means are, in principle, reasonably related to the ends. The means and ends relationship . . . is observably a close and real one.'[28] While the Appellate Body did not expand on the 'disproportionate' test, it does appear to provide some scope for panels to examine the nature of the measure and its relation to the end goal with the possibility of rejecting a measure that appears to the Appellate Body to be too broad for the given end.

In summary, in terms of the contribution of the measure to the goal, Article XX(b) establishes a potentially high hurdle, particularly where the

---

23 *Brazil – Tyres AB Report*, ibid. at para. 145.
24 Ibid. at para. 151.
25 *US – Reformulated Gasoline AB Report*, *supra* note 2 at 18–19.
26 *US – Shrimp I AB*, *supra* note 15 at para. 141.
27 Ibid. at para. 141. Steve Charnovitz, 'The WTO's Environmental Progress' (2007) 10 (3) *Journal of International Economic Law* 685 at 701.
28 *US – Shrimp I AB*, *supra* note 15 at para. 141.

trade impacts of the measure are severe. However, the Appellate Body has provided some room for deference to the opinions of the regulating government where the objective of the measure is important, there is some uncertainty concerning effectiveness, or the measure is part of a broader plan. Climate change policies in general appear to fulfil each of these factors and therefore a panel or the Appellate Body would seem likely to provide scope for (although not complete deference to) a domestic government's determination of an effective measure. For Article XX(g) the test plays a more limited role, with at most a weak proportionality requirement between any climate change policy and the objective specified by the government – that is, the measure cannot be overly broad relative to the objective.

9.2.3 Searching for Alternatives

Even if the objective is important and the measure is reasonably related to this objective in some fashion, there is the further question of how the measure fits with other potential policies. The measure may be effective but create more significant impacts on trade than another equally or more effective measure. Further, there may be a range of policies that are as effective and less costly to trade but are not feasible because of either cost or political concerns. The approach to alternatives by the Appellate Body or in the WTO agreements is an important factor in delimiting the regulatory policy space enjoyed by Members.

Article XX(b) most directly addresses this issue of alternatives. According to the Appellate Body in *Brazil – Tyres*, if the measure passes the initial 'weighing and balancing' discussed in the previous sections, it still has to be compared with possible alternatives.[29] There are three key requirements. First, the alternative must 'preserve for the responding Member its right to achieve its desired level of protection with respect to the objective pursued'.[30] This condition is particularly important as it affirms the right of the Member to set its own desired level of protection and appears to negate the possibility that a panel could find that a Member should have taken a measure which is considerably less harmful to trade and only

---

[29] *Brazil – Tyres AB Report, supra* note 8 at para. 156. The complaining party must identify possible alternatives and the responding party has the opportunity to show that these are not reasonable.

[30] *US – Measures Affecting the Cross-Border Supply of Gambling and Betting Services* (2005) WTO Doc. WT/DS285/AB/R (Appellate Body Report) at para. 308.

marginally less effective.[31] To give an example of what this reasoning could mean in practice, where country A claims that country B should have chosen a labelling scheme rather than a renewable portfolio standard, a panel would allow country B to maintain its specified objective in terms of reducing GHGs despite the very different impacts on trade.

Second, the alternative must be less trade restrictive than the impugned measure.[32] Combined with the first condition, this requirement of being less trade restrictive in effect makes the test one of cost-effectiveness, where the cost is that imposed on other Members. Different measures have very different impacts on trade – from complete import bans to significantly less trade restrictive labelling policies. Any alternative to the dispute measure must in effect provide the same marginal benefit (that is, the same marginal reduction in emissions for example), but must do so at a lower cost.

Third, even if an alternative measure provides the same benefit and is less trade restrictive than the impugned measure, it must also be 'reasonably available'. The Appellate Body stated that 'an alternative measure may be found not to be "reasonably available" . . . where it is merely theoretical in nature, for instance, where the responding Member is not capable of taking it, or where the measure imposes an undue burden on that Member, such as prohibitive costs or substantial technical difficulties'.[33]

The *Brazil – Tyres* decision provides an interesting application of these requirements. The EC proposed a range of alternatives to Brazil's import ban on imported retreaded tyres that would meet its goal of reducing the health and environmental risks from accumulation of waste tyres. The alternatives included better management and storage of the tyres. The Appellate Body, however, found that the panel was correct in rejecting this alternative. This alternative posed risks to human health 'similar to or additional to those Brazil seeks to reduce through the Import Ban' and, '[b]ecause these practices carry their own risks, and these risks do not arise from non-generation measures such as the Import Ban, we believe, like the Panel, that these practices are not reasonably available alternatives'.[34] Further, it held that Brazil was already taking some of the measures proposed by the EC and 'substituting one element of this comprehensive policy for another would weaken the policy by reducing the synergies between its components, as well as its total effect.'[35]

[31] Regan, *supra* note 6.
[32] *Brazil – Tyres AB Report, supra* note 8 at para. 156.
[33] *US – Gambling AB Report, supra* note 30 at para. 308.
[34] *Brazil – Tyres AB Report, supra* note 8 at para. 174.
[35] Ibid. at para. 172.

This interpretation of 'necessary' has implications for climate change policy. First, countries may set their own environmental impact targets and need not sacrifice those targets for a policy that is less trade restrictive. Second, if the alternatives proposed by the complaining Member are not feasible, because of resources, cost, or technical capabilities, the regulating Member does not need to take them. This requirement provides scope for developing countries to take different policies from those of developed countries. It does, however, provide panels and the Appellate Body with considerable discretion in determining whether the costs are 'excessive' for the responding country. Third, in *Brazil – Tyres* the Appellate Body explicitly took into account the similar and additional risks from the alternative, particularly compared with a policy that provides for non-generation of pollution. Panels and the Appellate Body may thus be open to arguments that measures aimed at imposing costs on fossil fuels or promoting alternative energy are reasonable (that is, aimed at non-generation of risks) as opposed to measures that require sequestration. Further, they may examine the entire life-cycle of the goods, which is particularly important for biofuels. If the goal relates to the reduction of GHG emissions, both the impacts of the production and use of the biofuel on emissions overall, as well as any other risks from its production, will be relevant. Finally, the Appellate Body has signalled that it will look at the place of the measure in the scheme of the country's entire policy package. If the regulating member includes alternatives as a part of the 'comprehensive' policy, the Appellate Body appears willing to defer to the regulating Member's view of its importance in the balance of measures. Climate policies are likely to be part of a comprehensive plan.

Article XX(g) has a more limited form of review of alternatives than Article XX(b). It requires that the measure be 'made effective in conjunction with restrictions on domestic production or consumption'. The Appellate Body has set a low threshold for this provision, requiring only 'even-handedness' in restrictions between domestic and foreign producers. The treatment does not have to be identical as long as some similar measures are imposed on domestic products.[36] It does not appear to provide scope for assessing alternative policies for trade impacts, but merely requires that the regulating country take some steps with respect to its own risks. Arguably a panel may view a measure as not 'relating to' the desired end, where, as noted above, it is found to be disproportionately wide

---

[36]   *US – Reformulated Gasoline AB Report, supra* note 2 at 20–22. This approach was followed in *US – Shrimp I AB Report, supra* note 15 at paras 143–5.

because there are other equally effective but less trade restrictive measures. However, this seems a large leap from the current interpretation.

There are, then, differences across the exceptions in how alternatives to the impugned measure are assessed. In many ways, the Appellate Body's approach to alternatives under Article XX(b) is compelling. It ensures that if the Member sets its own level of protection, it does not have to reduce that level in order to adopt other less trade restrictive measures. The Member must only ensure that there are no other less trade restricting means of achieving that end and, even then, only take them if the cost is not too high. The Appellate Body has further emphasized the need to consider other risks that arise from the alternatives.

9.2.4   Examining how the Measure is Applied

Up to this point, the focus has been on the nature of the measure itself. However, measures can be justified on their face but applied in a protectionist manner. Article XX(b) and (g) relate to the measure itself while the chapeau of Article XX addresses how that measure is applied. The chapeau prohibits measures from being 'applied in a manner which would constitute a means of arbitrary or unjustifiable discrimination between countries where the same conditions prevail, or a disguised restriction on international trade'. The Appellate Body has held that the chapeau is focused on abuse of the exceptions and that it requires good faith between the parties. The chapeau involves a search for

> a line of equilibrium between the right of a Member to invoke an exception under Article XX and the rights of the other Members under varying substantive provisions (e.g. Article XI) of the GATT 1994, so that neither of the competing rights will cancel out the other and thereby distort and nullify or impair the balance of rights and obligations constructed by the Members themselves in the Agreement.[37]

In *US – Shrimp I*, a key decision on the chapeau, the Appellate Body examined whether the conditions of the chapeau were met. First, the Appellate Body examined whether there was flexibility in the standard that was applied or whether the US standard was rigidly applied to other countries. It found that it was rigidly applied as it essentially required the complainants to implement the same regulatory scheme as the US, despite their different circumstances. As part of its finding, the Appellate Body found that there was 'arbitrary discrimination' because the US

---

[37]   Appellate Body, *US – Shrimp I*, paras *supra* note 15 at 158 and 159.

certification processes did not comport with 'basic fairness and due process'.[38] In particular it noted that the US measure was procedurally defective because complainants were not given an opportunity to be heard, to respond to arguments, to receive reasons or to have an avenue of appeal.[39] It found that under the GATT there were 'certain minimum standards for transparency and procedural fairness' that were not met.[40]

Second, the Appellate Body in *US – Shrimp (Article 21.5)* found that there was a need for good faith efforts to reach an agreement between the parties to the dispute. In the initial challenge to the US measures, the Appellate Body concluded that the US had not adequately engaged in such negotiations. In the subsequent challenge to the revised US measures, the Appellate Body noted that the requirement was not that agreement be reached but that the regulating party must engage in 'serious and good faith efforts' to reach an agreement.[41]

More recently, in *Brazil – Tyres* the Appellate Body expanded on this interpretation of the requirements of the chapeau. It noted that if there is discrimination between countries in the application of the measure, the measure will violate the chapeau 'when the reasons given for this discrimination bear no rational connection to the objective falling within the purview of a paragraph of Article XX, or would go against that objective'.[42] In the event, it found that Brazil's justification for allowing certain tyres into the country despite the general ban (as it was required to do under a MERCOSUR dispute ruling) bore no relationship to the objective under Article XX(b) of reducing risk from tyres and in fact went against this objective. It also concluded that it did not matter that the effects of the discrimination were small where the reason for the discrimination bore no rational relationship to the objective.

As a result, in discussing the chapeau of Article XX, the Appellate Body has incorporated some procedural and some substantive elements. It recognizes that imposing requirements on imports from other countries gives rise to some transparency and procedural obligations. These 'fairness and

---

38 Ibid. at para. 181.
39 Ibid. at para. 180.
40 Ibid. at paras 182 and 183.
41 *United States – Import Prohibition of Certain Shrimp and Shrimp Products – Recourse to Article 21.5 of the DSU by Malaysia* (2001) WTO Doc. WT/DS58/AB/R (Appellate Body) at para. 134.
42 *Brazil – Tyres AB Report, supra* note 8 at para. 227. Similarly it stated that 'we have difficulty understanding how discrimination might be viewed as complying with the chapeau of Article XX when the alleged rationale for discriminating does not relate to the pursuit of or would go against the objective that was provisionally found to justify a measure under a paragraph of Article XX' (para. 227).

due process' concerns (including the requirement of negotiations) seem aimed at providing greater assurance that the measures are not being applied in a manner that is in effect protectionist. Further, more recently the Appellate Body has focused on the rational relationship between the reason for any discrimination and the objective at which the country is aiming. It is therefore not sufficient to have some apparently non-protectionist reason for the discrimination. The reason has to be rationally related to the objective. Any climate change policies will have to comport with these requirements.

9.3   WHO DECIDES?

The Appellate Body's interpretation of Article XX therefore provides some scope for regulatory and tax measures aimed at addressing climate change. It has read a number of the requirements under Article XX broadly, deferring in many ways to the decisions of domestic governments on appropriate policies.[43] The main restrictions relate to ensuring that the measure is the least trade restrictive available given the objective and that there are appropriate procedures in place to reduce the possibility of protectionist application of the measure.

The focus of these requirements on trade restrictiveness and protectionism is positive from a climate change perspective as trade liberalization in the climate change area has many benefits. These include lower prices for and increased consumption of alternative energy if lower cost producers are not disadvantaged by trade barriers. There are still, however, concerns about these requirements. They only partially address concerns that countries may be free-riding in addressing climate change by claiming to be reducing GHG emissions while, in whole or in part, actually seeking to protect local industry. Tightening of the rules may both increase action on climate change (by reducing barriers to action and opportunities to free-ride) and reduce protectionism.

An important question in this regard is whether the Appellate Body should review the Member's objectives. Regan argues that, no matter how the importance of the goal is taken into account in the 'necessity' test under Article XX(b), the focus should not be on how important the goal

---

[43]   See Robert Howse, 'Subsidies to Address Climate Change: Legal Issues' (International Institute for Sustainable Development, August 2009) (arguing that the Appellate Body has signalled it will be relatively deferential to climate change measures).

is in the eyes of the Appellate Body but on its importance to the Member. He argues that, while determining this importance may be partially influenced by such matters as international agreements, 'the real question is about the importance of the purpose to the Member, and if it is clear that the Member has an eccentric view, that view should nonetheless be respected.'[44] On one view, Regan's approach makes sense. The concept behind Article XX(b) could be that the measure merely has to be necessary to some end relating to life or health (including the environment) since it may not then primarily be protectionist. It is the importance to the Member that matters.

The difficulty with this view is that accepting even completely eccentric views of the category of 'human, animal or plant life or health' makes the provision significantly less effective, if not meaningless, as a means of establishing a legitimate exception. If any view, even if not based on any evidence, is permissible as a goal and there is in effect no review of the importance of that goal, the ability to police for legitimacy of the measure is significantly reduced. The state may, for example, claim a stringent target for GHG restrictions through alternative energy policies is its legitimate objective but really be responding to interest group pressure for protectionist measures. Further, the state may be taking action on a measure because of public fear concerning risks (for example, from nuclear power) where no such risks exist. As Chang notes, fears relating to risks may be sparked by interest groups seeking favourable regulatory action.[45] These protectionist concerns point to the need for some form of review of the legitimacy of the goals and the level of protection sought.

Regan argues that no scrutiny or balancing of the objective against trade effects is desirable as it focuses the test inappropriately on the marginal benefit to the Member versus the cost to foreign exporters. He states that these costs to foreign exporters are irrelevant as 'domestically rational regulation is globally efficient'.[46] However, as he notes, this is only true if the regulation is domestically rational and will not work if there are concerns about irrationality including either 'protectionism, or well-motivated regulation that is unnecessarily trade-restrictive (which is domestically irrational because it harms domestic consumers unnecessarily, over and above harming foreign producers)'.[47] As we noted in Chapter 2, domestic

---

44   Regan, *supra* note 6 at 353.
45   Howard Chang, 'Risk Regulation, Endogenous Public Concerns, and the Hormones Dispute: Nothing to Fear but Fear Itself?' (2004) 77 *Southern California Law Review* 743.
46   Regan, *supra* note 6 at 367.
47   Ibid.

regulation may be motivated by the private interests of those in power (or with access to power), not necessarily the public interest.

In this regard, the importance of the objective may then be a (perhaps bad) proxy for domestic rationality. If the objective is important in terms of collectively determined ends and the measure contributes significantly to one or more of these ends, it may be more likely that the measure is domestically rational (and not protectionist). Further, if the trade effects are not great given the importance of the desired end and the contribution of the measure, it seems less likely that it is irrational in the sense of imposing unnecessary costs on consumers and other parties. The test then is related to whether there is protectionism, through the (weak) signal of common values and the level of contribution of the measure to the end. The importance of the goal, as measured by some means, is relevant to rationality, though perhaps not the best signal.

How can panels or the Appellate Body legitimately scrutinize policy goals and their relation to the means chosen? As noted in Chapter 2, it is difficult for the Appellate Body to determine the legitimacy of an objective related to climate change because of the different costs and benefits of alternative policies. Further, the chosen policy is based in part on ethical determinations deriving from the preferences of the citizens of a country for fairness and equity in the distribution of the costs of climate change. Panels and the Appellate Body seem more likely to make errors in assessing such preferences than domestic governments.[48] A panel will also require information about the effectiveness of the measure, the trade effects of the measure, and the feasibility of alternatives. The information required by these tests raises concerns about the ability of panels (and the parties) to obtain the required information, as well as the ability of WTO panels and the Appellate Body to evaluate the information they receive from the parties.

The Appellate Body has not yet had to deal with a minimal or non-existent level of risk directly in such a context. As discussed in Chapter 16, one possibility (similar to the SPS Agreement) is to require a minimum level of scientific evidence for an objective and, if it exists, then allow broad deference to the domestic decision on the level of protection. The next chapter discusses a series of questions related to these concerns with the tests under Article XX and other constraints on domestic climate policies.

---

[48]   Andrew Guzman, 'Food Fears: Health and Safety at the WTO' (2005) 45 *Virginia Journal of International Law* 1 (arguing that panels and the Appellate Body are not likely to be as good at identifying the preferences of the citizens of a state as the domestic government).

What form of review should panels or the Appellate Body take in analysing measures such as those aimed at climate change that involve scientific and other forms of uncertainty and information about the preferences of individuals in different member states? Who should bear the burden of proof in assessing these claims? Are we asking too much of generalist trade panels to make these assessments of climate policies?

10. Judging domestic policy

10.1 CERTAINTY, FLEXIBILITY AND ENFORCEMENT

Addressing climate change is likely to involve a combination of all the instruments discussed in Part III – regulations, taxes, subsidies, and border adjustments. Governments can use these instruments to overcome the market failure at the centre of climate change. The difficulty, as mentioned in various ways for the different instruments, is that these instruments also provide opportunities for protectionism and the WTO has to determine when the policies are legitimate and when they are essentially forms of cheating on trade commitments. It is critical that panels and the Appellate Body are able to sort out these different motivations. It is particularly important for developing countries, who have a large stake in ensuring that the climate change system develops in a manner that is compatible with a fair, open, and rules-based international trading system that affords them opportunities to further their growth and development.[1] The discussion in the previous chapters has shown that the existing rules do not optimally allow this sorting out to happen in the context of climate change. This chapter sets out some of the general concerns with the status quo and then discusses the value of changes to how panels and the Appellate Body review domestic policies.

The prior chapters on domestic policy indicate that flexibility and decentralization are essential to addressing climate change. Climate change is a global challenge and it makes no difference to the atmosphere whether GHGs are emitted in one country or another. However, efficient and effective policies require that the context for action in each country be taken into account by policy-makers. The policies must take into account the costs and benefits of different types of actions in each country – perhaps not in the form of strict cost–benefit analysis, but at least roughly taking into account the direct costs of action and the opportunity costs of different policies. Moreover, in deciding on the stringency of action, countries

---

[1] World Bank, *World Development Report 2010: Development and Climate Change* (Washington, DC: The World Bank, 2010) at 255.

will take into account the values of their own citizens. In some cases these values will push towards stringent action and in some, less stringent; however it is difficult to imagine legitimate and sustainable policies that do not take into account the differences in values across countries. Finally, information is changing – both about what action is required and about the efficacy of different policies. Governments must be allowed to adapt to new information as well as to innovate on the basis of existing knowledge (or uncertainty).

The difficulty with existing WTO rules concerning domestic policies is that they do not adequately permit flexibility and decentralization, or allow adequate enforcement of existing requirements. There are three main concerns with existing WTO rules concerning domestic policies. First, there is a lack of sufficient flexibility to allow countries to develop effective climate policies. Second, there is a lack of certainty, which may hinder Members' willingness to take effective and efficient action on climate change. Third, there is a lack of effective enforcement rules and procedures, which undermines the ability of developing countries to rely on the WTO rules. These will be discussed in turn.

10.1.1 Lack of Flexibility

We have discussed throughout the book the need for flexibility – in terms both of adapting measures to the circumstances of particular countries and of responding to changing information. This flexibility could come from finely tailored ex ante rules designed to cover all the different types of measures that could be used and to specify in advance whether they are permissible or not. However, such tailoring, to the extent it is possible, comes at a potentially high cost including the cost of the information necessary to specify these measures with any accuracy and the high bargaining costs as parties seek to shape these rules to suit their own interests.

The WTO chooses a different form of flexibility – through the use of standards that set out the basic requirements for measures (such as national treatment) and the exceptions to those requirements (and, in particular, Article XX). The standards for national treatment attempt to ensure that whatever measures are put in place are not discriminatory – that is, countries can take whatever measures they wish but they cannot discriminate between domestic products and imports. The degree of flexibility it provides depends on how broadly the requirements are interpreted. For example, the more narrowly the 'like' test is set in economic terms, the more types of measures it will capture as discriminatory and therefore the less flexibility will be built into the WTO rules. As discussed in Chapter 5, the breadth of the current test for 'like' in the regulatory context, for example, depends on the willingness of panels or the Appellate Body to look to factors such as idealized consumer preferences.

If the measures are discriminatory, they may be saved by the exceptions under Article XX, which do not specify exactly which measures are permissible but rather the type of measures that are permissible. Article XX does not provide sufficient flexibility, at least as it has been interpreted until recently. This concern can be linked back to the concern about certainty. First, if a measure falls under Article XX(b), it must satisfy the stringent 'necessary' test, which, depending on the evidence required to satisfy the test, may limit the ability of Members to adopt certain measures. Further, it is an open question whether climate measures would fall under Article XX(g) as relating to the conservation of exhaustible natural resources. The Appellate Body has provided signals of its willingness to provide considerable deference to domestic environmental policies, such as in *US – Shrimp* and *Brazil – Tyres*. However, the interpretation under Article XX will determine how flexible the WTO rules actually are with respect to climate policies.

Beyond these concerns with taxes, regulations and BTAs, there is the further concern about flexibility and subsidies. The SCM Agreement places restrictions on subsidies but does not contain an Article XX-type exception clause. The lack of an exception limits the ability of countries to use subsidies where they are an important component for a plan for addressing climate change in a particular country. For example, while taxes and emissions trading are in general superior to subsidies from an efficiency and effectiveness standpoint, there may be occasions or issues for which subsidies are the only politically feasible option. It does not make sense to deny Members the ability to use subsidies (or impose a cost on the use of subsidies) if alternate measures are not politically feasible. The Appellate Body has developed fairly strict rules around subsidies but the lack of appropriate flexibility is a matter of concern. As we noted in Chapter 7, it may be that this lack of flexibility leaves countries without a politically feasible (perhaps, in some contexts, the only politically feasible) climate measure.

There is therefore the potential for flexibility depending on how panels and the Appellate Body interpret these provisions going forward. There appears to be some evolution in the decisions towards greater scope for domestic measures. If this evolution continues, there is some flexibility under national treatment for regulations and taxes, though much less flexibility under the rules on subsidies. There is also expanding scope for saving measures under Article XX. Much will depend on how panels or the Appellate Body engage with individual challenges on these issues.

10.1.2 Lack of Certainty

Very closely related to the concern about flexibility is the considerable uncertainty under existing WTO rules for governments wishing to put in place climate policies. Consider the rules about national treatment. In the context of regulations, the decisions concerning national treatment raise uncertainties about whether the domestically produced product and the import are 'like' products, about whether there has been 'less favourable treatment' of the import if they are 'like', and whether the rules permit distinctions based on PPMs. For tax measures, there is an even greater array of questions, including whether the domestic and imported products are 'like', whether instead they are 'directly competitive and substitutable', and whether the products are 'similarly' taxed. These issues also underlie examinations of BTAs. Review of subsidies raises different concerns but more uncertainty such as whether the subsidy causes an adverse effect.

It is not just that this is a factual inquiry that is difficult for a panel to sort out, which it clearly can be. Panels and the Appellate Body have not settled on a clear set of tests to deal with these issues. For example, the role of consumer preferences is unclear yet quite important in the climate change area as products with different carbon footprints can be viewed differently. The Appellate Body also lacks a coherent, or at least clearly articulated, approach to PPMs in each of these contexts. The lack of an articulated, consistent approach makes it difficult for countries to determine how their measures will be treated if challenged.

This uncertainty also extends to Article XX. For example, any climate measure must be shoe-horned into one of the exceptions that were not set with climate change in mind. As noted in Chapter 9, a Member defending a climate measure may rely on Article XX(b), which will depend on the nature of the balancing test in determining 'necessity'. For Article XX(g), it is not clear whether climate measures would be found to relate to an 'exhaustible natural resource'. Moreover, to satisfy the chapeau will require some form of negotiations with other Members, which, while seemingly broad, is not entirely clear in the climate area.

There may be good reasons to prefer broader standards over detailed rules, with the content of the broader standards to be developed and articulated through case-by-case dispute settlement.[2] However, to obtain

---

[2]   See Chapter 2 for a discussion of rules and standards. A key framework for this distinction is found in Louis Kaplow, 'Rules Versus Standards: An Economic Analysis' (1992) 42 (3) *Duke Law Journal* 557.

the benefit of the standards there must be some degree of certainty about what is entailed over time. The general guidance about the standard gives parties confidence and predictability about future decisions and investments. The uncertainty about how a panel will apply the provisions discussed in this Part may lead to a reduced willingness to adopt certain climate measures (those that may be subject to challenge). It increases the cost of climate action. Moreover, this uncertainty may also increase the number of challenges and the cost of each challenge as Members will also be uncertain both about the legality of the particular measures and about what evidence is necessary.

10.1.3   Lack of Enforcement

The lack of certainty and of flexibility is exacerbated by the concerns about the WTO enforcement system. The WTO has one of the most developed enforcement systems in the international arena. However, both the nature of remedies under WTO law and the costs (direct and indirect) of the dispute resolution system raise problems about the efficacy and fairness of the system. Interestingly, these concerns about the remedial provisions have different implications for flexibility and uncertainty. On the one hand, they lead to even greater uncertainty about the rules as it is not clear whether the existing rules will be followed. On the other hand, the lack of enforcement provides a form of flexibility, although perhaps not in an optimal fashion.

The issues of remedies and costs of enforcement stem from the remedial provisions of the Dispute Settlement Understanding (DSU). Members can bring complaints about measures of another Member under the DSU. The complaint goes through a consultation process and if it is still not resolved it goes to a dispute resolution panel. If the panel (or the Appellate Body on appeal) finds that the measure does not comply with the Member's WTO obligations, the Member taking the measure is required to remove the measure. If it fails to do so, the Members can attempt to agree on compensation but if no agreement is reached the complaining party may seek permission to impose countermeasures against the Member taking the measure. These countermeasures take the form of the complaining party withholding concessions, such as by increasing tariffs.[3]

---

[3]   The remedial provisions for export subsidies are somewhat stricter both in the actual remedies and the timelines; see Andrew Green and Michael Trebilcock, 'Enforcing WTO Obligations: What Can We Learn From Export Subsidies?' (2007) 10 (3) *Journal of International Economic Law* 653.

These remedial provisions potentially lead to differing abilities and willingness of Members to use the WTO dispute settlement system.[4] Consider first the nature of the remedies for non-compliance with WTO commitments. As the countermeasures generally take the form of increased tariffs, the Member imposing the countermeasures must have sufficient trade with the violating country to actually induce action. It is difficult to have any economic effect from the sanction if the country imposing the countermeasure cannot significantly harm the exporting industry of the non-complying Member. As a result, large importing countries, such as the US and the EU, have much greater ability to use these countermeasures to induce compliance by others. This difficulty in finding leverage for some Members has led to calls to revamp the remedies system to allow, for example, monetary sanctions against non-compliant Members, or to allow successful complaining countries to auction off to other Members the right to take countermeasures.[5]

Moreover, the remedies under the WTO dispute settlement system are prospective.[6] In ordinary civil litigation, any remedies for breach of

---

[4] There is a debate in the literature about the nature of WTO sanctions. They may be viewed as a form of liability rule – that is, a rule that allows the responding (violating) party to determine whether the harm it is causing is greater or less than the benefits it receives. Such a view would allow for efficient breach (non-compliance with the WTO rules where it is efficient). The alternative is that there would be a very high penalty for non-compliance with WTO rules, indicating that there is a strict prohibition on non-compliance. The nature of WTO remedies (including their prospective nature) appears to point towards the sanctions being a form of liability rule. See, for example, Warren Schwartz and Alan O. Sykes, 'The Economic Structure of Renegotiation and Dispute Resolution in the World Trade Organization' (2002) 31 *Journal of Legal Studies* S179; Joel Trachtman, 'The WTO Cathedral' (2007) 43 (1) *Stanford Journal of International Law* 127. But see John H. Jackson, 'International Law Status of WTO Dispute Settlement Reports: Obligations to Comply or Option to "Buy Out"?' (2004) 98 (1) *American Journal of International Law* 109, and Joost Pauwelyn, 'Optional Protection of International Law: Navigating Between "European Absolutism" and "American Voluntarism"' (University of St Gallen Law and Economics Working Paper, No. 27, 2007).

[5] See, for example, Trachtman, ibid.; Schwartz and Sykes, ibid.; Marco Bronckers and Naboth van den Broek, 'Financial Compensation in the WTO: Improving the Remedies of WTO Dispute Settlement' (2005) 8 (1) *Journal of International Economic Law* 101; and Green and Trebilcock, *supra* note 3.

[6] Schwartz and Sykes, ibid., argue that the prospective nature of remedies allows efficient adjustments as new circumstances arise. There is an exception to the prospective nature of remedies in the area of subsidies: *Australia – Subsidies Provided to Producers and Exporters of Automotive Leather – Recourse by the United States to Article 21.5 of the DSU* (2000) WT/DS126/R (Panel Report). However, this decision has not been followed by other panels.

contract would in most cases at least equal the harm that the breaching party has caused to the complaining party. The remedies may be such as to put the complaining party in the position it would have been but for the breach. However, in the case of the WTO, the countermeasures can only relate to the level of harm at the time that the Member was found to be in violation of its WTO commitments – that is, it does not cover any of the harm that the Member caused from the time it implemented the measure up to the finding of non-compliance.

There are a number of reasons given for this prospective nature of WTO remedies. It may be, for example, that Members are presumed to be acting in good faith such that any non-compliance is merely a good faith disagreement over an uncertain agreement. However, the result is that countries do not face any immediate costs (beyond reputational costs) for putting in place a non-compliant measure. The costs only start once another Member has complained and a panel has found non-compliance. This prospective nature of WTO remedies reduces the incentives against non-compliance with the Agreement, and may in some circumstances encourage countries to take short-term measures that can be removed in the event of a finding of non-compliance.[7]

Finally, with regard to the nature of the remedies, countermeasures are intended to impose a cost on the non-compliant Member – the loss of access to the complaining Member's markets. However, even significant countermeasures may not be enough to induce some countries to change where the issue is particularly politically salient. For example, in the dispute over the EU banning imports of meat grown using hormones, the EU ban was found to be non-compliant with its WTO obligations and Canada and the US imposed significant countermeasures against the EU.[8] Due to local political pressure, the EU did not change its measure but instead sought to build further evidence that the ban was justified.[9] The climate change context may be similar. If the US public, for example, feels sufficiently strongly about either climate change or the unfairness of

---

[7] See, for example, Green and Trebilcock, *supra* note 3, discussing how the prospective nature of WTO remedies allows countries to use one-time export subsidies to gain control of a market without facing direct countermeasures, and A. Green, 'Carbon Pricing, the WTO and the Canadian Constitution', in Thomas J. Courchene and John R. Allan (eds), *Canada: The State of the Federation 2009, Carbon Pricing and Environmental Federalism* (Montreal and Kingston: Institute of Intergovernmental Relations, McGill-Queen's University Press, 2010).

[8] *EC – Measures Concerning Meat and Meat Products (Hormones)* (1998) WTO Doc. WT/DS26/AB/R, WT/DS/48/AB/R.

[9] *Canada – Continued Suspension of Obligations in the EC – Hormones Dispute* (2008) WTO Doc. WT/DS321/AB/R.

the US taking action on climate change while other countries appear not to be, the US government may not respond to countermeasures by removing non-compliant BTA provisions.[10] Moreover, the public may even call for greater protectionism and public officials can respond without fear of public backlash. They may therefore make a politically advantageous decision to implement measures despite the threat (and even in the event) of retaliation by another country.

These aspects of the nature of the remedies reduce the willingness of Members to complain and/or reduce the effectiveness of the remedies. There is, relatedly, a concern about the costs of the remedies to the complaining party. As the countermeasures take the form of increased tariffs, they in effect harm the complaining party at the same time as they impose costs on the non-compliant party. Countries that increase tariffs in general face a welfare loss as the tariff aids domestic competing industries, but this benefit is outweighed by the harm to consumers and others from the higher prices.[11] There may, of course, be political benefits from the increased tariffs, particularly where those harmed domestically by the increased tariffs (such as consumers) face collective action problems. However, any country that wishes to take action under the WTO must be willing to consider harming itself to take action against the non-compliant Member. Developing countries may be unwilling to bear such costs of applying WTO remedies.

In addition, there may be indirect costs of Members taking remedial action. For example, reputation may play a significant role in Members' decisions. Developed countries may be hesitant to impose severe countermeasures against developing countries to the extent that they face a reputational cost (either at home or abroad) from harming their chances of economic growth. Developing countries, for their part, may not bring complaints against developed countries if they fear that the developed country will retaliate in other ways such as through reduced aid.[12] These

---

[10] Andrew Guzman and Beth Simmons, 'To Settle or Empanel? An Empirical Analysis of Litigation and Settlement at the World Trade Organization' (2002) 31 *Journal of Legal Studies* S205. Guzman and Simmons describe disputes as 'lumpy' where they do not admit of a continuous form of solution (such as removing a ban on imports of a harmful substance) and find some empirical evidence that 'lumpy' cases are less likely to settle than 'continuous' cases (such as lowering of a tariff level), at least where the dispute involves a pair of democratic countries.

[11] P. Krugman and M. Obstfeld, *International Economics: Theory and Policy*, 7th edn (London: Pearson, 2005) (discussing loss of welfare from tariffs, particularly if the country is small in the sense of not being able to affect the world price of the good).

[12] See, for example, Joel P. Trachtman, 'The WTO Cathedral' (2077) 43 (1)

reputational effects may be muted by the fact that it is an independent panel that found the non-compliance. Such an independent finding may raise the cost to the non-compliant Member taking retaliatory action against the complaining Member as other countries may view any such retaliation in the face of an independent finding to be unfair and evidence of bad faith.[13] However, the forms of retaliation may be sufficiently difficult to monitor for these indirect costs (or at least the threat of such costs) of taking remedial action to deter complaints by smaller countries.

These aspects of the nature of the remedies and the costs from the remedies have been argued to reduce both the effectiveness of the WTO dispute resolution system and its usage by developing countries. As Barrett has noted, any action taken to induce other countries to act where there is free-riding must be both severe and credible.[14] The action must be severe enough to cause the non-participating country to act and must be credible enough for the non-participating country to believe that the action to be taken. The same concern arises in the case of one Member attempting to address non-compliance by another such as in the case of BTAs that do not comply with WTO commitments. The reduced incentives from the inability of small countries to impose sufficient harm to induce larger countries to act, as well as the prospective nature of the remedies and the lumpiness of the issue (that is, their all or nothing character), all reduce the severity of the remedies. Moreover, developing countries or smaller WTO Members may not be willing to bear the costs or may view the potential outcomes as insufficiently effective to justify these costs. There is some evidence that developing countries use the dispute settlement system at a lesser rate than would be expected given their involvement in international trade.[15]

These concerns about the effectiveness and use of the remedial provi-

---

Stanford Journal of International Law 127. But see Andrew Guzman and Beth Simmons, 'Power Plays and Capacity Constraints: The Selection of Defendants in WTO Disputes' (2005) 34 *Journal of Legal Studies* 557 (arguing that reputation or fear of retaliation is as important to origin of WTO challenges as the lack of resources for developing countries).

[13]   Sykes and Schwartz, *supra* note 4.

[14]   Scott Barrett, *Why Cooperate? The Incentive to Supply Global Public Goods* (Oxford: Oxford University Press, 2007).

[15]   For discussions of the difficulties of developing countries using the dispute settlement system, see, for example, Chad P. Bown and Bernard M Hoekman, 'Developing Countries and Enforcement of Trade Agreements: Why Dispute Settlement is Not Enough' (2008) 42 (1) *Journal of World Trade* 177; Guzman and Simmons, *supra* note 12, and Chad Bown, *Self-Enforcing Trade: Developing Countries and WTO Dispute Settlement* (Washington, DC: Brookings Institution Press, 2009).

sions influence both the certainty and the flexibility of the WTO agreements. Non-compliance with provisions of the WTO agreements may not be often challenged, particularly in the context of complaints by developing countries. There is then continued uncertainty about the scope of the rules. This uncertainty does not exist because conflicts do not arise, but because they do not get addressed.

Perhaps more importantly, these concerns actually increase the flexibility of the agreements, something we have argued for, because they reduce the likelihood that Members will be challenged for non-compliance with (inflexible) rules or standards. However, such flexibility is not likely to be either efficient or fair. Flexibility is desirable to the extent it allows Members to take legitimate action to address climate change even where there may be some trade impact. In the case of flexibility arising from the ineffectiveness or lack of use of the remedial provisions under the DSU, the policy space exists not only for legitimate measures to be expanded but also for measures that are protectionist either in whole or in part. There is no reason to believe that this form of flexibility is on net welfare enhancing. Moreover, this flexibility will be greater for measures taken that harm particular Members – developing countries – which is unfair to those members.

10.2 PROCEDURAL VERSUS SUBSTANTIVE REVIEW

If the status quo creates difficulty because of a lack of certainty, flexibility and effective enforcement mechanisms, is it possible to address these concerns by altering the role the Dispute Settlement Body plays in reaching decisions on domestic measures? A considerable literature has developed on the form of review by the WTO.[16] Should panels or the Appellate Body defer to scientific (or other) determinations of Members' governments? Are the error costs of strict review so high that they should not even attempt such a review?

---

[16] See, for example, Andrew Guzman, 'Dispute Resolution in SPS Cases', in D. Horovitz, D. Moulis and D. Steger (eds), *Ten Years of WTO Dispute Settlement* (London: International Bar Association, 2007); Andrew Guzman, 'Determining the Appropriate Standard of Review in WTO Disputes' (2009) 42 (1) *Cornell Journal of International Law*; Robert Howse, 'Democracy, Science and Free Trade: Risk Regulation on Trial at the World Trade Organization' (2000) 98 *Michigan Law Review* 2329; and Alan O. Sykes, 'Domestic Regulation, Sovereignty and Scientific Evidentiary Requirements: A Pessimistic View' (2002) 3 (2) *Chicago Journal of International Law* 353.

The WTO can undertake either a procedural or a substantive review. Under a procedural review, the WTO requires the regulating member to take certain procedural steps prior to putting the measure in place. These measures can be more or less onerous. They may include notice of the proposed measure, an opportunity for the public and other states to respond, a requirement to provide reasons for the decision and some avenue of appeal. More onerous requirements may involve the completion of a specified form of risk assessment, as is required under the WTO's SPS Agreement.[17] These assessments can entail extensive scientific analysis and data collection. As discussed in Chapter 9, the Appellate Body has required such procedural requirements under the chapeau for the application of a measure. They could also be required for the establishment of the measure itself under Article XX.

Procedural requirements may aid in overcoming the principal–agent problem underlying regulatory measures. The principal–agent problem arises because the executive of a particular government takes actions on behalf of legislators or the public more generally.[18] The legislators or the public delegate these powers because the executive has greater expertise and more time and can take action relatively quickly. However, the problem arises because the executive may use this power to fulfil its own policy preferences as opposed to those of the 'principal' – that is, take the action that it feels is best rather than the action that the principal would have chosen. It may also use the power to obtain rents from regulated parties, obtaining personal benefits rather than regulating in the public interest. Procedural steps that increase transparency and reason-giving may overcome these concerns in whole or in part. They increase the probability that the executive actor making the decision obtains information

---

[17]   For an overview of these requirements under the SPS Agreement, see Tracey Epps, *International Trade and Health Protection: A Critical Analysis of the WTO's SPS Agreement* (Cheltenham, UK and Northampton, MA, USA: Edward Elgar, 2008). See also Howard Chang, 'Risk Regulation, Endogenous Public Concerns, and the Hormones Dispute: Nothing to Fear but Fear Itself?', (2004) 77 *Southern California Law Review* 743, and A. Guzman, 'Food Fears: Health and Safety at the WTO' (2005) 45 *Virginia Journal of International Law*.

[18]   Guzman and Simmons, *supra* note 12 (arguing that panels and the Appellate Body are not likely to be as good at identifying the preferences of the citizens of a state as the domestic government and arguing for the benefits of procedural review and not substantive review under the SPS Agreement), and A. Green, 'Regulations and Rule-Making: The Dilemma of Delegation', in Colleen Flood and Lorne Sossin (eds), *Administrative Law in Context* (Toronto: Emond Montgomery, 2008) (discussing the benefits of such procedural requirements in the domestic context).

from the public on their preferences and that interest group pressure will be exposed to public scrutiny.[19] Further, depending on the manner in which the regulating state fulfils these procedural requirements, the deliberation on the measures may aid in building collective values on the issue at the core of the measure.[20] In addition, the procedural requirements may provide information on the nature of the chosen measure.[21] Under these theories of procedural requirements, then, the decisions of the agency are improved.[22]

Unfortunately, regulating Members may fulfil these procedural requirements but not attend to the information obtained in them. This may occur if the accountability mechanisms thought to underpin procedural requirements (such as public pressure on the executive) are not effective. For example, if the public are boundedly rational (such as being unable to fully understand a small risk of large harm) or are subject to fears created by particular interest groups, the use of procedural requirements may not lead to improved regulations.[23]

---

[19]   Howse, *supra* note 16. See also A. Green and T. Epps, 'The WTO, Science and the Environment: Moving Towards Consistency' (2007) 10 (2) *Journal of International Economic Law* 285 (arguing that there is no principled justification for scientific requirements for SPS measures and not for environmental measures and that review of such scientific evidentiary requirements should focus on minimum procedural requirements) and Guzman and Simmons, *supra* note 12.

[20]   A. Green, 'Creating Environmentalists: Environmental Law, Identity and Commitment' (2006) 17 *Journal of Environmental Law and Practice* 1.

[21]   Stephenson, for example, develops a model in which courts can use the quality (as opposed to the informational content) of agency explanations of their regulatory decisions as a signal of the level of benefits from the decisions. The model requires that agency and court preferences are somewhat aligned and that when the court cannot evaluate substantively the agency's reasons, the quality of the reasons given provides evidence that the agency views the measure as of high value. Matthew Stephenson, 'A Costly Signaling Theory of "Hard Look" Judicial Review' (2006) 58 *Administrative Law Review* 753.

[22]   Ethan Bueno de Mesquita and Matthew Stephenson, 'Regulatory Quality Under Imperfect Oversight' (2007) 101 (3) *American Political Science Review* 605 (examining the impact of domestic oversight on the quality of regulatory decision-making where the overseer can observe some forms of effort but not others). For more general discussions of the use of decision-costs to control agency behaviour, see Matthew McCubbins, Roger G. Noll and Barry Weingast, 'Administrative Procedures as Instruments of Political Control' (1987) 3 (2) *Journal of Law, Economics and Organization* 243, and Matthew Stephenson, 'Bureaucratic Decision Costs and Endogenous Agency' (John M. Olin Center for Law, Economics and Business, Harvard University, Discussion Paper No. 553, 2006).

[23]   See Chang, *supra* note 17, and Cass Sunstein, *The Law of Fear* (Cambridge: Cambridge University Press, 2005) discussing the underlying rationality issues as well as public fear.

Instead of imposing procedural requirements, the WTO may rely on some form of substantive review. Substantive review is controversial, in part because there seems to be a significant risk that panels will make errors either in the review of the science or in relating the science to the underlying preferences of the citizens of the state (such as preferences for risk).[24] The panels either may not have the information required to make these decisions or may not be able to fully understand the evidence that has been provided to them. The error costs are therefore potentially high given that the panel or the Appellate Body is attempting to determine the true reason for the policy measure.

Substantive review gives rise to another concern. If the measures are at least in part based on ethical considerations, or require some form of threshold consideration about the proportionality of the measure, the panels or the Appellate Body may substitute their views on these issues for those of the regulating Member – that is, there is a principal–agent problem involved in having these decisions made by a set of particular panel or Appellate Body members. There has been considerable empirical and theoretical work undertaken about the extent to which judges in domestic courts vote in accordance with their own policy preferences or 'attitudes'.[25] While the extent of such attitudinal decision-making depends on the underlying institutional structure, there may be concerns about the preferences of panel or Appellate Body members such as where, for example, they tend to be drawn from trade circles. These preferences may represent a particular view of the importance of trade versus other values.

The nature of WTO review relates to the discussion of flexibility, certainty, and enforcement. Procedural review provides more flexibility for domestic governments. It allows governments to take whatever actions they wish provided they can satisfy the procedural hurdles. The hope is that the accountability mechanisms for the domestic government provide a check on protectionism as WTO review would not involve examination of the substance of the measure. Procedural review also provides more certainty for the regulating government as there is less discretion for panels or

---

[24]   See Guzman and Simmons, *supra* note 12 (arguing against any substantive review of risk assessments under the SPS Agreement in part because of the error costs from mistakes by panels or the Appellate Body).

[25]   There is a large and growing literature examining whether justices vote in particular cases in line with their own personal policy preferences (for example, for discussion of these models in the US context, see J. Segal and H. Spaeth, *The Supreme Court and the Attitudinal Model Revisited* (Cambridge: Cambridge University Press, 2002)).

the Appellate Body in reviewing the measure. Finally, procedural review makes challenges less costly and therefore more accessible for developing countries.

The difficulty is that the value of procedural review depends on the strength of accountability mechanisms. These accountability mechanisms will differ significantly between WTO Members, for example, between developing and developed countries or democratic and non-democratic governments. The issue of accountability is a particularly acute concern in the climate change context as it is very difficult for individuals to understand central features such as the small risk of potentially catastrophic harm. If individuals cannot fully understand the underlying issue, the accountability mechanisms will be weak and the connection between the procedures and the level of protection similarly weak. Further, the increased costs from these procedures may either lead to reduced environmental benefits or, if they are sufficiently large or the benefits and costs are sufficiently close, may lead the country to not regulate. These costs will also differ significantly between various WTO Members and will have differential impacts across countries (with developing countries obviously most likely to be constrained by the costs).

The value of substantive versus procedural review therefore depends on a number of factors including the extent of divergence between the preferences of panels (or the Appellate Body) and regulating countries, the cost of challenges, and the extent to which procedural requirements actually constrain the ability of Members to provide protectionist benefits to domestic industry. In the end, some form of mixed strategy (that is, mixed procedural and substantive review) may be preferred. However, these factors cause considerable concern in the climate area and, given the proliferation of climate measures and the pressure for protectionist measures during the recent global economic crisis, challenges to climate measures are likely to strain the WTO review process in the very near future.

10.3   BEYOND FORMS OF REVIEW

Unfortunately, relying on decisions in particular cases is a piecemeal approach that is subject to both the vagaries of which cases are brought before the Dispute Settlement Body and the time it takes for cases to be brought to conclusion. The concerns about uncertainty and lack of flexibility (to the extent related to the uncertainty) remain in the near term when action on climate change is urgently needed. Addressing these concerns, along with the concerns about the enforcement of WTO rules, may require other solutions.

These other solutions will be discussed further in Chapter 16. They include a Peace Clause under which Members would agree not to challenge the climate change measures of other Members for a certain period of time (for example, five years); an explicit climate change agreement within the WTO in the same way as the SPS Agreement covers measures related to the plants and animals; and a multilateral agreement covering trade and climate measures negotiated under the UN process. Before we further assess the relative advantages of different options for improving the interaction between trade and climate change, we discuss the other types of interactions. Part IV addresses the impact of WTO rules on unilateral action by members against countries they believe are not taking sufficient action on climate change. Part V then turns to the existing interaction between multilateral agreements on climate and WTO rules.

PART IV

Unilateral action to force other countries to
take climate change action

11.   Carrots – positive inducements

One suggestion for overcoming the problem of persuading countries to participate in and/or comply with an international climate change agreement is through the use of positive incentives, often known as 'carrots'.[1] Positive incentives may be contrasted with 'sticks' (discussed in Chapter 13), where threats of actions such as trade sanctions or withdrawal of aid are employed if target countries do not follow a particular course. Possible means of providing positive incentives or carrots include technical assistance and capacity building, technology transfers, increased investment, foreign aid, and debt forgiveness. There is also at least some scope for developed countries to use trade measures as carrots by offering preferential market access or other trade concessions to developing countries to persuade them to take action to mitigate climate change. This chapter focuses on the unilateral use of trade measures as carrots.

Unilateral trade measures used as carrots raise questions not only as to their potential environmental benefits but also as to their legality under WTO rules. In this chapter, we briefly canvass the legal issues that will arise as a result of these measures and note the uncertainties and difficulties they present.[2] We then ask, even if they may be used in a WTO-consistent manner, is it desirable to use unilateral trade measures as carrots? We conclude that trade measures used as carrots are, by themselves, unlikely to provide sufficient motivation to developing countries to take the climate change action desired of them and thus are not likely to achieve the goal of climate change mitigation. More importantly, justice and equity concerns will arise; carrots may be seen as being unfairly coercive if the only way a

---

[1]   Robert F. Housman and Durwood J. Zaelke, 'Making Trade and Environmental Policies Mutually Reinforcing: Forging Competitive Sustainability' (1993) 23 *Environmental Law* 545 at 561.

[2]   For further analysis of WTO rules, see Andrew Green and Tracey Epps, 'The WTO, Science and the Environment: Moving Towards Consistency' (2007) 10 (2) *Journal of International Economic Law* 285–316; Joost Pauwelyn, 'US Federal Climate Policy and Competitiveness Concerns: The Limits and Options of International Trade Law' (prepared by the Nicholas Institute for Environmental Policy Solutions, Duke University, 2007); and Thomas L. Brewer, 'The WTO and the Kyoto Protocol: Interaction Issues' (2004) 4 *Climate Change* 3–12.

country can receive a certain benefit is to take action that it does not wish to take or that does not serve its interests. One issue will be in determining whether a 'benefit' is really a benefit or simply represents market access that the recipient would argue ought to have been accorded to it under the multilateral trade regime in any event. We conclude that trade measures used as carrots are only likely to be helpful if used in combination with both sticks and non-trade carrots, and that in any event multilateral action is preferable to unilateral measures.

11.1   WHY USE CARROTS?

Unlike sticks, which punish countries for failure to act, carrots hold the prospect of additional benefits for countries over and above those already due. The desirability of using carrots rather than sticks was endorsed by the World Bank and the GATT Secretariat in the early 1990s. Both organizations called for countries to resist coercing other countries into environmental action by threats. A 1992 World Bank report suggested that countries coerced into action by threats are unlikely to comply 'either very thoroughly or for very long'.[3] The then Vice-President and Chief Economist of the Bank, Lawrence Summers, stated that:

> when consumption in the petitioning country is 20 times that of the country asked to bear additional costs for environmental improvement, or when countries are asked to forgo the benefits of their natural resources, equity more than economic logic suggests that threats to reduce poor countries' incomes further by trade restrictions are inappropriate.[4]

Similarly, in a 1990 report on trade and the environment, the GATT Secretariat wrote that 'trade measures are seldom likely to be the best way to secure environmental objectives and, indeed, could be counter-productive.'[5] The Secretariat concluded that positive incentives for countries to join multilateral agreements are likely to be far more effective than any negative approach, particularly one involving discriminatory trade restrictions.[6]

---

[3]   David Dodwell, 'Environment Better Served by Free-trade Carrot than Protectionist Stick', *Financial Times* (13 May 1992) 4.

[4]   Ibid.

[5]   GATT Secretariat, *Trade and the Environment* (Geneva: *International Trade*, vol. 1, General Agreement on Tariffs and Trade, 1990).

[6]   Ibid.

The current climate change regime does not provide any direct guidance as to what trade measures may or may not be used to induce countries to take mitigating action. Article 3.5 of the UNFCCC requires the Parties to avoid any trade measures that 'constitute a means of arbitrary or unjustifiable discrimination or a disguised restriction on international trade'. As we discuss in Chapter 13, it is possible that trade restrictions (sticks) could be designed that would not violate either this provision or WTO rules. However, Article 3.5 also asks Parties to promote a 'supportive and open international economic system that would lead to sustainable economic growth and sustainable development in all Parties, particularly developing country Parties, thus enabling them better to address the problems of climate change'. Carrots that confer additional benefits on countries such as trade preferences have the potential (unlike sticks) to produce economic benefits for those countries and, to this extent, may be seen as furthering the UNFCCC's goal of economic growth and sustainable development.[7]

11.2   TRADE MEASURES AS CARROTS

Carrots in the form of trade measures offer some form of additional benefit to the recipient country above and beyond those already enjoyed under existing trade arrangements. The most plausible unilateral use of carrots in the climate change context will involve the extension of preferential treatment over and above existing levels of market access to a less developed country, depending on its participation in and/or compliance with relevant climate change agreements.[8] The most important rules regarding such preferences are those concerning the Generalized System of Preferences. These are discussed in the next sub-section. Other trade concessions offered on a non-preferential basis are then discussed.

---

[7]   Robert Hudec, *Developing Countries in the GATT Legal System* (London: Gower, 1987) at 151. As noted above, trade benefits might not accrue from use of carrots. There are also downsides to the use of preferential trading arrangements, including supply-side constraints such as lack of physical infrastructure, education, well-functioning financial markets and modern technologies, which mean that a number of developing countries simply do not have the ability to take advantage of market openings, even where they exist.

[8]   Charnovitz uses the term 'trade conditionality'. Steve Charnovitz, 'The Environmental vs. Trade Rules: Defogging the Debate' (1993) 23 *Environmental Law* 475 at 492.

11.2.1   Generalized System of Preferences

In 1971, a temporary MFN waiver was adopted under the auspices of the United Nations Conference on Trade and Development (UNCTAD) to allow developed countries to establish a Generalized System of Preferences (GSP) whereby they could provide preferential tariff treatment to developing countries.[9] This waiver was made permanent under the GATT in 1979, with adoption of the 'Differential and More Favourable Treatment, Reciprocity and Fuller Participation of Developing Countries' framework agreement (the 'Enabling Clause'). The Enabling Clause created, *inter alia*, a permanent legal basis for preferential tariff treatment to exports from developing countries. Currently, most developed countries operate GSP schemes that provide preferences to a wide range of developing countries, including the larger and growing GHG emitters such as China, India, and Indonesia.[10]

The prospect arises that developed countries might wish to condition their GSP schemes on developing countries taking action to mitigate climate change.[11] There are questions, however, as to whether such conditionality would be legitimate under the Enabling Clause. In particular, it is unclear exactly to what extent a preference-giving country may differentiate among beneficiaries.[12] Some guidance has been provided by the Appellate Body in *EC – Tariff Preferences*. In this case, India challenged the EU's GSP arrangements, which offered special preferences to countries involved in efforts to fight drug production and trafficking. India's challenge arose from the fact that it did not benefit from the scheme while other countries did. It argued that the EU's scheme violated WTO

---

[9]   Resolution 21(II) of the Second UNCTAD Conference, in UNCTAD, Proceedings of the Conference of 1968, Report and Annexes (United Nations, TD/97). Bartels notes that the term 'generalized' probably reflects an early view that there should be a common scheme adopted by all major developed countries. However, he finds that the term 'generalized' in relation to preferences should be treated as legally redundant. Lorand Bartels, 'The WTO Enabling Clause and Positive Conditionality in the European Community's GSP Program' (2003) 6 (2) *Journal of International Economic Law* 507 at 523.

[10]   China is listed as a beneficiary under the EU GSP Scheme, but not under the US Scheme. US Generalized System of Preferences Guidebook, available at the Office of the US Trade Representative, online: http://www.ustr.gov/assets/ Trade_Development/Preference_Programs/GSP/asset_upload_file666_8359.pdf and Council Regulation (EC) No. 732/2008 of 22 July 2008, *Official Journal of the European Union*, 6 August 2008.

[11]   Michael McKenzie, 'Climate Change and the Generalized System of Preferences' (2008) 11 (3) *Journal of International Economic Law* 679 at 688.

[12]   Ibid.

rules because the Enabling Clause does not allow a preference-granting country to accord preferential tariff treatment to any beneficiary of their GSP schemes without granting identical preferential tariff treatment to all other beneficiaries. The Panel and the Appellate Body were thus required to consider what, if any, discrimination is permissible under the Enabling Clause. That is, must all developing countries be treated alike, or can countries that grant preferences discriminate among beneficiaries on the basis of different types of criteria?

Paragraph 2(a) of the Enabling Clause provides that developed countries may accord preferential tariff treatment to products originating in developing countries in accordance with the GSP, which is described in footnote 3 to the paragraph as involving 'generalized, non-reciprocal and *non-discriminatory* preferences beneficial to the developing countries' (emphasis added). The Panel accepted India's arguments that the description in the footnote is in effect a requirement that preference-giving countries provide identical benefits to all developing countries without differentiation.[13] Based on this interpretation, it found that the EU was in violation of the Clause because it had granted additional preferences to some countries and not to others (including India).

On appeal, the Appellate Body concurred with the Panel that, pursuant to paragraph 2(a), preferential tariff treatment must be non-discriminatory.[14] However, unlike the Panel, it considered that some differentiation between beneficiaries is nevertheless permitted. The Appellate Body held that it would not be discriminatory for preference-giving countries to differentiate between developing countries if they have different needs so long as a number of conditions are met. First, pursuant to paragraph 3(c), preferential treatment must be designed to respond positively to the development, financial and trade needs of developing countries. Second, when determining the existence of development, financial and trade needs, preference-giving countries must have reference to an objective standard. In this regard, the Appellate Body considered that 'broad-based recognition of a particular need, set out in the WTO Agreement or in multilateral instruments adopted by international organizations', could serve as such a standard.[15] Third, the preference-giving country must show that tariff preferences are an effective means of addressing the needs identified.[16]

---

[13] *EC – Conditions for the Granting of Preferences to Developing Countries* (2003) WTO Doc. WT/DS246//R (Panel Report) at para. 7.161.

[14] *EC – Conditions for the Granting of Preferences to Developing Countries* (2004) WTO Doc. WT/DS246/AB/R (Appellate Body Report) at para. 145.

[15] Ibid. at para. 163.

[16] Ibid. at para. 164.

Finally, the Appellate Body held that the preference-granting country must ensure that identical treatment is available to all *similarly-situated* GSP beneficiaries, that is, to all GSP beneficiaries that have the need to which the treatment in question is intended to respond.[17] Where these conditions are met, preference-giving countries may treat different developing countries differently.[18]

Thus, there are several issues that would have to be considered by a country wishing to use its GSP scheme to incentivize climate change action. We consider two simplified scenarios. The first is where a country decides to make its entire GSP scheme contingent on climate-related action (a 'negative' condition). For example, it might require developing countries to ratify and implement a climate change agreement or, alternatively, it might require them to take action such as adopting and meeting a set emissions target. The closest that any country's current scheme comes to such a scenario is that adopted by the US. Its GSP scheme utilizes a form of negative conditionality by specifying various bases of ineligibility for its preferences, including, *inter alia*, where a country has not taken steps to afford internationally recognized labour rights to workers in their territory, and where a country has not implemented its commitments to eliminate the worst forms of child labour.[19]

In the second scenario, the preference-giving country would maintain a basic GSP scheme available to all developing countries, but would provide additional benefits to those countries that comply with climate-change-related conditions (a 'positive' condition). This scenario would be comparable to the current EU GSP arrangements. Through its GSP scheme, the EU provides preferences to 176 countries.[20] The scheme includes a component known as GSP+ where additional preferences are provided over and above those ordinarily granted in the course of the scheme. To qualify for the additional preferences, countries must 'ratify and effectively implement' a set of key international conventions, including the Kyoto Protocol.[21] They will, however, only be eligible for the preferences

---

[17] Ibid. at para. 173.
[18] Ibid. at paras 162 and 163.
[19] U.S. Code Title 19 – Customs Duties, Chapter 12 – Trade Act of 1974, Subchapter V – Generalized Scheme of Preferences, Section 2462, paras (b)(2)(G) and (H).
[20] Council Regulation (EC) No. 732/2008 of 22 July 2008, *Official Journal of the European Union*, 6 August 2008.
[21] European Union, Factsheet: EC Generalised Scheme of Preferences (GSP), available online: http://trade.ec.europa.eu/doclib/docs/2008/july/tradoc_139988.pdf (date accessed: 9 January 2009). These particular arrangements will have little if any impact on climate change policies. As discussed, developing countries do not

if they are 'vulnerable while assuming the special burdens and responsibilities' resulting from the ratification and effective implementation of those conventions.[22]

There would prima facie be no discrimination between beneficiaries in either scenario due to the fact that all countries are given the opportunity to qualify for the preferences (in other words, there is no *de jure* discrimination). However, there may be *de facto* discrimination if some countries, due to lack of resources, find it more difficult to comply with the conditions than other countries. In the first scenario, the first group might then be denied preferences altogether and, in the second scenario, the additional preferences. The remainder of this discussion will take the position that there would at least be the potential for discrimination in either scenario.[23]

Looking at the conditions stipulated by the Appellate Body in *EC – Tariff Preferences*, the first question is whether the preferences would be considered a positive response to 'development, financial, and trade needs', while the second question asks whether those needs can be objectively identified. In *EC – Tariff Preferences*, the Appellate Body treated the paragraph 3(c) requirement as providing alternatives (referring to development, financial *or* trade needs), despite the fact that the wording used in the paragraph is 'development, financial *and* trade needs'.[24] The Appellate Body did not provide any explanation for this interpretation. It may be that they simply took the view that 'or' means 'and', and 'and' means 'or' in the context of a list such as this. In the following discussion we take the approach that only one of the identified needs must be met. To a large extent, these needs are interconnected and something that responds to one will necessarily respond to the others. This will not always be the case, however, and it

---

currently have binding emission reduction commitments under the Kyoto Protocol. This significantly limits the effectiveness of the EU's current GSP+ arrangements as an incentive to take action to mitigate climate change. In addition, the incentive effect is reduced by the fact that only 'vulnerable' countries are eligible.

[22]   Council Regulation (EC) No. 732/2008 of 22 July 2008, *Official Journal of the European Union*, 6 August 2008 at Article 8.

[23]   India referred to this problem in the context of the EC's GSP program, arguing that 'the special incentives were discriminatory with respect to countries unable to follow the standards, and which were consequently unable to benefit from the supplementary benefits'. Cited in Robert Howse, 'India's WTO Challenge to Drug Enforcement Conditions in the European Community Generalized System of Preferences: A Little Known Case with Major Repercussions for "Political" Conditionality in US Trade Policy' (2003) 4 (2) *Chicago Journal of International Law* 385 at 525.

[24]   *EC – Tariff Preferences*, *supra* note 14 at para. 164.

would be desirable for the Appellate Body to offer some rationale for its interpretation. From a policy and development standpoint, it is valid because it ensures a wide range of needs are considered.

The first question raises a slightly confusing issue, namely, in asking whether the preference would be a positive response, do we look at the preference alone or do we look at the preference *and* the condition taken together as a 'package'? The answer will probably depend upon the precise manner in which the condition is drafted. Where it is a 'negative' condition that countries will not be eligible for preferences if they do not take steps to mitigate climate change (such as the US provision that makes countries ineligible for preferences should they not take steps to eliminate child labour), it is arguable that the proper interpretation is the first and that the preference-giving country would only have to show that the preferential tariff would respond to a development need. This is because the overriding purpose of the preference is separate from the condition imposed upon its availability. (This conclusion would of course be subject to the precise wording of the regulation authorizing the preferences.) Showing that such a preference responds to a development need ought to be a fairly simple matter, as the purpose of granting preferential tariff access is widely considered to be a means of promoting economic growth and the need for economic growth is commonly seen as a development need.

On the other hand, in the second scenario of a 'positive' condition, a more likely interpretation of the requirement is that it refers to the preferential tariff *and* the condition taken together as a package. This is because the type of positive condition illustrated is where a preference-giving country offers additional preferences for countries with certain needs over and above those met through the ordinary tariff preferences granted through the scheme. Thus, for example, in the case of the EU's GSP+ scheme, additional preferences are explicitly stated to be an incentive for 'sustainable development and good governance'. The EU has arguably identified a development need (ratification and implementation of certain conventions in order to promote sustainable development and good governance) and seeks to enable 'vulnerable' developing countries to address that need through preferential tariffs that will enable them to ratify and implement the said conventions.

Thus, if a country's GSP scheme provided additional preferences on the condition that beneficiaries take climate change action, the preference-giving country would presumably have to show that this conditionality is itself a response to a development need. This would require a conclusion that addressing climate change is a development need. That this is the case was accepted by the parties to the Copenhagen Accord, which represents the outcome of the December 2009 Conference of the

Parties at Copenhagen. The Copenhagen Accord states in paragraph 3 that 'a low-emission development strategy is indispensable to sustainable development'.[25] This conclusion is supported by the 2010 World Development Report which finds that, unmanaged, climate change will reverse development progress and compromise the well-being of current and future generations.[26]

It might be argued that, despite these links between development and climate change, taking action to mitigate climate change is not a development need as envisaged by the Enabling Clause. Many of the countries that seek to benefit from preferential trade arrangements will experience losses as a result of climate change regardless of any steps they take to mitigate emissions.[27] This is because many developing countries – especially the poorest – have contributed very little to global warming and the majority of GHG emissions will continue to emanate from other countries. In 2004, countries that were members of the OECD accounted for 46 per cent of total carbon dioxide emissions (the US alone accounted for 20.6 per cent and Canada 20.0 per cent), followed by Central and Eastern Europe and the Commonwealth of Independent States (CIS) (11 per cent). While developing countries accounted for 42 per cent, China alone accounted for 17.3 per

---

[25]   UNFCCC, Conference of the Parties, Fifteenth Session, Copenhagen, 7–18 December 2009, Draft Decision -/CP.15, Copenhagen Accord, FCCC/ CP/2009/L.7, 18 December 2009.

[26]   World Bank, *World Development Report 2010: Development and Climate Change* (Washington, DC: The World Bank, 2010) at 37. See also Michael McKenzie, 'Climate Change and the Generalized System of Preferences' (2008) 11 (3) *Journal of International Economic Law* 679 at 691. McKenzie notes the IPCC's finding that climate change may slow the pace of progress toward sustainable development and impede achievement of the UN Millennium Development Goals (including eradicating extreme poverty and ensuring environmental sustainability). If, he argues, climate change is an impediment to meeting the development needs identified by the UN, it follows that responding to climate change will help address those needs. Further, the UN Millennium Goals serve as an appropriate 'objective standard' as required by the Appellate Body. Second, he argues that responding to climate change is itself a development need given that climate change poses a significant threat to development. He suggests that the UNFCCC could serve as the required objective standard to establish the existence of the need, referring to its goal of achieving stabilization of GHG concentrations in the atmosphere at a level that would prevent dangerous anthropogenic interference with the climate system, and its statement that such levels should be met within a time frame sufficient to 'enable economic development to proceed in a sustainable manner'.

[27]   As Gordon argues, if wealthy nations decide not to take action, poorer nations will suffer with absolutely no recourse within the international system. Ruth Gordon, 'Climate Change and the Poorest Nations: Further Reflections on Global Inequality' (2007) 78 *University of Colorado Law Review* 1559 at 1564.

cent of this total. Other than China, the largest developing country emitters in 2004 were still only responsible for small shares, including: India (4.6 per cent), Korea (Republic of) (1.6 per cent), Mexico (1.5 per cent), South Africa (1.5 per cent), Iran (1.5 per cent), Indonesia (1.3 per cent) and Brazil (1.1 per cent). As a region, sub-Saharan Africa only accounted for 2 per cent of emissions (the majority of this coming from South Africa), while least developed countries (LDCs) accounted for 1 per cent.[28]

One could take the case of a small, non-industrialized developing country that contributes only a minuscule amount to global emissions. Is emission reduction by this country necessary to address climate change and therefore to further development? Even if the country was completely carbon neutral, unless OECD members and China drastically reduced their emissions, it would continue to be negatively affected. This does not necessarily invalidate the argument that taking mitigation action is a development need. As stated, climate change is a collective action problem and every country has a role to play (however small) and, eventually, collective action will help all countries.

Assuming then that climate change mitigation is a development need, the next question is whether preferential tariffs conditioned upon ratification and implementation of an international agreement constitute a 'positive response' to that need. In relation to the EU GSP+ scheme, Bartels notes a paradox that would also be applicable to both scenarios suggested here. The stated purpose of the GSP+ arrangement is to promote sustainable development and good governance and, in order to do so, to enable countries to meet the cost of ratifying and implementing certain conventions.[29] The problem Bartels identifies is that the preferences are only made available once the conventions have been ratified, which means that countries are required to bear the costs of ratification before they receive benefits in the way of preferential tariffs. This, he argues, raises the issue of how the imposition of a cost on a country can be considered a 'positive response' to a development need, even if compensated for later by the benefits flowing from preferential tariffs. Indeed, those benefits may only be enough to enable the country to 'break even' – they may not be enough to benefit it above and beyond implementing the convention in question, causing it to have to overlook other pressing development needs. This

---

[28]   Human Development Report 2007/2008, 'Fighting Climate Change: Human Solidarity in a Divided World' (New York: United Nations Development Program, 2007) at 69.

[29]   Council Regulation (EC) No. 732/2008 of 22 July 2008, *Official Journal of the European Union*, 6 August 2008 at Preamble, para. 8, and Article 8. Vulnerability is defined in Article 8(2).

raises the question, what is a carrot? Clearly it would include an incentive that resulted in more than enough economic benefits to cover the costs of the required climate change action. Yet would it cover an incentive where the benefits received only covered the costs of the required climate change action but nothing more? And what about beneficial flow-on effects of taking action to mitigate climate change, such as improved (or stabilized) agricultural productivity? On the one hand, the effects may be negative, such as leakage of industry or loss of international competitiveness. In addition, prices might rise for consumers as business looks to pass on mitigation costs, causing a welfare loss. On the other hand, to the extent that climate change mitigation helps tackle the negative effects of climate change, this can be considered a positive effect and thereby a benefit. It is possible there would also be flow-on benefits such as potential economic diversification. Further, even if there was a zero fiscal benefit in the first year, this may change over the long term.

The third requirement in *EC – Tariff Preferences* is that tariff preferences be an effective means of addressing the development need in question. In the first scenario (where the development need is not specifically climate-related), this is likely to be reasonably simple to show because tariff preferences are recognized as being a contributor to economic growth. In relation to the second scenario – assuming that responding to climate change is found to be a development need – McKenzie suggests that this requirement could be met by showing that tariff preferences will provide economic benefits for developing countries that will allow them to meet the costs of adopting measures to address climate change, and that such measures will assist developing countries to advance their development goals.[30]

Finally, a country wishing to use either negative or positive conditionality in its GSP scheme to incentivize climate change action would be required, following the *EC – Tariff Preferences* case, to ensure that the special benefits were available to all developing countries similarly affected, and that its regulations specified the criteria or standards that a developing country would have to meet in order to qualify for the benefits. This much would not appear to unduly hinder countries in designing their GSP schemes related to climate change. The failure of the EC to do so regarding the drug arrangements that were at issue in *EC – Tariff Preferences* suggests that, in that case, considerations were at issue other than the development needs of the beneficiary countries.[31]

---

[30]   McKenzie, *supra* note 11 at 692.

[31]   The EC wanted to protect its *own* citizens from drugs, not to further the beneficiary countries' development needs. Robert Howse, 'India's WTO Challenge

Where a country's GSP scheme fails to meet the requirements of the Enabling Clause, its only other option is to justify it under GATT Article XX, which allows measures that are otherwise in violation of GATT rules to be justified where they are, *inter alia*, necessary to protect human, animal or plant life or health, or are related to conservation of natural resources. Article XX was discussed in detail in Chapter 9.

11.2.2   Trade Concessions

Outside their GSP schemes, countries might use the promise of improved market access as a carrot to induce other countries to implement desired climate change measures. However, GATT rules require that trade concessions be offered to all WTO members without discrimination. Article I (the most-favoured-nation obligation) precludes a country from discriminating among its trading partners to the benefit of one at the expense of another. Thus, countries are fairly limited in what they can do in terms of using the promise of trade concessions to force desired behaviour by other countries. First, any concessions would have to be offered to all WTO members, even if only the original negotiating partner effects the desired behaviour change. For example, if the EU extracted a commitment from China to reduce its GHG emissions in return for reduced tariffs on certain agricultural products, it would have to provide the same lower tariff rate to third countries. This would open up potential for such countries to free-ride off China's actions and would thus reduce the leverage available to force action by those third countries. Second, there would be political and diplomatic repercussions if developed countries used WTO negotiations as a means to force developing countries into accepting climate change obligations. Trade carrots may be seen as an unfair form of coercion, as opposed to other forms of positive incentives such as side payments or favourable allocation of emission entitlements.[32] Already, developing countries legitimately feel that they have not benefited as they should have from multilateral trade liberalization. Any perception of coercion would

---

to Drug Enforcement Conditions in the European Community Generalized System of Preferences: A Little Known Case with Major Repercussions for "Political" Conditionality in US Trade Policy' (2003) 4 (2) *Chicago Journal of International Law* 385 at 401. Citing First Written Submission of the European Communities in *EC – Tariff Preferences, supra* note 13 para 166.

[32]   See discussion of positive incentives in Robert N. Stavins and Scott Barrett, 'Increasing Participation and Compliance in International Climate Change Agreements' (Fondazione Eni Enrico Mattei Working Paper No. 94.2002; Kennedy School of Government Working Paper No. RWP02-031, 2002) at 17.

only serve to diminish trust in the multilateral trading system among those countries even further.

11.3   SHOULD CARROTS BE USED?

Assuming countries are able to implement trade measures as carrots in a WTO-consistent manner (or at least justify their decision under Article XX), the question arises as to whether this use of trade measures is desirable from a broader policy perspective. This requires consideration of the overarching goals discussed earlier, namely climate change mitigation, deterring protectionism, and furthering development.

In theory, unilateral trade preferences would further environmental goals by providing some incentive for countries to refrain from free-riding. A further advantage is that, unlike straight cash payments, trade measures that involve granting greater market access or trade preferences may have beneficial effects in terms of economic growth from trade liberalization, thus furthering the goal of development.[33] The expectation of economic growth is, after all, the basis of preferential access arrangements under the Enabling Clause.[34] The assumption is based in part on the argument that (unlike infant industry protection) the use of preferences allows for extra-national economies of scale, at least to the extent that the major competitors preventing the realization of economies of scale in the short run are located outside the countries enjoying preferential access.[35]

However, there are a number of concerns about the use of trade measures as carrots other than the possibility that they would violate either the GATT or the Enabling Clause. First, it is probable that carrots would simply not be that environmentally effective. In order to truly impact the climate change behaviour of a target country, the actual incentives (in the absence of other measures) would have to be sufficiently large to overcome the difference between the costs and benefits of climate action for a particular country. The difficulty is that, at least in the short term, this difference appears very large for some countries and it would be

---

[33]   See Robert Hudec, *Developing Countries in the GATT Legal System* (London: Gower, 1997).

[34]   Ibid. at 151.

[35]   The Danish Institute for International Studies and the Food and Resource Economics Institute, *Special and Differential Treatment and Differentiation between Developing Countries in the WTO* (Copenhagen and Frederiksberg: The Danish Institute for International Studies and the Food and Resource Economics Institute, 2005) at 6.

difficult to tailor sufficiently large incentives to induce their participation and compliance.[36] Carrots may, however, have some impact where the difference is not large or is negative (the benefits exceed the costs) but the country requires resources (or in this case revenue) to finance change. It is likely that, to have any real effect, preferential tariffs under a GSP scheme would have to relate to sectors of significant export interest to developing countries, otherwise the benefits would probably not be that large. This may involve granting preferences in respect of sectors that are currently classified as 'sensitive'.[37] Thus, preferences that are truly environmentally beneficial (and helpful to development) are unlikely to be politically feasible in granting countries.

Second (and related to the last point), the country providing preferential market access faces a political risk in the form of a loss of political support from the industries that now face greater foreign competition. [38] This is particularly likely to be the case where preferences are provided in respect of 'sensitive' industries. On the other hand, the granting country potentially gains from the benefit to consumers in the form of cheaper imports due to the lower trade barriers, and satisfaction of any 'green' preferences from helping to address climate change. The gain in terms of either welfare or political support from consumers (both from cheaper 'green' products and from action on climate change) must be greater than the loss to the industry that is no longer protected for the preferences to be politically feasible.

Third, countries have different reasons for not entering into a climate change agreement. For some developed countries, such as the US (and even China), the benefits (at least in the short term) of climate change action may seem to be outweighed by the costs.[39] For others, particularly developing countries, there are significant benefits from action but

---

[36]   Cass Sunstein, 'The Complex Climate Change Incentives of China and the United States' (John M. Olin Law & Economics Working Paper No. 352, The Law School, University of Chicago, 2007).

[37]   The US classifies a number of product lines as 'import sensitive': U.S. Code Title 19 – Customs Duties, Chapter 12 – Trade Act of 1974, Subchapter V – Generalized Scheme of Preferences, Section 2462, para. 2463(b)(1).

[38]   Although, preferences will not be as difficult to sustain as monetary transfers, which tend to be zero sum, that is, there is a winner and a loser. Carrots in the form of trade preferences in one sense reduce this risk because reducing trade barriers actually increases national welfare in the compensating state, thereby ensuring that both parties 'win' in terms of increased welfare from reduced barriers. Stavins and Barrett, *supra* note 32 at 18.

[39]   Sunstein, *supra* note 36.

they face either resource constraints or a large cost due to lost economic opportunities.

Finally, Chang argues that the use of 'carrots' to foster environmental protection actually creates incentives to harm the environment, at least in the short run.[40] Countries that are potentially eligible for incentives may be induced to pollute in new ways in order to gain eligibility for the carrots on offer (for example, engaging in an activity such as coal-fired electricity production in order to gain market access preferences).[41] Further, if the size of the incentive depends on the amount of pollution, eligible countries may be induced to pollute more to gain a greater benefit (larger carrots). Chang suggests that, in this scenario, countries could use the threat of continuing these levels of environmentally harmful activities to extort carrots from other countries. This concern may not be so great in the context of GSP schemes unless the larger emitters are eligible to be beneficiaries. This concern about the incentive effects of preferences may have greater resonance for preferences relating to process and production methods (PPMs) than for products that emit GHGs, as the former are likely to be more open to manipulation.

11.4 CONCLUDING REMARKS

Increasing developing countries' participation in and compliance with climate change agreements may be aided by using trade measures as carrots under a GSP scheme. However, these are not likely to become the central plank in a strategy to increase participation and compliance. They are likely to have only limited potential due to difficulties in making them significant enough and to have perverse incentive effects where countries increase emissions to obtain the carrots. They will certainly be insufficient on their own. Countries wishing to use trade measures as carrots must first ensure that they do not violate the GATT's MFN obligation or the requirements of the Enabling Clause.

Even if WTO-compliant, carrots that look like positive incentives may actually function more like a sanction if compliance with climate change conditions becomes the only way in which developing countries can

---

[40] Howard Chang, 'An Economic Analysis of Trade Measures to Protect the Global Environment' (1995) 83 *Georgetown Law Journal* 2131. Howard F. Chang, 'Carrots, Sticks, and International Externalities' (1997) 17 *International Review of Law and Economics* 309. He finds this perverse incentive particularly likely in multilateral agreements.

[41] Chang, ibid. at 313.

obtain preferential treatment. Serious equity and justice concerns will then arise – developing countries may view the so-called incentives as another condition imposed by the West that will further restrict their development efforts. Even if portrayed as extra special treatment, market access to products of export interest to developing countries has been so limited to date that such treatment may be more properly viewed as access that is long overdue than as any kind of 'special privilege'. Thus, the very idea of using preferences to induce participation and/or compliance with a climate change agreement may be seen as a retrograde step in a multilateral system that has to date failed to deliver to developing countries.

The Enabling Clause, then, does not provide a particularly helpful framework for achieving the threefold set of goals we have laid out. Yet attempting to revise the clause to forbid the use of carrots would probably not be helpful either. There may be occasions where carrots would be beneficial and may aid development in a way money would not. Further, attempting to delineate cases where they are not beneficial would probably be ineffective, as well as imposing high costs to make and enforce the rule. The granting of preferences is at best based on need and at worst on political expediency – something that is extremely difficult to influence through legal rules.

12. Dismantling roadblocks

Thus far we have considered the scope for unilateral trade measures to be used as 'carrots'. Trade measures may also be used by one country to dismantle roadblocks that are preventing other countries from participating in and/or complying with a climate change agreement. Here we identify four roadblocks. First, most developing countries lack the technical and financial capacity to implement mitigation measures. Second, many countries see the costs of action as outweighing the benefits. Developing countries in particular have an overriding imperative to promote economic growth and development, and to the extent that these goals are considered incompatible with climate change mitigation activities, they are unlikely to be willing participants in a climate change agreement that requires them to take such action. Third are equity and justice issues that lead developing countries to argue that developed countries must take the primary responsibility to reduce emissions. Fourth, there are concerns in both developed and developing countries about a loss of international competitiveness should domestic measures (such as regulations or taxes) be implemented to reduce GHG emissions.

Trade measures are not likely to play a significant role in dismantling the first three roadblocks. Nevertheless, it is important to consider them as part of the broader context within which trade measures might be used.

12.1 LACK OF CAPACITY

Many developing countries simply do not have the economic or technical capacity that would allow them to take measures necessary to reduce GHG emissions.[1] The Kyoto Protocol's Clean Development Mechanism (CDM) has an important role to play in this regard. The CDM allows emission reduction projects in developing countries to earn Certified Emission Reduction (CERs). These CERs can be traded and sold, and

---

[1] David Weisbach, *Responsibility for Climate Change, by the Numbers* (John M. Olin Law & Economics Working Paper No. 448 (2nd Series), Public Law and Legal Theory Working Paper No. 255, 2009) at 25.

used by industrialized countries to meet part of their emission reduction targets under the Kyoto Protocol. While the CDM is widely seen as one means of improving technology transfer and diffusion, a continuing lack of technical capacity has led developing countries to place a strong emphasis on the need for enhanced capacity building provisions to form part of any post-Kyoto agreement.[2]

12.2   COSTS VS BENEFITS

Countries – both developed and developing – may decide that it is not in their self-interest to participate in a climate change agreement that requires emission reductions if the costs of doing so outweigh the benefits. Sunstein suggests that the costs of Kyoto for the US would be $325 billion, with anticipated benefits of only $12 billion.[3] This is in part because the US is not expected to suffer major adverse impacts from global warming for several decades.[4] Rather, it is actually predicted to enjoy benefits in the short term in the form of enhanced agricultural productivity due to warming and carbon fertilization.[5] Further, the ecological impacts in the

---

[2]   See generally Raymond Clémençon, 'The Bali Road Map: A First Step on the Difficult Journey to a Post-Kyoto Protocol Agreement' (2008) 17 *The Journal of Environmental & Development* 70. The preamble to the Bali Action Plan states that the Conference of the Parties will 'launch a comprehensive process to enable the full, effective and sustained implementation of the Convention through long-term cooperative action by addressing', *inter alia*, 'nationally appropriate mitigation actions by developing country Parties in the context of sustainable development, supported and enabled by technology, financing and capacity-building, in a measurable, reportable and verifiable manner.' Regarding the CDM, see Antoine Dechezleprêtre, Matthieu Glachant and Yann Ménière, 'The Clean Development Mechanism and the International Diffusion of Technologies: An Empirical Study' (Fondazione Eni Enrico Mattei Note de Lavoro Series Index: http://www.feem.it/ Feem/Pub/Publications/WPapers/default.htm (date accessed: 3 March 2010)).

[3]   Sunstein calls this a 'plausible if rough projection' of the benefits and costs. Cass R. Sunstein, 'Montreal vs. Kyoto: A Tale of Two Protocols' (2007) 31 *Harvard Environmental Law Review* 1 at 34.

[4]   Richard B. Stewart and Jonathon B. Wiener, *Reconstructing Climate Policy: Beyond Kyoto* (Washington, DC: The AEI Press, 2003) at 41.

[5]   Cass R. Sunstein, *The Complex Climate Change Incentives of China and the United States* (John M. Olin Law & Economics Working Paper No. 352 (2nd series), Public Law and Legal Theory Working Paper No. 176, The Law School, University of Chicago, 2007) at 12. Citing Olivier Deschenes and Michael Greenstone, 'The Economic Impacts of Climate Change: Evidence from Agricultural Output and Random Fluctuations of Weather' (2006), available at: www.aei-brookings.org/publications/abstract.php?pid=1031.

US are not predicted to be as severe as those in some other regions.[6] It is also expected to be better able to adapt to the effects of climate change.[7] China also has strong disincentives operating on it in regard to taking on emission reduction commitments. Like the US, China may perceive a benefit from warming over the next several decades because of longer growing seasons, carbon fertilization, and consequent improved agricultural productivity.[8] Further, it has strong incentives to continue to release emissions due to the importance to its economy of manufacturing and the comparative advantage it obtains from low energy costs derived from its large coal reserves.[9]

Many developing countries are just as likely to consider that the costs of climate change mitigation outweigh the benefits. One of the strongest disincentives is the fact that, as noted in Chapter 11, their overriding priority is usually to promote economic growth and development goals. Taking action to reduce GHG emissions is likely to be considered incompatible with, or at least secondary to, these goals. Even where some fiscal and technical capacity exists, many developing countries will choose to prioritize economic growth and development over climate change mitigation. For some, the likely harms from climate change are not considered to pose a significant threat in the short term.[10] In contrast, persistent under-development is

---

[6] Stewart and Wiener, *supra* note 4 at 52. Although it should be noted that some of the more extreme projections of harm would see many major US coastal cities and nearly all of Florida being flooded. See, for example, James Hansen, *The Threat to the Planet* (2006) 53 (1) *New York Review of Books* 4–5.

[7] Michael P. Vandenbergh, *Climate Change: The China Problem* (Vanderbilt University Law School: Public Law & Legal Theory Working Paper No. 08-09; Law & Economics Working Paper No. 08-15, 2008) at 18.

[8] Stewart and Wiener, *supra* note 4 at 42. Russia's agricultural sector is also projected to benefit from climate change; India, on the other hand, is expected to suffer large losses both in terms of health and agriculture. Eric A. Posner and Cass R. Sunstein, *Climate Change Justice* (University of Chicago, John M. Olin Law & Economics Working Paper No. 354 (2nd series), 2007) at 13.

[9] Vandenbergh, *supra* note 7 at 14. Vandenbergh also highlights (at 14–15) incentives operating in the opposite direction, including some projections that China would suffer harm including flooding of coastal areas if sea levels were to rise 5 metres, as well as the economic harm that would follow if, due to climate change, trading partners were to reduce demand for Chinese goods.

[10] Gordon writes for example that many African nations view climate change as a distant problem that does not affect them directly, at least in the short term, and view mitigation efforts as another mandate from the West that will further dampen their development efforts. Ruth Gordon, 'Climate Change and the Poorest Nations: Further Reflections on Global Inequality' (2007) 78 *University of Colorado Law Review* 1559 at 1603. Citing Anil Agarwal, 'A Southern Perspective on Curbing Global Climate Change', in Stephen H. Schneider et al., *Climate*

causing significant harm today. In order to grow their economies, these countries argue, they must be allowed to maintain and even grow their GHG emissions, just as the industrialized world has already done.[11] Indeed, developing countries only joined the UNFCCC on the understanding that doing so would not hurt their development prospects.[12]

12.3   EQUITY AND JUSTICE CONCERNS

Issues of equity and justice are central to any discussion of multilateral action to address climate change.[13] To begin with, the standard account of responsibility finds that developed countries are responsible for the majority of past emissions.[14] Based on this, the argument is made that it is unfair that industrialized countries grew economically through reliance on GHG emissions, yet developing countries are now constrained in their growth by the need to reduce emissions. Further, because carbon dioxide and other GHGs persist for so long in the atmosphere, many of the historical emissions generated by industrialized countries are still in the atmosphere and remain the largest contributor to current global warming.[15]

Change Policy: A Survey (New York: Cambridge University Press, 2002) at 375, 388–90.

[11]   See, for example, Liu Jiang, Vice-Chairman, National Development and Reform Commission of China, Keynote Speech on the Round Table Meeting of Energy and Environment Ministers from Twenty Nations (2005). Cited in Eric A. Posner and Cass R. Sunstein, *Climate Change Justice* (University of Chicago, John M. Olin Law & Economics Working Paper No. 354 (2nd series), 2007) at 33.

[12]   Ruth Gordon, 'Climate Change and the Poorest Nations: Further Reflections on Global Inequality' (2007) 78 *University of Colorado Law Review* 1559 at 1601. Citing Anil Agarwal et al. (eds), *Green Politics: Global Environmental Negotiations* (New Delhi: Centre for Science and the Environment, 1999).

[13]   Paul Harris, 'The European Union and Environmental Change: Sharing the Burdens of Global Warming' (2006) 17 (2) *Colorado Journal of International Environmental Law and Policy* 309 at 351.

[14]   The Pew Center on Global Climate Change reports that 'industrialized countries have been historically responsible [for climate change] since they as a group have some of the highest per capita energy use and also have benefitted from emitting vast quantities of greenhouse gases over the last century.' Eileen Claussen and Lisa McNeilly, 'Equity and Global Climate Change – The Complex Elements of Global Fairness' (Arlington, VA: Pew Center on Global Climate Change, 29 October 1998). See also the United Nations Environment Programme, which states that 'historically the developed countries of the world have emitted most of the anthropogenic greenhouse gases'. United Nations Environment Programme, 'Vital Climate Change Graphics' (UNEP, 2005).

[15]   About half the carbon dioxide emitted in 1907 still remains in the atmosphere

When the EU and the US joined the UNFCCC, they acknowledged that the majority of the blame for climate change lies with them and that they have some responsibility to help countries that will be negatively affected.[16] Yet a recent study by Weisbach disputes this standard account of responsibility. Weisbach reviews data contained in the Climate Analysis Indicators Tool (CAIT)[17] and finds that responsibility for climate change (including past emissions) is spread far more widely than commonly suggested. He finds that a number of poor countries are near the top of the list in respect of both comprehensive measures of contributions to the stock of GHGs in the atmosphere and emissions measured on a per capita basis or an intensity basis. He finds that countries such as Indonesia, Brazil and Malaysia are in the top 20 of total GHG emissions, while others such as Belize, Guyana, Qatar and Brunei appear in the top 10 of per capita emissions.[18] Weisbach's explanations for this are as follows. First, standard data tends to average poor countries with high and low emissions, thus masking those with high emissions. So, for example, Belize and Guyana are combined with low emitting Central and South American countries so they do not show up in the lists. Likewise, treating the Middle East as a single data point hides the high per capita emissions of Qatar, the UAE and Kuwait.[19] Second, there is a tendency to use narrow measures of emissions, such as emissions from energy use only, and poor countries often do

---

today. Posner and Sunstein, *supra* note 11 at 83. See also Stewart and Wiener, *supra* note 4 at 42.

[16]   Harris, *supra* note 13 at 321. The Preamble to the UNFCCC says that most current and historical emissions of GHGs have originated in the developed world. The convention calls on all parties to share the burdens, but to do so in such a way that those most responsible for historical emissions and those most capable of taking action bear the bulk of the burden. Thus, Article 3(1) says that countries should protect the world's atmosphere from climate change 'on the basis of equity and in accordance with their common but differentiated responsibilities and respective capabilities', with the economically developed countries taking the lead in addressing the problem and its effects. The understanding is that the economically less developed countries would not be required to undertake commitments until developed countries did so.

[17]   CAIT was developed by the World Resources Institute, an environmental think tank. It draws data from various sources, including the carbon inventories required for developed countries under the UNFCCC, the International Energy Agency and the Energy Information Administration, and the Carbon Dioxide Information Analysis Center. See www.cait.wri.org.

[18]   David Weisbach, *Responsibility for Climate Change, by the Numbers* (John M. Olin Law & Economics Working Paper No. 448 (2nd Series), Public Law and Legal Theory Working Paper No. 255, 2009) at 10 and 13.

[19]   Ibid.

better on these narrow measures, whereas they do worse on measures such as land use change. Thus, measures that exclude land use change will show higher relative emissions from developed countries.

Weisbach's findings do not necessitate a conclusion that developing countries should take equal responsibility for mitigation even though he argues that there is no reason why a measure of responsibility for climate change should be limited to only some types of emissions.[20] As he also notes, if the poor countries that have contributed significantly to climate change were held responsible on the same basis as rich countries, the resulting obligations would be likely to cause significant hardship.[21] Further, not only do many developing countries lack the financial and technical capacity to take mitigation action but many of the emissions were probably caused at the behest of the developed world and may not even have had significant benefit to their own societies. This has occurred through supply of goods to developed country markets, and through resource extraction that has fuelled development in the industrialized world. Thus, a finding that certain developing countries have contributed more to the GHG stock than commonly accepted does not translate into an obvious finding that they should therefore take the same level of responsibility.

Questions of justice and equity are critical because, as Wiegandt argues, part of the rationale for inclusion of social justice goals in a climate change regime is the notion that countries will only agree to do what is fair.[22] In other words, compliance with a climate change agreement will not be achieved if the agreement is not perceived as being fair and equitable.[23] The *real politik* of the situation is that developing countries have clearly said they will not join any future agreement that is not fair and equitable and based on commonly accepted notions that developed countries are most responsible for the problem historically.[24] Further, even the revised account provided by Weisbach does not necessitate concluding otherwise.

---

[20]   Ibid. at 16.

[21]   Ibid. at 25.

[22]   Ellen Wiegandt, 'Climate Change, Equity, and International Negotiations', in Urs Luterbacher and Detlef F. Sprinz (eds), *International Relations and Global Climate Change* (2001). Cited in Paul Harris, 'The European Union and Environmental Change: Sharing the Burdens of Global Warming' (2006) 17 (2) *Colorado Journal of International Environmental Law and Policy* 309 at 352.

[23]   Harris, ibid.

[24]   Ibid. at 326.

12.4 ADDRESSING THE FIRST THREE ROADBLOCKS

Regarding the *capacity* issue, various measures will be necessary at an international level, including intensive efforts to build capacity within developing countries, financial assistance, and technology transfers to ensure that developing countries are able to take steps to reduce emissions. Such measures will probably have to be taken on a multilateral (and regional) basis, and may include reforms to the CDM.[25] There is also potential for such requirements to be incorporated into WTO obligations, possibly through the TBT Agreement's provisions on technical assistance, or the Aid for Trade programme, which aims to provide development assistance to help developing countries take advantage of trade opportunities.[26] The amount of finance required is enormous and it was one of the key stumbling blocks in the Copenhagen negotiations. The 2009 World Development Report estimated that developing countries will require between $US140 billion and $US175 billion annually to help them implement the mitigation measures required to prevent the world from warming more than 2 degrees Celsius.[27] The Copenhagen Accord only affirms commitment of $US30 billion in funding over three years and sets a goal of $US100 billion in annual funding by 2020.

Regarding *economic and development goals*, there will remain a need for foreign aid to flow to developing countries (although this falls outside the scope of trade law and policy as such). The industrialized world must find ways to assist developing countries in pursuing growth and development, while still contributing to a collective effort to address climate change. It is only once economic growth and development goals are met that developing countries will consider fully participating in climate change agreements. Equity and justice concerns are absolutely critical and must primarily be addressed through design of a climate change regime that spreads the burden in an appropriate and equitable manner.

---

[25] On problems with, and potential reforms to, the CDM, see Michael W. Wara, 'Measuring the Clean Development Mechanism's Performance and Potential' (available online at http://ssrn.com/abstract=1086242).

[26] International Centre for Trade and Sustainable Development (ICTSD), Trade and Climate Change Briefing, Issue 2, Climate Change Financing, UNFCCC COP 15, Copenhagen 2009, 5 December 2009.

[27] Ibid. Additional funds would also be required for up-front investments. McKinsey and Company estimates that, because the economic savings associated with energy efficiency and the use of renewable energy sources only appear over time, an extra $US563 billion would be required above and beyond business-as-usual investments.

12.5   COMPETITIVENESS-RELATED ROADBLOCKS

The remainder of this chapter addresses two competitiveness-related roadblocks that stand in the way of climate change action. One roadblock arises from industry concerns at losing international competitiveness and broader concerns about 'leakage'. Chapter 8 discussed the concerns of industries that they will lose competitiveness if they are required to incorporate the price of carbon into their production costs, and the associated concerns about leakage of production to third countries with no carbon pricing. That chapter discussed the concern in the context of taxes. However, the same concern will arise in the face of domestic regulations designed to achieve emission reductions. Affected industries and interest groups will pressure governments not to adopt measures that may result in a competitiveness loss. This pressure may present a roadblock to the government taking climate change action.[28]

A further problem is that countries with no commitments (or those that are failing to comply with commitments made) will want to maintain the competitive advantage held by their own industries due to their lack of commitments and will be reluctant to make future commitments, as doing so would negate their advantage. This reluctance to give up their advantage presents a second roadblock to climate change action.

One way to dismantle these two roadblocks, and persuade both sets of countries to take on commitments, would be to eliminate the disadvantages faced by participating and complying countries, along with the advantage held by those that do not participate or comply.

12.6   ADDRESSING THE COMPETITIVENESS-RELATED ROADBLOCKS

Unilateral trade measures might play a role in helping to dismantle the competitiveness-related roadblocks. First, countries may address concerns over loss of competitiveness and leakage by using either border tax adjustments (BTAs) or internal regulations that impose costs on foreign producers equal to those faced by domestic producers. BTAs would allow

---

[28]   For a survey of competitiveness issues, see Aaron Cosbey and Richard Tarasofsky, *Climate Change, Competitiveness and Trade* (A Chatham House Report, London: The Royal Institute of International Affairs, 2007); Joost Pauwelyn, *US Federal Climate Policy and Competitiveness Concerns: The Limits and Options of International Trade Law* (Nicholas Institute for Environmental Policy Solutions, Duke University, 2007) at 2.

them not only to keep their own competitors on a 'level playing field' but also to remove any competitive advantage held by non-participating or non-compliant countries, thus reducing the opportunity costs of future participation and compliance.

Regulations aimed at the physical characteristics of domestic and imported products (such as the level of GHG emissions or energy efficiency) can help ensure that purchases in the domestic market are not distorted by differential costs where foreign producers do not have to meet the same standards. Measures related to process and production measures (PPMs) will also help to reduce distortion. For example, a BTA on imported cars made in a factory using coal-fired electricity could equalize the impact of a domestic tax on the carbon emissions of locally generated electricity. More severe would be a ban on imports or sales of products according to their embedded carbon.

There are a number of concerns with BTAs and regulations targeted at imports. The first two discussed here relate to the practicality and cost of implementation, while the third relates to broader issues of politics and fairness.

First, as noted in Chapter 8, there is a potentially high cost associated with sorting among imported products to determine the appropriate tax adjustment or impose the relevant regulatory requirement.[29] Some regulatory requirements will be easier to design and implement than others, such as certain product standards that can be more easily monitored (for example, an automobile emission limit). For measures to be targeted to specific products, an assessment would have to be made of the levels of carbon emitted in their PPMs, similar to the idea of determining the carbon footprint for products. However, this raises questions as to how the carbon emissions for any given product would be measured and this is likely to be extremely contentious and costly, particularly in the context of global supply chains.[30] It would be particularly difficult to attempt to get credible information on PPMs in some countries. Further, any comprehensive climate change agreement will inevitably cover an enormous range of goods and services. The manufacture of almost all goods results in GHG emissions and even some services (for example, tourism) – making

---

[29] See Robert N. Stavins and Scott Barrett, *Increasing Participation and Compliance in International Trade Agreements* (Working Paper No. RWP02031, Kennedy School of Government, Harvard University, 2002) at 21. Stavins and Barrett argue that it is very costly to attempt to use BTAs on all relevant products and attempting to impose them on a subset of products would be ineffective. Also see Chapter 8.

[30] See ibid. at 22, for a discussion of possible means of calculation.

it extremely difficult to determine what products should be covered by any BTA or regulation.

Second, the impact of BTAs or regulations on the domestic market will depend on the size of that market and the particular measure used. A BTA on imports would ensure domestic products remained competitive with imports, while a BTA on exports would ensure their competitiveness in foreign markets. However, while regulations may level the domestic playing field in an importing country, they may make exports uncompetitive. For example, if a standard (as opposed to a tax) were used to influence emissions from domestically produced goods, an equivalent standard for all imported products would ensure that all products in the domestic market faced similar constraints. However, if the standard is applied to a product that is exported, the domestic industry may lose out in international markets if its competitors in certain markets are not required to meet similar standards.

Third, it cannot be assumed that governments invoke BTAs or regulations purely to increase domestic and/or global welfare. Political officials may take actions that benefit themselves (by leading to funds for re-election or future employment opportunities), rather than actions that explicitly aim at increasing national, let alone global, welfare. This public choice view of state action may mean that states do not impose sanctions to merely offset the costs of climate action. They will do so to protect or favour certain domestic industries.[31] Distinguishing such protectionist action from legitimate environmental measures is difficult for both trading partners and the WTO's Dispute Settlement Body. This difficulty arises, for example, in determining whether a measure violates the national treatment principle or whether it can be justified as a legitimate environmental measure under Article XX. To the extent panels and the Appellate Body cannot draw such a distinction, and protectionist measures slip through, trade may be unnecessarily reduced or distorted. (Conversely, of course, measures may be improperly characterized as protectionist when they have genuine and justifiable environmental objectives and this result should be avoided, which only heightens the difficulties described.) Attempting to further clarify WTO rules is not likely to be helpful due to the difficulties of identifying in advance the parameters of a rule specific to the kinds of measures in question.

---

[31] See generally Jide Nzelibe, 'The Case Against Reforming the WTO Enforcement Mechanism' (2008) *University of Illinois Law Review* 319; Alan Sykes, 'The Economics of Public International Law' (University of Chicago Law and Economics Olin Working Paper, No. 216, 2004).

A further problem is that even if a panel or the Appellate Body can determine that certain measures are illegitimately protectionist, the remedies for violation of WTO agreements may be too weak to adequately deter such protectionism. Chapter 10 discussed the problems with enforcement in the WTO dispute settlement system, including in particular the use of liability rules so that countries using climate change as an excuse for protectionist measures will not necessarily be forced to remove them. They may decide that bearing the suspension of concessions or other obligations is worth the cost. It also noted the high likelihood of protectionism in the climate change context. In general, protectionist action has a negative welfare effect on the country that is taking the protectionist measure.[32] Producers gain while consumers lose, but because the losses to individuals are smaller and more diffuse, consumers face a collective action problem that limits their ability to pressure government not to take the action. This is due to the fact that if the public supports action on climate change, its opposition to protectionist measures may be muted. The public may not realize the measure is protectionist and not object as they view it as furthering environmental goals. Further, the public may even call for protectionist measures. This situation provides the possibility for political officials to respond to protectionist pressures with little risk of political backlash from the general public. They may thus make a politically advantageous decision to implement measures despite the threat (and even in the event) of retaliation by a third country.

Developing countries may face a particularly strong likelihood of their trading partners imposing protectionist measures. This is because developing countries may not be able to use the WTO enforcement system effectively. They tend to lack the resources to effectively identify and challenge protectionist measures by other countries. Moreover, they may be unwilling to challenge measures by more powerful countries due to fear of retaliation either in trade or in other areas such as foreign aid. Even if they can use the system, developing countries will often lack the power to actually force change. For the WTO remedy of retaliation to be effective, the complaining party must have the ability to harm exporters in the protectionist country. However, developing countries often do not have sufficiently large or valuable enough trade volumes to be able to cause such harm in developed countries. As a result, developing countries tend

---

[32] P. Krugman and M. Obstfeld, *International Economic Theory and Policy*, 7th edn (London: Pearson, 2005) at 184–6 (discussing loss of welfare from tariffs, particularly if the country is small in the sense of not being able to affect the world price of the good).

to use the WTO enforcement system much less than would otherwise be expected.[33] This reduced use of the WTO dispute settlement mechanism may mean that developed countries will not be as constrained in taking protectionist measures against developing countries as they would be in taking such measures against other developed countries. The risk thus exists that the use of trade measures to dismantle the two roadblocks to climate change action discussed here will fail to meet all three goals cited in Chapter 1 – climate change mitigation, deterring protectionism, and furthering development.

12.7   CAN TRADE MEASURES HELP DISMANTLE ROADBLOCKS?

Unilateral trade measures have some potential to help dismantle the road-blocks that stand in the way of both developed and developing countries taking action on climate change. However, the potential is small due to the political factors that make their use largely undesirable. The use of BTAs to remove pressure from trade-exposed industries or to eliminate non-participating and non-compliant countries' competitive advantage would be likely to undermine the principle of common but differentiated responsibilities and invite trade friction and broader political and diplomatic tensions. Such tension has already been brewing, with the US and France suggesting that border adjustments be used not only to protect local industry but *explicitly* to force the hand of other countries. For example, in 2009, Democrat Senator John Kerry and Republican Senator Lindsey Graham wrote in the *New York Times* that

> there is no reason we should surrender our marketplace to countries that do not accept environmental standards. For this reason, we should consider a border tax on items produced in countries that avoid these standards. This is consistent with our obligations under the World Trade Organization and creates strong incentives for other countries to adopt tough environmental protections.[34]

---

[33] For discussions of the difficulties of developing countries using the dispute settlement system, see, e.g., Chad P. Bown and Bernard M. Hoekman, *Developing Countries and Enforcement of Trade Agreements: Why Dispute Settlement is Not Enough* (2008) 42 (1) *Journal of World Trade* 177, 177–203; Andrew T. Guzman and Beth A. Simmons, *Power Plays and Capacity Constraints: The Selection of Defendants in World Trade Organization Disputes*, (2005) 34 *Journal of Legal Studies* 557.

[34] Cited in International Centre for Trade and Sustainable Development

In France, President Sarkozy has stated that

> if large economies of the world do not engage in binding commitments to reduce emissions, European industry will have incentives to relocate to such countries ... the introduction of a parallel mechanism for border compensation against imports from countries that refuse to commit to binding reductions therefore appears essential, whether in the form of a tax adjustment or an obligation to buy permits by importers. This mechanism is in any case necessary in order to induce those countries to agree on such a commitment.[35]

Responses to this and similar suggestions have been unequivocal. At Copenhagen, India's chief climate change negotiator said of border adjustment: 'We are totally against it – totally against it'.[36] Previously, India's environment minister had suggested that allowing border adjustments would be a 'pernicious' move.[37] China's Minister Cheng has been quoted as saying that the move would probably trigger retaliatory action, in the worst case leading to a trade war.[38] China's opposition to the use of BTAs was formally expressed at a climate change negotiating session in June 2009 when, together with India, and supported by a number of other developing countries, it introduced language into the draft climate change text to prevent the use of border measures. The language included the provision that:

> developed country Parties shall not resort to any form of unilateral measures including countervailing border measures, against goods and services imported from developing countries on grounds of protection and stabilization of the climate. Such unilateral measures would violate the principles and provisions of the Convention [UNFCCC], including, in particular, those related to the principle of common but differentiated responsibilities (Article 3, paragraph 1); trade and climate change (Article 3, paragraph 5); and the relationship between mitigation actions of developing countries and provision of financial resources and technology by developed country Parties (Article 4, paragraphs 3 and 7).[39]

(ICTSD), Trade and Climate Change Briefing, Issue 3, Border Carbon Adjustment, UNFCCC COP 15, Copenhagen 2009, 5 December 2009.

[35] Letter to EU Commission President Jose Manuel Barroso, January 2008.

[36] International Centre for Trade and Sustainable Development (ICTSD), Trade and Climate Change Briefing, Issue 2, Climate Change Financing, UNFCCC COP 15, Copenhagen 2009, 5 December 2009.

[37] Amy Kamin, 'India Lambasts "Pernicious" US Carbon Tariffs', *Financial Times*, 20 June 2009. See also 'China Joins Carbon Tax Protest', *Financial Times*, 3 July 2009.

[38] Ibid.

[39] Ibid.

The drawbacks of using origin-specific BTAs have also been recognized in developed countries. The then European Union Trade Commissioner, Peter Mandelson, has suggested that their use would be 'bad politics' and that 'a punitive approach to pursuing international cooperation on climate change would be politically and strategically clumsy, igniting a carbon war'.[40] In a reference to a French proposal to impose BTAs, the German State Secretary for the Environment said their imposition would amount to a 'new form of eco-imperialism'.[41]

The failure to reach agreement at Copenhagen led to a flurry of speculation about trade wars. For example, the *Financial Times* suggested that 'if threats of carbon border tariffs emanating from parts of the European Union and the US are implemented, the world could enter the biggest trade war since the Great Depression'.[42]

BTAs might possibly be used in the context of a specific bilateral relationship. However, the potential for their useful invocation would need to be reviewed on a case-by-case basis.[43] Imposing regulations on imported products may be less blatant, but would still have potential to cause trade and political tensions.

In addition to undermining the common but differentiated responsibilities principle, BTAs would provide a vehicle for countries to sneak through protectionist measures. Such action would lead to its own loss to global welfare. This welfare loss may be reduced to the extent that states adhere to international product standards, or panels and the Appellate Body are able to distinguish between protectionist measures and legitimate environmental measures. However, much uncertainty remains in this regard. The key roadblocks faced by developing countries – lack of capacity, negative benefit to cost ratio, equity and justice concerns – can only be addressed through a combination of both unilateral and multilateral measures.

---

[40]   Peter Mandelson, 'How Trade Can be Part of the Climate Change Solution', Comment by Peter Mandelson, European Union Trade Commissioner, Brussels, 18 December 2006, p. 17.

[41]   Mia Shanley and Ilona Wissenbach, 'Germany Calls Carbon Tariffs Eco-imperialism', Reuters.com, 24 July 2009.

[42]   Editorial Comment, 'One Easy Way to Start a Trade War', *Financial Times*, 9 December 2009. The author opined further that 'as a ruse to keep trade lawyers in gainful employment, carbon border taxes are perfect. As policy, they would likely be a disaster.'

[43]   They would only be useful to the extent they assisted in securing an effective policy signal for emissions mitigation. John Stephenson and Simon Upton, *Competitiveness, Leakage, and Border Adjustment: Climate Policy Distractions?* (Paris: Organisation for Economic Co-operation and Development (OECD), Round Table on Sustainable Development SG/SD/RT(2009)3, 2009).

Finally, the prospect of using BTAs or regulatory measures with the explicit goal of inducing another country to take climate change action is extremely troublesome from political and fairness standpoints. As discussed in Chapter 8, using such measures to remove the roadblock created by competitiveness concerns is likely to lead to trade friction. Using BTAs to persuade or force countries to take measures is even more problematic. This would represent a bold unilateral move by one country to alter another country's comparative advantage. Between developed countries (or between developing countries) this would create trade friction of varying degrees. Between developed and developing countries it would serve to heighten already existing tensions and further reduce already dismal prospects of international cooperation.

The most useful role that unilateral trade measures could play would be for countries to engage in unilateral liberalization to help foster economic growth and development. Trade measures do have a further role to play. It is crucial that developed countries adopt trade policies that help poor countries grow economically and that allow developing countries to take the necessary steps to help their industries adjust to the costs of climate change mitigation. Most significantly, developed countries must begin to take seriously the goals articulated at the outset of the so-called Doha Development Round. Developed countries should make good on their commitment to development in the Doha Round by extending market access in products of export interest to all developing countries (particularly agricultural products), with particular focus on reducing tariffs, tariff peaks and tariff escalation.[44] Such market access commitments should be extended to all countries on a most-favoured-nation basis. It is not enough to offer preferential treatment to the most vulnerable economies. Further, developed countries should eliminate subsidies that distort world markets and make it difficult for developing countries to integrate their economies into the world market.[45]

---

[44] T. Epps and M. Trebilcock, 'Special and Differential Treatment in Agricultural Trade: Breaking the Impasse', in Chantel Thomas and Joel P. Trachtman (eds), *Developing Countries in the WTO Legal System* (Oxford: Oxford University Press, 2009).

[45] The issue of subsidies was discussed in Chapter 7.

13. Negative incentives: using 'sticks'

13.1 WHY USE STICKS?

As we noted earlier in this book, a core concern in addressing climate change is the incentive for countries to free-ride on the efforts of others. One solution to the free-rider problem is for the parties to enter into a multilateral international agreement relating to the issue at hand. However, as can be seen from the case of the Kyoto Protocol and the more recent post-Kyoto negotiations, there are difficulties with both participation and compliance. With the Kyoto Protocol, some countries refused to participate (at least in the sense of agreeing to binding commitments under the Protocol). Others, such as Canada, have signed on and taken binding commitments but, at the end of the compliance period, will not have met these commitments. These issues will be discussed in Chapter 14. This chapter discusses the use of unilateral 'sticks' where such agreement has not been reached or complied with – that is, measures taken by a country not as part of a climate change agreement but on their own to force other countries to act.

'Sticks', or negative incentives, could be used either to force countries to take domestic action on climate change (or a particular form of action) or to attempt to force participation in and compliance with a multilateral agreement. These sticks include very high tariffs and bans on trade with particular countries, either generally or in certain products or sectors. They could be based on the characteristics of the products themselves or on how these products are produced. According to Barrett, 'a treaty that sustains real cooperation must deter both non-compliance and non-participation.'[1] In part, this need for deterrence arises because there is no central government to force countries to sign on to agreements and accept commitments.[2] They must be willing to sign on and comply or to otherwise live up to norms of behaviour such as taking climate change action.

---

[1] Scott Barrett, *Why Cooperate? The Incentive to Supply Global Public Goods* (Oxford: Oxford University Press, 2007) at 82–3.

[2] Barrett, ibid. Scott Barrett, *Environment and Statecraft: The Strategy of Environmental Treaty-Making* (Oxford: Oxford University Press, 2003) and Henrik Horn and Petros Mavroidis, 'International Trade – Dispute Settlement' in Alan O. Sykes and Andrew Guzman (eds), *Research Handbook in International*

To be effective, these negative incentives must be both severe and credible.[3] They must be sufficiently severe to induce the other countries to take the desired action (such as to join in or comply with a treaty or to adopt climate policies). The non-participating state must see itself as better off bearing the cost of taking climate change action than the cost of the negative incentive. In one sense, it is not difficult to make trade measures this severe as they do not necessarily need to be tailored to the nature of the non-compliance or non-participation.[4] It would be very costly to determine which goods contain or are made from GHGs and to design a tariff or other measure to balance out these costs. However, if the intention is merely to set the tariff or ban in a manner that punishes the other countries then it may be relatively straightforward to do so, provided there is sufficient trade between the countries.

In fact, the issue with severity is often that the measures may be overly severe. The theory behind trade sanctions is for the sanctioning party to impose costs on the non-participating/non-complying state. The hope is that the sanctioning state will act with global welfare in mind. However, as we have noted before, government officials may not act to further national, let alone global, welfare but instead their own political self-interest, favouring concentrated interests that can provide them with some form of benefit. The result may be protectionism, in this case in the guise of fostering participation in climate goals or compliance with pre-existing commitments. Import-competing industries tend to be concentrated while consumer groups hurt by protectionism are more diffuse and harder to organize.

In addition, the pressure from the public not to put in place protectionist measures will arise only if they perceive a negative welfare effect from the measures. The climate change context may mean this pressure is even further reduced. The public may not realize the measure (the 'stick') is protectionist if they view it as furthering environmental goals and so may not object to strong measures. The public may even push for stronger measures to foster climate change action. In such a situation, there is a heightened risk of a country taking protectionist measures – political officials can

Economic Law (Cheltenham, UK and Northampton, MA, USA: Edward Elgar Publishing Ltd, 2008).

  [3] See Barrett (2003), ibid. and Scott Barrett and Robert Stavins, 'Increasing Participation and Compliance in International Climate Change Agreements' (2003) 3 *International Environmental Agreements: Politics, Law and Economics* 349.

  [4] Scott Barrett, 'Climate Treaties and the Imperative of Enforcement' (2008) 24 (2) *Oxford Review of Economic Policy* 239.

indulge protectionist demands from domestic industry without fear of a political cost from the general public.

There then may be a bias in favour of strong action where it benefits domestic industry and its competitiveness. In one sense, this bias is beneficial as it makes the negative incentive or stick more severe (and, as noted below, credible as it does not impose major costs on the sanctioning country, at least politically). The difficulty is that such strong measures unnecessarily hinder trade liberalization. They impose short-term costs that are higher than necessary until the target state participates or complies.

These risks from protectionist measures are even greater for developing countries. As discussed in Chapter 10, most developing countries lack the ability to effectively enforce WTO rules. They may not have the resources to undertake a complaint, and even if they are successful, they may be unwilling or unable to impose a sufficiently large countermeasure to induce developed countries to change their measures. Further, while severe measures may induce developing countries to participate, they may impose high short-term costs until they do so. These costs harm economic development and the efforts to alleviate global poverty. Moreover, as will be discussed in Chapter 15, severe measures may induce developing countries to enter into agreements that do not fairly distribute the burden of reducing emissions. Fairness in the distribution of burdens is obviously difficult to determine.[5] However, there is a risk of developing countries bearing a high cost of action if they are forced to enter into an agreement they did not negotiate or had only a limited role in negotiating.

In addition to being severe, negative incentives must be credible. That is, they cannot impose too great a cost on the sanctioning state or it will seem unlikely that the state will use the stick.[6] Barrett and Stavins argue that 'to be credible, countries threatening to impose restrictions must be better off when they carry out their threats than when they do not, given that non-participation has occurred.'[7] They point to the success of the Montreal Protocol on ozone depleting substances (ODS), which provided for the suspension of trade in cases of non-compliance. They argue that this threat was credible because the benefits of curtailing the possible leakage of industry to non-members were sufficiently large for the parties to have an incentive to bear the costs of sanctioning non-participating or non-complying countries.

---

5   Barrett, ibid.
6   See Barrett, *supra* note 2, and Barrett and Stavins, *supra* note 3.
7   Barrett and Stavins, ibid.

As in the case of the Montreal Protocol, there are fears of leakage of industry to countries that do not have strong climate policies. However, unilateral sanctions against countries not taking action on climate change may still be too painful to be credible. First, there may be high administrative costs of trade measures, such as those of determining where particular goods are from and monitoring and enforcing the tariff or ban. These costs will be less than attempting to tailor measures to the precise conditions in each target state but can still be significant.

Second, any such measures may not be credible, as the more extensive the trade measures, the greater the costs to the country imposing them in the sense of loss of consumer surplus.[8] The Montreal Protocol had only small negative welfare effects due to trade restrictions on ODS because there were viable alternatives to these. There are currently no alternative products or production processes for many of the products and services that result in carbon emissions, giving rise to a greater risk of welfare loss if trade restrictions are imposed. However, there is a caveat. As noted above, these sticks only lack credibility in public choice terms if the public senses the welfare loss and places pressure on the government either to not adopt them or to remove them. Further, as discussed in the last section, they may be focused on particular sectors in order to increase their credibility. The losses to consumer welfare may not be so high with sectoral-based agreements that consumers would object.

Unilateral trade measures must therefore be both severe and credible enough to foster action by other countries. While there are costs from such measures, the concern may be not whether they are possible but whether they can be contained. We discuss this further in the last section, but first we outline the constraints placed on the use of unilateral measures by WTO rules.

13.2   WHAT TYPES OF STICKS COULD BE USED?

The most severe form of stick that could be used is a ban or restrictive quota on particular products, such as banning all imports from a country not taking climate change action or just imports from a particularly harmful sector. A stick could also take the form of a punitive tariff, which

---

[8]   Barrett, *supra* note 2. Consumer surplus represents the difference between what a person is willing to pay for a product, rather than go without it, and the market price which has to be paid. It can be considered 'bonus utility', satisfaction people feel when prices are less than they are willing to pay.

is a tariff that is so high that it can restrict the importation of a product by making it uncompetitive in the domestic market. It is different from the border tax adjustments discussed in Chapter 12 in that BTAs are aimed at equivalency with domestic measures. In general, punitive tariffs need not have any such necessary connection to particular domestic policy instruments or equivalency to any domestic action by the country applying the stick. Punitive tariffs could have the equivalent effect to a ban or quota, although with the added benefit to the Member of revenue if the tariffs are not so high as to completely stop trade. Countries may base these measures either on the characteristics of the products themselves (such as the emission level of cars) or their process and production methods or PPMs (such as the amount of energy used in producing the car). As discussed below, any such sticks would, in general, be difficult for Members to justify under WTO rules.

Let us first consider bans or other quantitative restrictions on products based on their characteristics (such as level of energy efficiency) or on their PPMs. Any such ban or quantitative restriction would have to comply with GATT Article XI, under which Members may not maintain any 'prohibitions or restrictions other than duties, taxes or other charges, whether made effective through quotas, import or export licenses or other measures'. These bans must relate to the importation of the product. For example, a panel found the US violated Article XI when it banned the importation of shrimp from countries the US had not certified as having sufficiently low levels of related sea turtle kills.[9] On the other hand, a panel found Article XI did not apply to France's ban on the manufacture, export, import or domestic sale or transfer of asbestos and certain asbestos-containing material. The panel found that the measure applied to both domestic and imported products (even though Canada argued there was no domestically produced asbestos) and therefore fell under Article III.[10] It could be that, as in the case of a substance like ODS, the

---

[9]   *United States – Import Prohibition of Certain Shrimp and Shrimp Products* (1998) WTO Doc. WT/DS58/R (Panel Report) (the finding on the violation of Article XI was not appealed).

[10]   The panel relied on the Ad note to Article III which states: 'Any internal tax or other internal charge, or any law, regulation or requirement of the kind referred to in paragraph 1 which applies to an imported product and to the like domestic product and is collected or enforced in the case of the imported product at the time or point of importation, is nevertheless to be regarded as an internal tax or other internal charge, or a law, regulation or requirement of the kind referred to in paragraph 1 and is accordingly subject to the provisions of Article III.' See *European Communities – Measures Affecting Asbestos and Asbestos-Containing Products* (2000) WTO Doc. WT/DS135/R (Panel Report).

stick could take the form of a domestic ban and an import ban, in which case the ban would seem to fall under Article III. However, bans used as sticks in the climate change context seem more analogous to the ban on the importation of shrimp. They are likely to apply to imports of products from certain countries, rather than be framed as a general ban on the use or production of a product, and therefore fall under Article XI rather than Article III.

Similarly, a punitive tariff imposed on imports of a product may be in non-compliance with GATT Article II, which essentially requires that Members' tariffs not exceed the tariff levels they have committed to in WTO negotiations (their bound tariffs). Sticks in the form of punitive tariffs that exceed these bound levels would therefore violate Article II. There are two instances in which punitive tariffs would not violate Article II. First, if the country has not bound its tariff for a particular product, Article II would not apply to the tariff. Second, if the bound rate is sufficiently high that it would itself be a punitive tariff (in the sense of stopping all trade in the product) and the actual tariff is below this rate, an increase above the actual rate but below the bound rate may then not violate Article II and yet have the desired impact on trade.

The key to WTO legality will therefore not be whether the measure complies with the substantive requirements of the WTO agreements, as they will probably not comply. The issue will be whether the ban or restrictive quota can be saved under Article XX. As we discussed in Chapter 9, an Article XX analysis has two parts – determining whether the measure falls within one of the exceptions and, if so, assessing whether it satisfies the conditions of the chapeau. The tests may be difficult for a regulating party to satisfy since the measures at issue are intentionally aimed at restricting or even stopping trade.

For Article XX(b) and XX(g), the analysis of whether the measure meets the aims of each exception remains the same as the general case discussed in Chapter 9; that is, whether the measure's goal relates to 'exhaustible natural resources' (Article XX(g)) or to 'human, animal or plant life or health' (Article XX(b)). The unilateral trade measure must also satisfy the tests for the connection of the measure to the goal. For Article XX(g), the measure has to be 'related to' the conservation of exhaustible natural resources. The Appellate Body has held that there must be a close relationship between the measure and the goal and seems to have imposed a weak proportionality test.[11] The panel or Appellate Body will have to consider

---

[11]   *United States – Import Prohibition of Certain Shrimp and Shrimp Products (US – Shrimp I)* (1998) WTO Doc. WT/DS58/AB/R (Appellate Body Report).

the nature of the measure and determine whether or not it is closely related to and not disproportionate to the goal of compelling the other Member to take climate change action. In *US – Shrimp*, the Appellate Body found a ban on the importation of shrimp caught without taking steps to protect turtles was not disproportionately wide and was closely related to the end of protecting sea turtles. It therefore is willing to consider complete bans on trade. However, in terms of a stick, whether or not it is saved under Article XX will depend on the nature of the measure and how it is designed. A blanket ban on all trade with a particular Member may be considered too broad. A target ban on products that are not 'climate friendly' may more easily pass scrutiny. Panels may even be willing to find that sticks applied to products based on their process and production methods (PPMs) may satisfy this exception – as they arguably did with the ban on shrimp based on how they were caught.[12]

The other aspect of Article XX(g) is that the measure must be 'made effective in conjunction with restrictions on domestic production or consumption', which the Appellate Body has taken to require 'even-handedness' between domestic and foreign producers. The burden would therefore be on the Member using the stick to show that it was also taking domestic measures equivalent to those it purported to demand of other Members. In theory, such a requirement makes sticks attractive in that the Member is only asking other Members to follow its lead. It imposes an upper bound on such measures. However, panels will have difficulty assessing this even-handedness as the scope of the climate plan considered becomes wider. For example, where a punitive tariff or ban is based on the lack of an overall climate policy (or of an effective climate policy) of another Member, a panel will have difficulty determining whether overall the domestic climate policy of the Member applying the stick is largely equivalent to what it is requiring of the other Member. A panel may have less difficulty if the stick is being applied in a particular sector (such as aluminum), as it may be easier to assess the equivalence of the measures in the two states relative to the one industry.

For Article XX(b), the measure will have to satisfy the necessity test, which the Appellate Body has recently stated involves assessing 'all the relevant factors, particularly the extent of the contribution to the

---

The Appellate Body noted that the measure was not 'disproportionately wide in its scope and reach in relation to the policy objective . . . The means are, in principle, reasonably related to the ends' (at para. 141).

[12] *US – Shrimp I*, ibid. Note that the Appellate Body also made a comment that the turtles were migratory and at times were within US waters, which makes the actual scope of the ruling uncertain.

achievement of a measure's objective and its trade restrictiveness, in the light of the importance of the interests or values at stake'.[13] A stick is by its nature at the extreme end of the trade restrictiveness scale. As noted in Chapter 9, the Appellate Body has stated that where a measure has severe effects on trade, such as in the case of an import ban (or, by extension, a punitive tariff), it will be 'difficult for a panel to find that measure necessary unless it is satisfied that the measure is apt to make a material contribution to the achievement of its objective'.[14]

The framing of the objective will be important to this determination. If the objective is framed as avoiding catastrophic climate change (for example, limiting increases in temperature to 2 °C), a panel may not view a ban on the imports from another Member as making a material contribution. It will depend on the viewpoint of the panel. A panel may view the emissions from some countries as too small to make a material contribution to the goal and therefore that the measure is not necessary. Alternatively, it may take into account that controlling climate change is an aggregate public good and therefore all countries must take some action for this public good to be produced. It may then be more willing to find a country's contribution important. However, the other aspect of this material contribution test is that the measure must actually have an impact on the emissions (or participation or compliance) of another Member. Werksman et al. argue that unilateral trade measures are unlikely to have a significant impact on the policy decisions of other Members because the trade in any given set of products will probably be too small with one country to force the exporting country to change its policies.[15] However, to the extent that the measure and the objective are more narrowly framed, such as the reduction of emissions from the cement sector by a certain amount, a ban related to that sector may more readily pass the necessity test. It may provide some leverage at least in specific areas that have high emissions and are subject to international competition.[16]

---

[13] *Brazil – Measures Affecting Imports of Retreated Tyres* (2007) WTO Doc. WT/DS332/AB/R (Appellate Body Report) at para. 156. See Chapter 9 for a discussion of the scope of the necessity test under Article XX(b).

[14] Ibid. at para. 150.

[15] Jacob Werksman, James Bradbury and Lutz Weischer, 'Trade Measures and Climate Change Policy: Searching for Common Ground on an Uneven Playing Field' (World Resources Institute Working Paper, December 2009). But see Gary Hufbauer, Steve Charnovitz and Jisun Kim, *Global Warming and the World Trading System* (Washington, DC: Peterson Institute for International Economics, 2009) (arguing that the Appellate Body has not closely examined the actual effectiveness of measures under Article XX(b) (at 84)).

[16] Barrett, *supra* note 4.

The other important aspect of the necessity test is that it involves a search for possible, less trade restrictive alternatives. The alternative must achieve the same level of protection, must be less trade restrictive than the 'stick', and must be reasonably available in the sense of not imposing prohibitive costs or substantial technical barriers.[17] The less trade restrictive requirement is obviously a concern in terms of sticks. If the measure is a complete ban or punitive tariff, other less trading restricting measures might be found to have the same effect. However, the Appellate Body has considered measures in the context of more comprehensive plans for meeting the goal and may, therefore, be unwilling to find another measure a reasonable alternative where the 'stick' is an integral part of such a plan.[18]

The chapeau of Article XX adds its own complications for the justification of sticks. It relates to how the measure is applied. The measure cannot be 'applied in a manner which would constitute a means of arbitrary or unjustifiable discrimination between countries where the same conditions prevail, or a disguised restriction on international trade'. There are three key elements to determining whether the application of a stick would be found to comply with the chapeau.[19] First, it must be applied flexibly. In this context, flexibility would mean that the basis for the stick could not be that the other country did not have exactly the same plan or policies as the Member applying the stick. Instead, it must be based on the lack of a policy which is comparable to that of the Member using the stick.[20] This comparability may be difficult for a panel to assess where the basis for the stick is the lack of an overall comprehensive climate change plan. It would be easier to the extent that the stick related to the lack of a measure relating to a particular sector or source of emissions. As discussed in Chapter 16, one benefit of a climate change agreement is that it may provide a basis for comparability. It may do so directly by specifying the conditions for comparability and the application of trade measures, or it may do so indirectly, as where panels or the Appellate Body use commitments within such agreements as the basis for finding a country is taking 'comparable' action.[21]

---

[17] See Chapter 9.

[18] *Brazil-Tyres AB Report, supra* note 13.

[19] See Chapter 9 for a more detailed description of these elements of the analysis under the chapeau.

[20] *US – Shrimp I, supra* note 11 (referring to the need to ensure the policy is comparable in effectiveness as opposed to exactly the same).

[21] See Werksman et al., *supra* note 15, discussing the US domestic legislation and the possibility of climate talks resulting in a basis for determining

Second, in applying the stick, the Member must comply with basic fairness and due process. This procedural review focuses on such issues as whether the Member allowed others the opportunity to be heard, the right to comment on the proposed measure, and possibly a right of appeal. In theory, such procedural rights should reduce mistakes in the use of sticks as the targets could provide evidence as to why the stick was unnecessary or unnecessarily punitive. They may also increase the accountability of the domestic government for protectionist measures by allowing target countries to tap into consumer or public pressure in the regulating state, or into international pressure (such as by harming the reputation of parties using sticks for protectionist purposes). The difficulty is, of course, even if these procedural rights are provided, it is impossible through such a review to ensure that the measure is not protectionist. The only hope is that the accountability regime through which the process operates has sufficient impact to reduce the probability of protectionist measures. As noted above, however, in the context of climate change, such accountability may be attenuated domestically where strong measures are seen by the public as a means of meeting climate goals. Further, many countries (particularly developing countries) may not be able to take advantage of these procedural opportunities because of a lack of resources.

Finally, to comply with the requirements of the chapeau, there is a need for good faith efforts to reach an agreement with the other parties to the dispute. Developed countries wishing to use trade measures to force action by other Members (including developing countries) might argue that the Kyoto Protocol (or post-Kyoto agreement) constitutes such an attempt and that the failure of other WTO members to make reduction commitments justifies the imposition of trade measures. However, these more general negotiations over targets may not in themselves be sufficient basis for the application of a stick. A panel may find there remains a need to further negotiate with particular countries that are not participating in the climate agreement or complying with their commitments. Further, at least for developing countries, fairness considerations will arise as

---

comparability for the purposes of imposing unilateral trade measures. They also discuss the extent to which 'comparability' may take into account the principle of common and differentiated responsibilities given that it appears to be an element of both the WTO agreements and the UNFCCC. See also Gary Hufbauer, Steve Charnovitz and Jisun Kun, *Global Warming and the World Trading System* (Washington, DC: Peterson Institute for International Economics, 2009) (arguing that unilateral measures are unlikely to be saved under Article XX). But see Barrett, *supra* note 4, arguing that the Kyoto emissions caps provide a very poor basis for determining comparability of effort.

they may raise a kind of estoppel argument given that, under the Kyoto Protocol in any event, they were not required to take on the same commitments as Annex I countries. The nature of the post-Kyoto negotiations would aid in determining whether this requirement of the chapeau would be met.

13.3   SHOULD UNILATERAL STICKS BE PERMITTED?

Unilateral sticks are therefore possible under WTO rules depending on how they are structured. However, the concern is that such measures will be overly severe. Given their trade restrictive impetus, such measures seem particularly open to protectionist influences. As discussed in the first section, such protectionism may not be tempered by domestic consumer pressure in the case of objectives such as climate change, which can be framed as necessitating strong action against 'free-riders'. The more trade restrictive the measure, the greater the cost to global welfare in terms of trade. The main caveat is that if the sticks are sufficiently severe and credible, they may never have to be used (that is, the target country will take climate change action) and there will be no trade effect.

The scope for the measures and the concerns about them depend on how close an examination panels are willing to take when these sticks are challenged. Closer scrutiny such as to the equivalency of domestic measures or the flexibility with which the measure is applied will make it less likely that the measures will survive review. Moreover, the narrower the scope of the stick, the more likely it is to be found to comply with WTO commitments. For example, if the measure is applied to a particular sector, it is easier for the Member using the stick to satisfy different elements of the test such as the equivalency of domestic measures and the necessity of the measure. Requiring proportionality and even-handedness requires considerable understanding of the nature of the costs to the parties and their respective regulatory systems. The broader the measure, the more difficult it will be for a panel to gather, understand and assess this information.

In addition to efficiency concerns about sticks, there is the problem of legitimacy. Sticks may be seen as one Member attempting to impose its values and preferences on others. The country using the stick may see it as necessary to avoid a global catastrophe or irreversible environmental loss, but the target Member may not have the same level of concern about the issue. This difference in preferences may result in the use of sticks increasing animosity between Members. Such animosity may harm both trade relations and international efforts to address climate change. It reduces the goodwill between countries and their willingness to find cooperative solutions.

The requirement under the chapeau of Article XX to engage in good faith negotiations prior to implementation of the measure may go some way to offsetting the animosity concerns. However, the fact that the negotiations were not successful if the measure is imposed points to continued concerns about the legitimacy, or at least perceived legitimacy, of the stick. Such animosity may be greater to the extent that one country is seen as imposing its preferences on others. The next chapter will explore whether these concerns are reduced if the measures taken to induce participation in climate action are taken under a multilateral agreement.

PART V

Multilateral solutions

14. Trade measures in a climate agreement

14.1 TRADE, PARTICIPATION AND COMPLIANCE

In the previous chapters, we have seen that there is a risk of a WTO challenge to any unilateral action by states trying to ensure that other countries take action on climate change. Moreover, there are questions of the legitimacy of any such action that can be viewed as one state imposing its preferences on another. The Appellate Body has indicated the advisability of multilateral negotiations prior to the use of any trade measures.[1] The question arises as to whether there is any hope of using trade measures on a multilateral basis rather than unilaterally, or at least whether there can be a multilateral agreement specifying when such action can be taken. This chapter examines the possibility of including trade measures within a multilateral climate agreement. The Kyoto Protocol and the more recent post-Kyoto negotiations illustrate the concerns about both participation and compliance.[2]

As international agreements depend on the consent of the parties, countries must view entering into and complying with any agreement as in their self-interest, or at least not significantly against their self-interest. In using any enforcement mechanism, the sanction must be severe enough for each state to view itself as better off bearing the cost of taking climate change action than the cost of the negative incentive.[3] However, the remedial provisions also have an impact on the participation rates and the commitments parties are willing to make. As Barrett notes, any post-Kyoto

---

[1] *United States – Import Prohibition of Certain Shrimp and Shrimp Products (US – Shrimp I)* (1998) WTO Doc. WT/DS58/AB/R (Appellate Body Report) .

[2] Scott Barrett, *Why Cooperate? The Incentive to Supply Global Public Goods* (Oxford: Oxford University Press, 2007).

[3] See Scott Barrett, *Environment and Statecraft: The Strategy of Environmental Treaty-Making* (Oxford: Oxford University Press, 2003), and Scott Barrett and Robert Stavins, 'Increasing Participation and Compliance in International Climate Change Agreements' (2003) 3 *International Environmental Agreements: Politics, Law and Economics* 349.

agreement has to achieve broad participation, provide incentives for compliance, and produce significant emission reduction commitments.[4] These are difficult targets to meet simultaneously because achieving any one makes the others more difficult to achieve. Increasing the incentives for compliance makes it more difficult to obtain broad participation without watering down the emission reduction targets (and possibly not even then).

Multilateral environmental agreements may include trade measures that impose restrictions or conditions on the ability of states to import or export certain products. They may limit trade in substances that are harmful to the environment. For example, the Basel Convention on the Transboundary Movements of Hazardous Wastes and their Disposal limits trade in hazardous waste. They may also restrict trade where the trade itself is harmful to the things sought to be conserved. The Convention on International Trade in Endangered Species of Wild Fauna and Flora (CITES) bans trade in endangered species. These trade measures have tended to be used as a last resort. For example, the CITES provides for suspension of trade with a non-complying party, but the focus is on working with the non-complying party to achieve remedial action. A recommendation for a suspension of commercial, or all, trade in specimens of one or more CITES-listed species tends to be used as a last resort where a party's non-compliance is unresolved and 'persistent'.[5]

Trade measures have also been used to deter free-riding and thereby to foster participation and compliance. An example is the Montreal Protocol on Substances that Deplete the Ozone Layer, which is probably the most evoked agreement in discussions of analogies for the use of trade measures in climate agreements. It aims at reducing the emissions of ozone depleting substances (ODS) and has been claimed to have been largely successful in limiting emissions through broad participation and significant commitments.[6] The Montreal Protocol involved a ban on trade between parties and non-parties in ozone depleting substances (ODS) and products containing ODS. It did not, as originally intended, also ban products made with ODS. There was an exception to the ban on trade with non-parties where the country in question is determined to be in full compliance with

---

[4] Scott Barrett, 'Climate Treaties and the Imperative of Enforcement' (2008) 24 (2) *Oxford Review of Economic Policy* 239.

[5] United Nations Environment Programme, *Trade Related Measures and Multilateral Environmental Agreements* (UNEP, Economics and Trade Branch, Division of Technology, Industry and Economics, 2007).

[6] Barrett, *supra* note 3.

the Protocol's control measures.[7] It therefore had trade measures that both constrained trade in the substances and differentiated between participants and non-participants.

As Barrett notes, the trade bans under the Montreal Protocol were never used and their mere threat was sufficient to make countries act.[8] There were other factors involved in the success of the Montreal Protocol, including the fact that there was potential economic self-interest for the countries entering into the deal; the cost–benefit analysis was generally in favour of taking action on ODS; and there were provisions to aid developing countries (including added time for compliance and financial aid).[9] As a result, it is difficult to know the role played by the trade measures in the Protocol.

The UNFCCC makes only passing reference to the connection between trade and climate change commitments. It states that '[m]easures taken to combat climate change, including unilateral ones, should not constitute a means of arbitrary or unjustifiable discrimination or a disguised restriction on international trade.'[10] Trade measures are therefore not generally contemplated as a means of enforcing participation or compliance with climate commitments.[11] Issues arise, however, over the extent to which the WTO would accept such trade measures in a climate agreement if states ever agreed to include them.

14.2 HOW DOES THE WTO VIEW MULTILATERAL ENVIRONMENTAL AGREEMENTS?

The question of the relationship between the WTO and MEAs has been the subject of long-running and as yet unresolved discussions in the WTO's Committee on Trade and Environment (CTE). The Vienna Convention on

---

[7] UNEP, *supra* note 5 at 12.

[8] Barrett, *supra* note 4.

[9] Barrett, *supra* note 3, and Cass Sunstein, *Worst-Case Scenarios* (Cambridge, MA: Harvard University Press, 2007).

[10] UNFCCC, Article 3.5.

[11] The closest the Kyoto Protocol comes to a trade measure is a proposed restriction on trading in emission permits if parties do not comply with their Kyoto commitments. However, whether or not this constitutes a trade measure depends on whether international trade in emission permits is covered by the WTO agreements which is controversial. See Duncan Brack and Kevin Gray, 'Multilateral Environmental Agreements and the WTO' (The Royal Institute of International Affairs and International Institute for Sustainable Development, September 2003).

the Law of Treaties provides that a state is not subject to rights and obligations from a treaty to which it has not consented.[12] As a result, a non-party to a climate agreement does not become subject to its obligations or provisions including those relating to trade measures for non-participation or non-compliance with its rules. The non-party to the climate agreement could therefore potentially bring a WTO challenge on the basis that any such measure did not comply with WTO rules where both the complaining state and the state taking the measures were WTO Members.

However, the climate agreement could be applicable if it is not used as directly determinative of the relationship between the parties but as a means of interpreting the provisions of existing WTO agreements (such as Article XX) in assessing whether the measure was WTO-compliant. The climate negotiations may then serve as the basis for the WTO's understanding of Members' arguments about the use of measures. The Dispute Settlement Understanding states that the Dispute Settlement Body cannot add to or diminish the rights and obligations under the WTO agreements, but does note that it is 'to clarify the existing provisions of those agreements in accordance with customary rules of interpretation of public international law'.[13] A key rule of international law in regard to international treaties is set out in Article 31(3)(c) of the Vienna Convention on the Law of Treaties, which provides that in interpreting treaties, account must be taken of 'any relevant rules of international law applicable in the relations between the parties'.

The Appellate Body has taken MEAs into account in interpreting some provisions of WTO agreements, in particular Article XX. For example, it used international environmental law to interpret the scope of the Article XX(g) exception to the GATT and to establish whether a living species is endangered for the purposes of Article XX(g).[14] Also in *US – Shrimp*, the Appellate Body referred to international law (the Rio Declaration) as being reflective of broader agreement in the international community, even where not all parties were bound by that law.[15]

However, more recently, a panel decision has muddied the waters on the use of other international treaties in interpreting WTO provisions. In *EC – Biotech*, the US, Canada, and Argentina challenged what they argued was effectively a ban by the EC on imports of genetically modified organisms.[16] The EC states had decided not to allow approvals of

---

[12]   Vienna Convention, Article 34.
[13]   DSU, Article 3.2.
[14]   *US – Shrimp I AB Report, supra* note 1 at paras 129–31, 132.
[15]   Ibid., para. 154.
[16]   *European Communities – Measures Affecting the Approval and Marketing*

biotech products pending new rules. Moreover, there were delays in dealing with some applications and some individual states took a different position on the approval of biotech products than the EC as a whole. The EC defended its actions on a number of grounds, the main one for the purposes of this chapter being that their actions were consistent with the Cartagena Biosafety Protocol, as well as the precautionary principle. The Cartagena Biosafety Protocol is a multilateral agreement covering trade in living modified organisms. The EC was a signatory to the Protocol, as were Canada and Argentina, but not the US.

The panel took a narrow view of Article 31(3)(c) and found that a rule of international law would only apply in the WTO context where it was applicable to all WTO Members. As the US was not party to the treaties in question, the Panel rejected the EC's call to take these treaties into account in interpreting the WTO rules at issue in the dispute. One of its key reasons was that a state should not be bound by rules to which it had not consented. This decision has been criticized and, as it is only a panel decision, it is not clear to what extent, if any, it will be followed in future cases.[17] As noted above, in other instances such as *US – Shrimp*, the Appellate Body has suggested that non-WTO legal norms have legitimate uses in WTO dispute settlement. These earlier decisions would imply that provisions of a climate agreement may be used to interpret WTO agreements.

However, there are other ways in which the provisions of an MEA and the WTO agreements could interact, in particular where both parties to a dispute are parties to both agreements. There are a number of rules in international law concerning how treaties that conflict are to be interpreted in such cases. For example, if the parties to the dispute are both parties to two different treaties that conflict, the later treaty prevails.[18] Further, if there is a conflict between two treaties, a more specific law prevails over a later more general law.[19] These rules are often difficult to apply in the context of MEAs and the WTO given the complex structure of the agreements. These difficulties can create considerable uncertainty between the

---

of *Biotech Products* (2006) WTO Doc. WT/DS291/R, WT/DS292/R and WT/DS293/R (Panel Report).

[17] See, for example, Caroline Henckels, 'GMOs in the WTO: A Critique of the Panels' Legal Reasoning in EC – Biotech' (2006) 7 *Melbourne Journal of International Law* 278 and Robert Howse and Henrik Horn, 'European Communities – Measures Affecting the Approval and Marketing of Biotech Products' (2009) 8 (1) *World Trade Review* 49.

[18] Vienna Convention, Article 30(4).

[19] See J. Pauwelyn, 'The Role of Public International Law in the WTO: How Far Can We Go?' (2001) 95 (3) *American Journal of International Law* 535.

parties. There may be clauses in an MEA that specifically attempt to delineate the relationship between the treaties, such as indicating which treaty
prevails in the event of a conflict.[20]

An alternative to a provision in the MEA specifying the nature of the relationship would be a WTO agreement about either the general relationship
between MEAs and the WTO or the relationship between the WTO agreements and specifically named MEAs.[21] The connection between MEAs and
the WTO is one of the areas of negotiation in the Doha Round. In particular, the negotiations are to focus on the 'the relationship between existing
WTO rules and specific trade obligations set out in multilateral environmental agreements'.[22] Specific trade obligations are trade measures such as bans
or tariffs that are explicitly included in the MEA.[23] However, the fate of the
Doha Round is uncertain at this time and, as noted, it only covers a portion
of the issue of the overlap between MEAs and WTO agreements.

A more narrowly tailored agreement is also possible. A form of agreement recently discussed is a waiver from WTO obligations for actions
taken under a climate change agreement.[24] There could be conditions
added to any such waiver such as that the measures taken would have
to be non-discriminatory or that they are subject to forms of oversight.
The waiver would not require consensus on the part of Members but only
approval from three-quarters of the Members.[25]

14.3 TRADE MEASURES AND CLIMATE AGREEMENTS

There is, therefore, at least the theoretical possibility of including in
some form of agreement rules about the overlap of trade measures and

---

[20] Brack and Gray, *supra* note 11. For example, the Cartagena Biosafety
Protocol states that it 'shall not be interpreted as implying a change in the rights and
obligations of a Party under any existing international agreements' (Preamble).
[21] Brack and Gray, ibid.
[22] Doha Ministerial Declaration, 2001, para. 31 (i).
[23] Brack and Gray, *supra* note 11.
[24] See R. Howse, 'Subsidies to Address Climate Change: Legal Issues'
(International Institute for Sustainable Development, August 2009) and Brack
and Gray, *supra* note 11. There is the possibility of formal interpretation under
Article XI of the WTO Agreement, although any such waiver must be taken by
three-quarters of the WTO Members.
[25] Gary Hufbauer, Steve Charnovitz and Jisun Kim, *Global Warming and
the World Trading System* (Washington, DC: Peterson Institute for International
Economics, 2009).

climate change. The Montreal Protocol, the main precedent given for trade measures in a climate agreement, may be difficult to apply to the climate context. The question of WTO-compatibility may not have been a practical problem for the Montreal Protocol because its membership is larger than that of the WTO. Where an MEA's membership is larger than the WTO's, and all parties agree to inclusion of the measures, the risk of a trade dispute is significantly reduced. It would be difficult for a WTO Member who is party to an MEA containing trade measures to challenge another Member's measures at the WTO.[26] The greater concern arises with trade restrictions in a climate agreement where not all WTO Members are parties to that agreement.[27] Such differences in membership raise serious concerns regarding the relationship of MEAs to the WTO.

Whether or not the trade measures in a climate agreement are effective will also depend both on the number of countries inside and/or complying with the agreement and on which countries are participating and complying. As Barrett notes, if the number of countries inside the agreement and attempting to impose trade bans on other countries is low, the countries outside the agreement may not have any real incentive to participate. However, as the number of countries participating (and complying) increases, participation becomes more beneficial to those outside the agreement and subject to possible trade measures.[28]

The UNFCCC had a very large number of parties. The Kyoto Protocol also had a large number of participants. However, it was hampered by the absence of some large players, in particular the US. The absence of the US in an agreement may mean that parties to a climate agreement may be less willing to take strong sanctions against non-participants. The costs of any trade measures to the sanctioning countries could potentially be quite large, particularly in some sectors. However, if the US and the other major developed economies were to join in a post-Kyoto agreement, and the parties were to agree upon some form of trade measures against non-participants, the sanctions could be extremely effective. It may, for example, be sufficient to force non-participating developing countries to enter the agreement.

One concern with such trade measures in a climate agreement is that they will be used to force participation in an unfair agreement. States inside the agreement may use protectionist measures not only to support their

---

[26] Risa Schwartz, 'Trade Measures Pursuant to Multilateral Environmental Agreements – Developments from Singapore to Seattle' (2000) 9 *RECIEL* 63.
[27] Barrett and Stavins, *supra* note 3.
[28] Barrett, *supra* note 3.

own producers but to essentially aid all members of the agreement – that is, there is a risk of the creation of a trading bloc with the type of harms that the GATT agreements attempt to avoid. There is a debate within the trade literature about the value of agreements that reduce trade barriers between groups of countries, such as regional trading blocs (like NAFTA or the EU) or bilateral trade agreements.[29] The proponents of these agreements argue that they lead to greater integration of like-minded nations and may foster greater and closer integration across all countries. However, critics maintain that the agreements lead to excessive administrative costs and factionalism as well as to more trade diversion than trade creation. The trade creation arises from reducing the barriers to trade between the parties to the agreement, while trade diversion is the shifting of trade away from the global least-cost producer to the members inside the trading bloc.

The GATT's most-favoured-nation principle is intended to create trade by ensuring that, if a country reduces its tariffs for one country, it does so for all so that trade goes to the least-cost producer. The GATT allows an exception to the MFN principle for regional trading blocs under Article XXIV. There are, however, two conditions – that the agreement cannot raise barriers to parties outside the agreement above the level prior to the formation of the trading bloc and barriers must be eliminated on substantially all trade between the parties to the agreement. These conditions are not strictly enforced by the WTO.

The fear about the use of trade measures within a climate agreement is that the parties may set the terms of participation in the agreement so high that it is extremely costly for non-participants to join, perhaps even more costly than for the original parties (including in terms of competitiveness). The non-participants then have a choice of bearing the high costs of protectionist trade measures or joining an agreement that imposes disproportionately high costs on them. The effect may be trade diversion or a perception that the agreement is unfairly coercive to those outside it.

The other concern about trade measures in a climate agreement is that, as with unilateral trade measures, there are very high administrative costs. The costs of negotiating the form of the measures will be significant. Getting a range of countries to agree on the nature and scope of any such measures may be difficult, particularly if they are to apply not only

---

[29]   See Jagdish Bhagwati, *Termites in the Trading System* (New York: Oxford University Press, 2008) and Razeen Sally, *New Frontiers in Free Trade: Globalization's Future and Asia's Rising Role* (Washington, DC: Cato Institute, 2008). See also Michael Trebilcock and Robert Howse, *The Regulation of International Trade*, 3rd edn (New York: Routledge, 2005) for a summary of the debates about preferential trade agreements.

to non-participating countries but also to non-complying parties to the agreement. As noted previously, an increase in the cost of non-compliance has potentially negative impacts on the level of participation and the level of commitments. It therefore entails a delicate and difficult set of negotiations to attempt to get commitment levels along with a sanction implicating economic growth. Perhaps even more costly will be the processes and institutions required to apply the necessary measures. It will be difficult to determine which imports are sufficiently tied to the non-participating state to be subject to sanctions. Broadening the scope of these trade measures and the number of countries subject to them is likely to significantly increase the costs of imposing them.

On the other hand, there are some virtues of including trade measures in a climate agreement compared with the use of unilateral measures. The key benefit is that the inclusion of such measures within a climate change agreement may provide a legitimacy that is absent for unilateral measures. In this sense, including trade measures in a climate agreement may have both an efficiency and a fairness benefit relative to unilateral measures. Countries must determine for themselves whether they wish to take climate action, depending on whether they wish to bear the costs of trade sanctions for not taking action. This flexibility allows countries to examine the costs and benefits of action, including in terms of domestic preferences. The costs they are facing depend not on the special preferences or balancing of a particular country, as under unilateral measures, but on those determined by a larger, hopefully more representative body of nations. These preferences may still be substantially different from those of the country facing sanctions for not participating.

However, the danger arises from the nature of the negotiating process for the particular agreement. As noted above, being a multilateral agreement does not necessarily make it fair. It depends on who is involved in the negotiations and how these negotiations are conducted. To the extent that a few countries negotiate the content of the agreement and attempt to force others to participate, the agreement can lose any apparent legitimacy. There was a concern, for example, over the negotiation process in Copenhagen as there was a sense that there was a lack of meaningful opportunities for participation and agreement by the majority of countries after the US and four other countries met in an attempt to find agreement. While potentially having greater legitimacy than unilateral measures, it still constitutes an imposition of the preferences of one set of states on others, particularly in the case of deterring non-participation as opposed to non-compliance.

There are other potential benefits to a multilateral climate agreement that includes trade provisions. One is that any negative incentives (sticks in the form of trade bans or tariffs) would be seen as antagonistic, and the inclusion of the trade measures in a climate agreement could result in pairing the 'sticks' with the 'carrots'. There is a need to ensure that developing countries have the financial ability to undertake whatever changes are asked of them while still being able to grow and provide an increased standard of living for their citizens. Commentators have argued that these financial incentives, along with the trade measures, were central to the success of the Montreal Protocol.[30]

Further, the inclusion of the trade measures within a climate agreement allows for the possibility that developing countries will be given some time to come into compliance with any requirements. Zhang argues, for example, that given the time that the US has taken to set up its climate policies, developing countries should be allowed at least ten years prior to trade measures taking effect.[31] The notion of common but differentiated responsibilities among states is already incorporated into the UNFCCC and WTO agreements.[32] The inclusion of trade measures within a multilateral climate agreement hopefully provides greater scope for allowing time for developing countries to take action.

Given the interpretation of Article XX, the WTO appears unlikely to allow trade measures against a Member merely because it is not participating in a multilateral climate agreement. As with unilateral measures, there would need to be some assessment that the state that is the target of the trade measures is not taking 'comparable' action to address climate to those within the treaty. This notion of 'comparability' will be very difficult to determine and the hope would be that a climate agreement could help define it.[33] Multilateral climate agreements may take different forms. There could be overall targets for all parties to the agreement, as with the Kyoto Protocol. Complying with these commitments or comparable levels of reductions may provide some basis on which to decide whether trade measures could be imposed, particularly if the UNFCCC parties explicitly

---

[30]   Zhong Xiang Zhang, 'Multilateral Trade Measures in a Post-2012 Climate Change Regime? What Can Be Taken From the Montreal Protocol and the WTO' (June 2009). Available at SSRN: http://ssrn.com/abstract=1328548; Barrett, *supra* note 3.

[31]   Zhang, ibid.

[32]   See UNFCCC, Article 3, along with the various provisions of the WTO agreements which allow developing countries added time in which to comply with commitments.

[33]   Zhang, *supra* note 30; Jacob Werksman, James Bradbury and Lutz Weischer, 'Trade Measures and Climate Change Policy: Searching for Common Ground on an Uneven Playing Field' (World Resources Institute Working Paper, December 2009).

agree that these commitments reflect what is meant by comparability.[34] However, given the uncertainty around the policy space and time to allow developing countries to comply, more definitive direction is likely to be needed about when trade measures can be taken either under a multilateral agreement or perhaps even unilaterally.

No real direction was provided in Copenhagen. Despite the fact that a number of developing countries went into Copenhagen wanting a ban on unilateral trade measures, the countries at the talks could not agree on any changes directly relating to trade measures in the Copenhagen Accord. [35] Moreover, even the 'commitments' the parties did agree to were minimal, based on a country's own self-declared target.[36] It seems possible that countries wishing to use border adjustments (such as the US) may not count hitting these 'targets' as 'comparable' efforts. In addition, the Copenhagen Accord lacks agreement on an international oversight process, leaving monitoring to individual countries. Such lack of independent monitoring also raises concern about objective determinations of compliance with commitments, and therefore the use of trade measures.

As Director-General of the WTO, Pascal Lamy, commented following the Copenhagen conference, while members were divided on the use of border measures, 'what I can say is that the more we move toward a multilateral framework on climate change, the more unilateral trade measures will be difficult to explain'.[37] Climate negotiations and agreement on what countries are responsible for undertaking should help on the issues of trade measures, competitiveness, and legitimacy. The extent of progress with these issues may define the scope of the agreement. For example, it may be easier to put in place trade restrictions to back a sectoral agreement.[38] They may be both credible to protect against leakage in sectors that are particularly open to leakage and able to be made sufficiently severe. We will return to this issue in the final chapter.

---

[34] Werksman, Bradbury and Weischer, *supra* note 33.

[35] Available online at http://unfccc.int/resource/docs/2009/cop15/eng/o7.pdf (date accessed: 22 January 2010).

[36] For example, the US committed to emissions reduction by 2020 'in the range of 17%, in conformity with anticipated US energy and climate legislation, recognizing that the final target will be reported to the Secretariat in light of enacted legislation' (see letter from Todd Stern, US Special Envoy for Climate Change, to the UNFCCC dated 28 January 2010).

[37] WTO, 'Lamy Praises Copenhagen Efforts, Calls for More To Be Done' (21 December 2009) (accessed 8 January 2010 at http://www.wto.org/english/news_e/news09_e/climate_21dec09_e.htm).

[38] Barrett, *supra* note 4.

15. Increasing environmentally beneficial trade

One of the pathways identified for achieving convergence between climate change and trade objectives is the development of multilateral measures. This chapter addresses the potential for multilateral agreement to increase trade in environmental goods and services (EGS). It begins by examining the case for liberalization, discusses what is meant by EGS, and considers developments in international negotiations to date. It concludes by considering what institutional framework might be most appropriate for liberalization of EGS given the overriding goals of climate change mitigation, deterrence of protectionism, and development.

15.1   WHY EGS LIBERALIZATION?

Liberalization of EGS was mandated in the Doha Ministerial Declaration of 2001, which called for the reduction or, as appropriate, elimination of tariff and non-tariff barriers of environmental goods and services.[1] Negotiations have taken place across various WTO committees. The Negotiating Group on Market Access for Non-Agricultural (NAMA) Products is responsible for negotiations on modalities for liberalization of environmental goods. The Council for Trade in Services in Special Session is responsible for environmental services, which are being negotiated as part of the broader services negotiations under the General Agreement on Trade in Services (GATS). Finally, the Committee on Trade and Environment in Special Session (CTESS) has the task of defining what is included in the category of EGS.[2] Progress on all three fronts has been slow. In particular, the NAMA negotiations cannot progress on environ-

---

[1]   Para. 31(iii).

[2]   In addition, at a meeting in 2002, it was agreed that the CTE in Special Session would keep track of the work undertaken in the Committee on Agriculture in Special Session, and there was broad support for the idea that a monitoring role could be played by the CTE in Special Session with regard to paragraph 31(iii). Committee on Trade and Environment in Special Session, *Summary Report of the*

mental goods until the CTESS has reached consensus on the definitional issue. Moreover, a general lack of progress on NAMA and agricultural liberalization has made many countries reluctant to engage deeply on EGS liberalization.

While liberalization of EGS is framed broadly in the Doha Declaration, it has particular significance for climate change in light of the goals cited in Chapter 2. First, it would deter protectionism through the elimination or reduction of tariff and non-tariff barriers to trade. Second, it can help in the mitigation of and adaptation to climate change. Many goods and services have the potential to contribute to climate change mitigation and adaptation, whether due to their nature and means of production (for example, zero carbon emitting steel), their consumption (for example, solar panels) or their disposal (for example, jute bags).[3] While (as discussed further below) defining EGS is a contentious matter, it is apparent that liberalization has significant potential to increase the accessibility to certain goods and services, through cost reduction and incentives for producers to expand their production.[4] This is illustrated in a study by the International Energy Agency (IEA) showing that by 2050, with moderately optimistic assumptions about development and diffusion of technologies for increasing efficiency or substituting non-fossil energy, reductions in GHGs of 28 per cent could be achieved from electricity generation and 19 per cent from industry.[5] To achieve this, EGS must not be overpriced or inaccessible due to trade barriers.

Third, liberalization of EGS can help further development. Developing countries will have a greater chance of building a sustainable and 'green' economy if they can increase local capabilities for innovation and adaptation of domestic technology rather than having to rely on transfer of

---

First Meeting of the Committee on Trade and Environment in Special Session 22 March 2002 (Committee on Trade and Environment in Special Session, 2002).

[3] Mahesh Sugathan, *Liberalization of Trade in Environmental Goods for Climate Change Mitigation: The Sustainable Development Context* (International Centre for Trade and Sustainable Development (Geneva), International Institute for Sustainable Development (Winnipeg), for the Trade and Climate Change Seminar, Copenhagen, Denmark, 2008) at 2.

[4] Ludivine Tamiotti et al., *Trade and Climate Change*: A Report by the United Nations Environment Programme and the World Trade Organization (Geneva: WTO, 2009) at 81.

[5] International Energy Agency 2008. Cited in Ronald Steenblik, Takenori Matsuoka and Jim Hight, *Facilitating Trade in Selected Climate Change-mitigation Technologies in the Electricity Generation and Heavy-industry Sectors* (OECD Global Forum on Trade: Trade and Climate Change, COM/TAD/ENV/JWPTE(2008)28, 2008) at 7.

foreign technology.[6] This will only happen if companies are able to access technologies at a reasonable cost. Further they will need to be able to access export markets for any EGS they produce. It has been suggested that if developing countries can enhance local capabilities and access export markets, benefits could include increased economic diversification, increased employment and poverty alleviation.[7] Increased local capabilities would also enable developing country firms to more easily comply with environmental standards in foreign markets. Domestically, improved market access for products derived from incorporating cleaner technologies could encourage the use of environmentally efficient products, thus supporting sustainable development.[8]

The potential value of EGS liberalization is widely recognized. In a 2005 report, the OECD suggested that reducing or eliminating tariff and non-tariff barriers to trade in EGS is a 'win-win' proposition: good for trade, and good for the environment.[9] More recently, the WTO-UNEP Climate Change Report suggests that this aspect of the Doha mandate provides 'an unprecedented opportunity for the multilateral trading system to contribute to furthering mutual supportiveness of trade and environment'.[10] As EU Trade Commissioner, Peter Mandelson, put it, a WTO-wide deal eliminating all tariffs on trade in green technologies and energy-saving

---

[6]   Tamiotti et al., *supra* note 4 at 81.

[7]   E. Claro et al., *Trade in Environmental Goods and Services and Sustainable Development: Domestic Considerations and Strategies for WTO Negotiations* (Geneva: ICSTD Environmental Goods and Services Series, Policy Discussion Paper, International Centre for Trade and Sustainable Development, 2007) at xvi. The *World Development Report 2010* noted that while traditionally developing countries have been importers of clean technologies, as a result of their improving investment climate and large consumer base, developing countries are in fact increasingly becoming major players in the manufacture of clean technologies. World Bank, *World Development Report 2010: Development and Climate Change* (Washington, DC: The World Bank, 2010) at 254.

[8]   CTE in Special Session, Environmental Goods for Development – Submission by Brazil – Paragraph 31(iii), WTO Doc. (TN/TE/W/59) 8 July 2005. See also E. Claro et al., *Trade in Environmental Goods and Services and Sustainable Development: Domestic Considerations and Strategies for WTO Negotiations* (Geneva: ICSTD Environmental Goods and Services Series, Policy Discussion Paper, International Centre for Trade and Sustainable Development, 2007) at 1.

[9]   Organisation for Economic Co-operation and Development (OECD), *Policy Brief – Opening Markets for Environmental Goods and Services* (Paris: OECD, 2005) at 3.

[10]   Tamiotti et al., *supra* note 4 at 80.

equipment would play an important role in furthering a 'business-friendly global solution to climate change'.[11]

It is difficult to establish exactly what barriers to trade in EGS currently exist due to the lack of consensus on what is included in the definition of EGS. However, several studies suggest that high tariffs and other trade and investment barriers currently impede access to GHG-reducing technologies, particularly in low- to middle-income countries.[12] One area where high tariffs are evident is biofuels, which currently face tariffs of over 40 per cent in the EU and the United States, while oil faces zero tariffs.[13] Further, non-tariff barriers exist across various sectors. In the electricity-generation and heavy-industry sectors, for example, non-tariff barriers include burdensome pre-shipment inspection and customs procedures; technical requirements and voluntary standards; burdensome conformity assessment, certification, and testing procedures; and non-transparent government procurement procedures.[14]

In the services sector, the OECD has identified various barriers including: allowing exports of services only through firms with a commercial presence in the importing country; limiting the scope of foreign business to specified activities; and requiring that a specified, significant proportion of staff of the foreign established company be nationals of the host country, regardless of experience or qualifications.[15]

Of course, reduction of trade barriers is not the only factor necessary to increase trade in EGS. Other important factors include level of gross domestic product, investment frameworks and levels of foreign direct investment, environmental regulatory frameworks, technical assistance, fiscal incentives, and intellectual-property-related costs.[16] Nevertheless, liberalization is an important piece of the jigsaw.

---

[11] The World Bank, *International Trade and Climate Change – Economic, Legal, and Institutional Perspectives* (Washington, DC: The World Bank, 2008) at 89.

[12] Ibid. at 80. A study by General Electric reports that the majority of WTO members levy tariffs on wind turbines and that solar panels and gas turbines also face significant tariffs. International Centre for Trade and Sustainable Development (ICTSD), 'GE Calls for Stand-Alone Deal on Environmental Goods and Services', (2009) 13 (37) *Bridges Weekly Trade News Digest*.

[13] ICTSD, ibid.

[14] Tamiotti et al., *supra* note 4 at 81. Steenblik, Matsuoka and Hight, *supra* note 5. In a recent study, General Electric reports that non-tariff barriers are particularly destructive to GHG reduction goals, citing 'buy domestic' requirements and other local content restrictions in China, the US, and Canada. ICTSD, *supra* note 12.

[15] OECD, *supra* note 9 at 5.

[16] Sugathan, *supra* note 3 at 75.

15.2   DEFINING EGS

The definition of EGS has proven to be a contentious issue, with most difficulty revolving around the definition of goods. There are two main alternatives: a narrow and a broad approach. The narrow approach focuses on identifying goods that would directly address environmental goals (sometimes known as 'traditional environmental goods').[17] The broader approach, on the other hand, extends the focus beyond end-use criteria to look at environmentally 'preferable' products.[18] The United Nations Conference on Trade and Development (UNCTAD) has defined 'environmentally preferable products' as those that cause significantly less 'environmental harm' at some stage of their life-cycle[19] than alternative products that serve the same purpose, or products whose production and sale contribute significantly to the preservation of the environment.[20]

The narrow approach is an absolute notion of environmental compatibility. Goods must have a positive impact on the environment. The broad approach, on the other hand, is a relative concept that depends upon a comparison between two goods. The benefit of a given good will depend upon how damaging the comparator good is. If the comparator product was a coal-burning stove, then a gas-burning stove may qualify as an environmental good, despite its own doubtful environmental qualities.

The *narrow* approach has the potential to incentivize innovation in the climate change context. However, it also presents certain problems.[21] Most contentious is what happens when a product has dual uses; that is, it is used for both environmental and non-environmental purposes.[22] Some products are inherently dual-use; for example, a pipe can be used as an input to a renewable energy plant but can also be used to transport oil.[23] Countries are divided in the negotiations as to whether or not EGS liberalization should extend to dual-use goods, with those for the proposition

---

[17]   Ibid. at 75.
[18]   Ibid. at 76.
[19]   Whether this be during production, consumption or other use, or disposal.
[20]   United Nations Conference on Trade and Development (UNCTAD), *Environmentally Preferable Products (EPPs) as a Trade Opportunity for Developing Countries* (Geneva: UNCTAD, UNCTAD/COM/70, 1995). Examples include improved solid-fuel cooking stoves and reusable shopping bags made of canvas rather than plastic or paper. OECD, *supra* note 9 at 2.
[21]   The World Bank, *International Trade and Climate Change – Economic, Legal, and Institutional Perspectives* (Washington, DC: The World Bank, 2008) at 84.
[22]   Ibid. at 77.
[23]   Ibid.

(generally developed countries) arguing that the benefits of liberalization would be limited if it was restricted to single-use goods.[24] Developing countries, however, worry about the impact that liberalizing dual-use goods would have on their domestic industries.[25]

Another problem with the narrow approach is that goods may be considered environmentally friendly in some countries but not so in others, due to differing stages of development and perceptions of what needs to be done to address climate change. There will also be debate within countries. By way of example, there is considerable domestic and international debate as to the environmental merits of certain biofuels.[26] Further, there is the constant evolution of technology. The OECD estimates that half of the environmental goods likely to be in use within the coming decade do not currently exist.[27] Environmental services will also evolve. Already, it has been noted that the current GATS list of services requires updating to represent the evolution of the environmental services industry from traditional end-of-pipe/pollution control/remediation/clean-up towards integrated pollution prevention and control, cleaner technology, and resources and risk management.[28] One possible solution to the problem of evolving technology is to have a 'living list' that would be amended as new EGS are developed.[29] However, this would present a significant administrative burden as countries would be required to conduct regular reviews of their commitments in light of new developments. Not only would new products need to be classified, but as products become older

---

[24]   Mahesh Sugathan, 'Environmental Goods: A Doha Round Deliverable for Climate Change?', in *Climate, Equity and Global Trade* (Geneva: International Centre for Trade and Sustainable Development (ICTSD), Selected Issue Briefs No. 2, 2007) at 1.

[25]   Sugathan, *supra* note 3 at 4.

[26]   See generally 'Biofuels for Transportation: Global Potential for Sustainable Agriculture and Energy in the Twenty-First Century' (Washington, DC: Worldwatch Institute, 2006).

[27]   Organisation for Economic Co-operation and Development (OECD), *The Global Environmental Goods and Services Industry* (Paris: OECD, 1999).

[28]   Members make commitments under the GATS according to the WTO Services Sectoral Classification List (W/120) which is based on the UN Provisional Central Product Classification (CPC). Sugathan, *supra* note 24 at 2.

[29]   New Zealand has supported this concept, noting by way of precedent the 1996 Ministerial Declaration on Trade in Information Technology Products (ITA) and the Uruguay Round 'zero-for-zero' initiative on Trade in Pharmaceutical Products which were both developed on the assumption that the lists of products they contained would need to stay current as technology advanced. New Zealand, WTO Committee on Trade and Environment Special Session, Submission by New Zealand, WTO Doc. TN/TE/W/45 (10 February 2005) at para. 14.

and no longer considered environmentally friendly, they may need to be removed from the list. There may be problems in this respect if countries want to raise tariff levels for such products as WTO rules do not contemplate raising of bound tariffs.

The narrow approach also presents practical problems due to the manner in which products are classified for tariff purposes. Most countries use the Harmonized System (HS) managed by the World Customs Organization. Under this system, each product is assigned a six-digit code based on product characteristics. Some countries also use *ex-outs*, where they identify goods nationally at an eight- or ten-digit level. These ex-outs are not universal and thus differ between countries. At the six-digit level, product descriptions are fairly broad and countries have limited ability to collectively isolate specific products. This is problematic because many HS six-digit categories contain both environmental and non-environmental goods. Administratively, it would be easier to liberalize an entire HS six-digit category, but this would result in unintended liberalization of a whole range of products.[30] Thus, easy administration is likely to be in tension with political feasibility. There would be enormous administrative costs involved in isolating environmental goods beyond the six-digit level as it would require harmonizing ex-out product descriptions across Members.

Looking at the *broader* definition, that is, goods that are 'environmentally preferable', it is not agreed whether a product ought to be so defined only on the basis of its characteristics, or whether its production and process methods (PPMs) should also be a consideration. If PPMs were a valid criterion, a washing machine that was responsible for less GHG emissions during its production process than another washing machine would obtain classification as an 'environmental good' (even if they were of equally low energy efficiency in terms of performance characteristics). In support of recognition of PPMs is the reality that in many cases the most detrimental environmental effects of a product arise from its production. While it is likely that technology will advance to the point where many products can be designed to have sound environmental characteristics in their performance, it will be critical that their PPMs are also environmentally sound if we are truly to reduce their environmental impact.[31] A

---

[30] The World Bank, *supra* note 21 at 90.

[31] Note in this regard a 2002 submission by Qatar to the CTE in Special Session in which it cautioned against establishing a distinction between product end-use and PPMs, arguing that energy has to do with processes of production. It queried whether an end-use criterion could take account of the entire energy life-cycle of a product. Committee on Trade and Environment in Special Session, *Summary Report of the Third Meeting of the Committee on Trade and Environment*

key question, however, is whether it is necessary to make this comparison between PPMs at the tariff classification stage, or whether it can be dealt with later at the point of sale through means such as eco-labelling. At what stage is consideration of PPMs likely to provide the greatest incentive to manufacturers to look at their production processes?

A number of problems augur against the broad approach to definition. How would the comparison be made? What benchmark would be used to determine what constitutes an environmentally sound method of production? And further, how much *more* environmentally sound would the method need to be before the product could be defined as *environmentally preferable*? The World Bank has noted difficulties associated with singling out goods that are *relatively* clean, giving the example of natural gas, which is a cleaner alternative to coal, but less so than wind power. What if wind power is only viable if subsidized by government?[32] Consideration of PPMs would make the comparison more difficult in the absence of an effective mechanism for calculating GHG emissions across different production processes. While such a mechanism is likely to be forthcoming, it will be critical to ensure that developing countries have the capacity to use it.

Not surprisingly, difficulties have plagued the Doha negotiations on the definitional question. While it may be possible to proceed with negotiations without a formally agreed definition of EGS, there would probably be numerous difficulties in so doing given that it would not be at all clear which products should and which should not be included.[33]

15.3   NEGOTIATING APPROACHES

Further to the difficulties of trying to reach consensus on a definition of EGS, countries have failed to agree on a negotiating approach, with delegations split between a *list* approach and a *project* approach.[34] The

---

in Special Session 10–11 October 2002 (Committee on Trade and Environment in Special Session, 2002). Qatar was supported in its efforts by Saudi Arabia. Committee on Trade and Environment in Special Session, *Summary Report of the Tenth Meeting of the Committee on Trade and Environment in Special Session 12–13 October 2004* (Committee on Trade and Environment in Special Session, 2004).

[32]   The World Bank, *supra* note 21 at 83.

[33]   New Zealand, WTO Committee on Trade and Environment Special Session, Submission by New Zealand, WTO Doc. TN/TE/W/45 (10 February 2005) at para. 5.

[34]   In 2008, the World Bank reported a negotiating deadlock as supporters

former would see the formulation of a list of goods followed by the negotiation of permanent tariff elimination and/or reduction. This approach
has been supported by developed countries as a response to the problem
of dual-use goods.

A suggested starting point for the *list* approach is a definition developed by the OECD and Eurostat (Statistical Office for the European
Communities) experts in the 1990s which defines the EGS industry as con-
sisting of 'activities which produce goods and services to measure, prevent,
limit, minimize, or correct environmental damage to water, air and soil, as
well as problems related to waste, noise and eco systems'.[35] Pursuant to
this definition, the OECD later categorized EGS under the headings of:
(i) pollution management; (ii) cleaner technologies[36] and products; (iii)
resource management; and (iv) environmentally preferable products.[37]
The OECD/Eurostat definition and categories do not fully resolve the
fundamental difficulty of defining a more specific set of goods and services
capable of informing market access negotiations. The categories cover
both the *narrow* and *broad* definitions – the first three could include 'traditional environmental goods', while the fourth covers 'environmentally
preferable' goods.

Different lists put forward by different delegations are not much more
helpful.[38] An attempt to consolidate the various proposals was made by
the so-called Friends of Environmental Goods group (Canada, the EC,
Japan, Korea, New Zealand, Norway, Chinese Taipei, Switzerland, and
the United States). This group jointly proposed a consolidated list of 153
goods, including a number of ex-outs, based on their own individual lists
(known as the 'Potential Convergence Set').[39] A particular source of dif-

---

of the list approach and the project approach have refused to compromise. The
World Bank, *supra* note 21 at 78.

[35]   OECD, *supra* note 9 at 2. This was suggested as a starting point by New
Zealand in 2002. The definition had also been used by APEC members who
came up with a list of products for inclusion in their Early Voluntary Sector
Liberalization initiative launched in 1997.

[36]   Interestingly, a fairly recent study found that of trade in environmental
products, only 1% was in cleaner technologies: Bora Bijit and R. Teh, 'Tariffs
and Trade in Environmental Goods', presentation to the WTO Workshop on
Environmental Goods, Geneva, 2004 – cited in OECD, *supra* note 9.

[37]   Ibid. at 2.

[38]   Countries to have made proposals include: the EC (TN/TE/W/47); Japan
(TN/MA/W/15); Korea (TN/TE/48); Qatar (TN/TE/W/14, W/19 and W/27);
Switzerland (TN/TE/W/57); Chinese Taipei (TN/TE/W/44); and the United States
(TN/TE/W/52).

[39]   WTO Doc. JOB(04)/98. This list was a reduction in the number of goods
listed as compared with a previous Friends list that included 400 products.

ference is the question of agricultural goods. Some low-carbon technologies such as sustainable biofuels may also count as agricultural products and trade liberalization in agriculture remains a contentious topic.[40] To date, no country has tabled any agricultural product as an environmental good, although Brazil has suggested for example that bioethanol (which is currently classified as an agricultural good) should be considered an environmental good.[41]

The *project* approach was proposed by India and would involve temporary liberalization for the duration of environmental projects.[42] Projects would have to be approved by a designated national authority.[43] The rationale behind the project approach is that, due to the nature of the Harmonized System and the dual-use issue, the list approach would lead to greater liberalization than intended, while the project approach would allow countries greater policy space.[44] However, the project approach has been criticized for lacking binding and predictable market access offered on a permanent basis, and for possible inconsistency with WTO rules.[45] Various other proposals have been put forward that combine elements of the two approaches. Brazil has suggested a *'request–offer'* approach whereby countries would request specific liberalization commitments from each other, extending tariff cuts as they deem appropriate equally to all WTO members.[46] Argentina has suggested an *integrated* approach that would incorporate aspects of the list and project approaches.[47] However, consensus remains elusive.

15.4 WHAT INSTITUTIONAL FRAMEWORK?

Liberalization of EGS must meet the criteria of fairness, efficiency, and political feasibility. The fairness criterion will be met if liberalization serves to meet developmental needs and goals. The way in which the definitional problem is resolved will be critical to this. As stated by Brazil, any

---

[40] The World Bank, *International Trade and Climate Change – Economic, Legal, and Institutional Perspectives* (Washington, DC: The World Bank, 2008) at 79.
[41] Ibid. at 87.
[42] WTO Docs. TN/TE/W/51, TN/TE/54, TN/TE/60, TN/TE/67.
[43] Sugathan, *supra* note 3 at 5.
[44] Ibid. at 78.
[45] Ibid.
[46] Sugathan, *supra* note 24 at 2.
[47] WTO Doc. TN/TE/W/62. See also Argentina and India Informal Submission: WTO Doc. JOB(07)/77, 6 June 2007.

definition of environmental goods should facilitate a triple-win situation, that is, trade promotion, environmental improvement and poverty alleviation.[48] EGS should be defined so as to cover products of export interest to developing countries. While some developing countries such as China, India and Brazil have become leaders in clean energy sectors, the reality is that many developing countries lack a comparative advantage in environmental goods (narrowly defined) that are capital- or technology-intensive. Some of the more low-tech environmental goods, such as parts and components, are likely to be dual-use goods. Ironically, as noted, it is with these goods that a number of developing countries have expressed concern because of possible impacts of such liberalization on their domestic industries.[49] Developing countries have, however, proposed the inclusion of agriculture or natural resource based products (such as ethanol) that fall into the broader category of *environmentally preferable* products.[50]

Our preferred institutional framework in which to achieve liberalization of EGS is through the current GATT tariff-reduction structure. Using the *narrow* definition would ensure that liberalized EGS were actually those that might objectively play a role in fighting climate change (as compared with a *wide* definition that would be inevitably subjective and potentially limit incentives to produce 'traditional environmental goods' if tariffs on those goods remained high). We recognize the difficulties presented by dual-use goods but there may be ways to overcome this, for example, through the use of customs declarations as to the intended purpose of the imported products, with preferential tariff rates only applicable where the goods are destined for an environmental purpose.[51] There are also administrative costs involved in the latter task, especially for developing countries, but some such costs are inevitable and they must be weighed up against the potential benefits from a climate change and development

---

[48]   Submission by Brazil, WTO Doc. TN/TE/W/59.

[49]   Sugathan, *supra* note 3 at 3.

[50]   See for example the submission by Kenya, WTO Doc. TN/MA/W/40, and Brazil's submission regarding ethanol.

[51]   Colombia has informally suggested an approach whereby Members would only have to liberalize trade in goods used in a project, programme, plan, or system deemed to have verifiable environmental benefits by a designated national authority. WTO Doc. JOB(06)149. See also Howse et al., who refer to a system of duty drawbacks where duty collected at the border is refunded based on an application by the ultimate purchaser certifying a particular use for the goods. Robert Howse, Petrus van Bork and Chartotte Hebebrand, *WTO Disciplines and Biofuels: Opportunities and Constraints in the Creation of a Global Marketplace* (Washington, DC: International Food and Agricultural Trade Policy Council, 2006).

perspective. Financial assistance can be used to assist developing countries without the administrative capacity.

It is critical that countries promote the use of environmentally preferable products, including in some cases, those with climate-friendly PPMs. However, this is best done on a unilateral basis with the incentive to do so coming from countries' binding emission reduction targets, and with institutional support from the WTO in terms of recognition of PPMs in certain climate-change-related circumstances. We refer in this respect to our discussion in Chapters 5 and 6 of the possibilities for internal regulations and taxes (and to our discussion of a possible Climate Change Agreement in the next chapter).

Unfortunately, the problems in reaching consensus on the definitional issue are proving difficult to overcome. Political feasibility appears to be lacking at the present time. A second-best option would be to negotiate a stand-alone plurilateral Environmental Goods and Services Agreement, perhaps modelled on the approach taken in the Information Technology Agreement (ITA).[52] The ITA is a tariff-cutting mechanism of which membership is voluntary. However, concessions made extend to all WTO Members on a most-favoured-nation basis. (Alternatively, an agreement could be reached that did not require most-favoured-nation extension of concessions.) While the ITA provides an example of a plurilateral approach, it also highlights the problems that such an approach can present. The ITA allows for the addition of new products as technology evolves but agreement has not been reached to add any new products since its inception. Further, a plurilateral approach would have limited scope unless a large number of Members were willing to join.[53] One of the weaknesses with either of these approaches is that they could lessen the incentive for WTO Members to work towards consensus. All efforts would need to be made, therefore, to keep EGS liberalization on the negotiating agenda.

A third-best option is that countries focus their efforts in the bilateral

---

[52]   The United States and EU have made a joint proposal for a similar agreement in the environmental area. It identifies 43 products directly relevant to climate change mitigation based on the consolidated list of 153 goods compiled by the Friends of Environmental Goods. Sugathan, *supra* note 24 at 2.2.

[53]   At the time of writing, it has been reported that frustration with the slow pace of the Doha Round negotiations has led the EU, the United States, China, and other OECD members to engage in 'closed-door talks' to negotiate a deal to liberalize environmental goods. International Centre for Trade and Sustainable Development (ICTSD), 'New Deal Could Slash Tariffs on Green Goods in OECD, China' (2009) 13 (36) *Bridges Weekly Trade News Digest*.

and regional arenas. Lack of agreement at the WTO level should not mean abandonment of the notion of EGS liberalization. If bilateral and regional agreements are to play a useful role in moving forward, one such role may be their potential to forge greater liberalization in the area of EGS liberalization.

PART VI

Conclusion

16.   Trade, climate protection and development

16.1   THE INTERACTION OF TRADE AND CLIMATE POLICIES

Two of the greatest crises facing the globe are climate change and widespread poverty. Our goal in this book has been to advance the fundamental premise that the international trading regime and efforts to address climate change are not only inextricably linked but that positive synergies can be found between them that will enable achievement of environmental, trade, and development goals. Throughout our analysis of the various ways in which the climate change and international trade regimes interact with each other, we have aimed to present an optimistic view of the connection between international trade and climate change policies by searching for solutions that foster trade liberalization while supporting climate change action and development. The effort to address both crises is critical. As Sir Nicholas Stern noted, we can achieve 'a safer, cleaner, quieter, more biodiverse world with growing incomes; a world where we can win the other major battle of our century, the fight against world poverty. We either succeed on both, or we fail on both; there is nothing that is stable in between.'[1]

We began the book by considering the underlying concerns about climate change and international trade. The core problem giving rise to climate change is its public goods nature and the consequent free-riding of individual countries that stand to benefit if others take action but have little incentive to join the international effort and take action themselves. The central concern with international trade is similar – the need to obtain cooperation on building a public good. The public good that the trading system is (or should be) aiming at is an increased standard of living for citizens of all countries.

The rest of the book has drawn out the relationship between WTO rules

---

[1]   Nicholas Stern, *The Global Deal: Climate Change and the Creation of a New Era of Progress and Prosperity* (New York: Public Affairs, 2009), at 204.

and domestic climate policies, noting that there are three main interactions between these regimes. The first is the relationship between international trade rules and domestic climate policies. Governments have a range of policy instruments to choose from when seeking to address climate change, including regulatory measures such as emissions trading schemes and energy efficiency standards, taxes, subsidies, and border measures. Part III analysed the various disciplines placed upon the use of these instruments by international trade rules. A number of WTO rules constrain countries in their instrument choice and design, including those contained in the GATT, SCM Agreement, and TBT Agreement. The design and interpretation of these rules must strike a delicate balance between, on the one hand, providing countries with the *flexibility* to innovate and experiment with domestic climate change policies and, on the other hand, *policing against protectionism*, which can hinder economic growth, action on climate change, and international relations. In addition, these rules must provide a degree of *certainty* that countries can take action on climate change without fear of facing a WTO challenge. Such challenges may damage their international reputation.

We favour decentralization to the extent possible as being the most efficient mechanism to allow innovation in policy instruments, variation in costs and benefits and values, and uncertainty of information. Decentralization permits countries to vindicate their own values on issues such as intergenerational equity and environmental protection. At the same time, there is a role for the WTO as a check on the protectionist impulses of domestic governments. The WTO's approach of focusing on standards, rather than more rigid centralized rules, is useful in this regard. Ex ante rules would be too costly (including the costs of negotiation and information), if not impossible, to set optimally given the rapidly changing information, technology and context in the areas of both climate change and trade. The chapters dealing with taxes, regulations, border adjustments and subsidies examined the standards laid out in the WTO agreements, highlighting the inevitable enforcement costs as well as the various uncertainties and attendant error costs in the current interpretations of these rules. There are greater signs of hope in the Appellate Body's more recent interpretations of Article XX. The efficiency and fairness of the future trading system will depend on building on such progress.

Part IV addressed the second interaction between trade rules and climate policies – the extent to which countries can use unilateral measures to induce other countries to take action on climate change. Countries can use trade measures as carrots to provide incentives to other countries to take action on climate change. While there are some possibilities for using trade preferences to this end, such action would probably have limited effectiveness. Moreover, it seems unlikely that the US or the EC would permit the offering of such trade preferences to the more advanced developing countries such as China and India.

At the other end of the spectrum, countries might be able to unilaterally invoke trade measures (such as sanctions) as sticks to force other countries to take climate change action. While such unilateral measures may be legally possible, there are serious concerns associated with such action, including the difficulty of enacting trade measures severe enough to force action by other countries, and the political undesirability of forcing any one country's set of values on another.

Trade measures may also be used to eliminate the roadblocks that stand in the way of climate change action in many countries, most notably competitiveness concerns. Where industry fears that it will lose international competitiveness if it is forced to face the costs of climate change regulation or taxation, it will pressure government to desist from taking action. Where the industry is powerful, its pressure on government can constitute a significant roadblock to taking climate change action. Trade measures such as border tax adjustments can help to eliminate these roadblocks, but would come at a potentially high political cost. As we discussed, the prospect of using border tax adjustments has prompted commentators to suggest that their use would provoke international friction, even possibly a trade war. Further, the difficulties associated with calculating border adjustments mean that they will be extremely difficult to monitor, thus increasing the possibility that they might be used as a protectionist tool

The third area of interaction between trade measures and climate change, namely multilateral solutions to climate change, was discussed in Part V. Trade measures could be included in a post-Kyoto multilateral climate change agreement. Using trade measures under a multilateral agreement has the potential to increase the fairness of attempts to induce participation in and compliance with a climate change agreement. Even without a broader multilateral agreement on trade and climate measures, some progress could be made through multilateral negotiations on liberalization of environmental goods and services. Such liberalization could foster efficiency as well as fairness in the sense of meeting development goals.

16.2   THE ROAD AHEAD

This book has aimed to show that while there are areas of conflict between trade rules and climate change, there are also a number of existing and potential synergies between the two regimes. This interaction of trade measures and climate measures can be used to aid developing countries, increasing both fairness and economic growth opportunities for these countries. Decisions that affect the way in which the trade and climate regimes interact must advance the ultimate goal of enhancing social welfare on a global scale. Global welfare is not composed solely of economic growth or of environmental protection, but includes both. Developing countries' ability to fully integrate into and benefit from the international trading system is hampered by protectionist policies adopted by both developed countries and other developing countries. Enforcement of international trade rules has the potential to deter protectionism and, to the extent that it is successful in doing so, it will aid in economic development for both developed and developing countries. It will also have beneficial effects for global efforts to address climate change through, for example, lowering the price of environmentally friendly goods and fostering expansion of green economies in developing countries. Further, mitigating climate change is obviously good for developing countries both directly, given projections of the adverse effects they are likely to face, and more indirectly by reducing the harm to their ability to grow and prosper by mitigating negative impacts on their agriculture and natural resources sectors.

The difficulty is in designing a trading system which provides at the same time deterrence of protectionism, policy space for addressing climate change, and fairness to developing countries. As discussed previously, the current system has some elements which are favourable for fostering this mix of aims. However, there are concerns about the current institutional structure and its current efficiency and fairness. A new or at least modified institutional framework is needed. There are a number of possible changes that could be made either solely or in combination including: a Peace Clause either under the existing WTO rules or in a new WTO agreement (or in a different multilateral agreement); a new WTO agreement which explicitly recognizes the relationship between trade and climate measures; changes in the existing trade rules to help either avoid or settle conflicts over trade and climate measures; and a new multilateral (that is, non-WTO) agreement which explicitly sets the terms of the relationship between trade and climate change. Each of these options will be discussed in turn.

16.2.1 A 'Peace Clause'

Some commentators argue that policy space needs to be fostered to encourage action on climate change. For example, Hufbauer, Charnovitz and Kim argue for a 'Peace Clause' which specifies that countries will not challenge climate measures by other countries where the violation is primarily technical.[2] They also argue that any such Peace Clause should contain some specification of the measures to which it would apply. For example, their Peace Clause would allow a certain number of emission permits to be distributed for free without these being regarded as a subsidy and would also permit certain research and development subsidies such as those related to sequestration and alternative energy. Relatedly, Howse argues that to address concerns about climate change subsidies, countries should report their subsidies to the UNFCCC and then the members should institute a waiver for these subsidies.[3] The waiver would mean that the covered subsidies would not be subject to WTO challenge.

The advantage of such a clause or a waiver would be that it makes the ground for challenges clearer, hopefully forestalling challenges or at least making any challenges easier to address. Such clarity would reduce dispute settlement costs. It would also provide members greater certainty, which would allow them to get on with the real work of setting up measures to address climate change.

However, there are a number of difficulties with any such Peace Clause or waiver. First, it may provide too much scope for protectionism. A Peace Clause or waiver would undoubtedly contain language that would seek to ensure that countries did not abuse it for protectionist purposes. Howse, for example, suggests a principle-based approach whereby the subsidies subject to the waiver must satisfy some basic WTO principles such as non-discrimination and transparency.[4] However, while such an approach provides some protection against protectionism, it seems to give rise to the same concerns about certainty and flexibility as the current WTO approach given that it is based on the WTO jurisprudence.

Moreover, the reality would probably be that protectionist measures would slip through. Where they do, they are likely to do so in forms that hurt developing countries. This would be a double loss for developing countries, who would not only face the losses caused by their trading partners' protectionist measures but would also be forestalled from taking action against those measures. If a Peace Clause provided too much space for domestic measures, there is thus a risk that developing countries would lose access to developed country markets. There is a potential gain from increasing policy space for taking climate action but it does not recognize

---

[2] Gary Hufbauer, Steve Charnovitz and Jisun Kim, *Global Warming and the World Trading System* (Washington, DC: Peterson Institute for International Economics, 2009).

[3] R. Howse, 'Subsidies to Address Climate Change: Legal Issues' (Winnipeg, Manitoba: International Institute for Sustainable Development, 2009).

[4] Ibid.

the synergies of a reduction in protectionism with both climate action and economic development. The result may be both a potential inefficiency (that is, there are unnecessary restrictions on trade, hindering economic growth and the diffusion of more climate friendly goods and technology) and a potential unfairness to developing countries.

Second, the negotiation of a Peace Clause seems unlikely given the protracted Doha negotiations and the consensus rule. Politically it would be difficult to get agreement on anything more than a broad statement of the desirability of not challenging legitimate climate measures. A more fulsome Peace Clause or waiver would be costly to develop in terms of time and information. Some developed countries may be willing to take the short-term political gain from enabling both climate action and pro-tectionism. However, the reduction in both growth and perceived fairness would mean that developing countries might resist any such clause unless it was connected to significant carrots such as financing. An alternative may be an agreement in which members agree not to challenge measures in exchange for an agreement not to impose border tax adjustments. Any such agreement may aid both developing countries interested in avoiding border measures and developed countries wishing to have some certainty in their policy measures.

Finally, the lack of adherence to the synergies of trade and climate change and the potential for the growth of protectionism compounds one of the greatest risks from a Peace Clause – that it may foster not peace but greater conflict. At best it may simply defer conflict until the end of the peace period, at which time all of the resentments from the building of protectionism are unleashed and challenges are brought. At worst, the Members may address the animosity from protectionist actions in other ways, either through elevating other trade disputes or by reducing their willingness to cooperate in other areas, including potentially on climate action. The result may therefore be the opposite of the aim of the Peace Clause.

16.2.2   A WTO Climate Change Agreement

Perhaps of greater long-term benefit than a Peace Clause would be a spe-cific agreement negotiated within the WTO addressing climate measures. The provisions within any such agreement would have to be designed to increase the clarity of the rules for Members in the sense of what climate measures are acceptable. The result would hopefully be an increase in the scope for parties to take climate action (that is, a reduction in the uncer-tainty about particular measures and an attendant reduction in regulatory chill) and a reduction in the amount and cost of dispute settlement.

The elements of such an agreement (ranked in increasing order of likely contentiousness among members) could include:

- *Committee for climate change*   A Climate Change Committee could be established that is similar to the SPS or TBT Committee. The SPS and TBT Committees are made up of Member States and at the meeting members can raise concerns in an effort to resolve matters even before the consultation stage. A Climate Change Committee could hear and attempt to settle disputes over the legitimacy of climate change measures prior to the panel stage. It could be composed of members but with the assistance of experts in the science of climate change as well as in the policy instruments that may be used to address it. Such an expert committee may reduce the likelihood of errors due to lack of understanding of the issues, thereby increasing the efficiency of the system. It may also have greater legitimacy because of the presence of experts. It would not mean that disputes could not proceed to the panel stage. It may, however, reduce the number and/or the scope of disagreements within any such challenges, thus reducing the costs of dispute settlement.

- *Notification of climate change measures*   Parties would be required to notify the Committee (and therefore the other parties) about any climate change measures they put in place that may impact trade. Again such notification is similar to provisions in the SPS and TBT Agreements.[5] It would allow transparency of domestic policies and possibly both lead to reduced incentives to take protectionist measures under the guise of taking action on climate change (as they would be more likely to be discovered) and reduce the number of such disputes as concerns can be addressed earlier in the process.[6]

---

[5]   There would be some overlap of reporting in the case of climate measures as they may, for example, have to be reported to the Climate Change Committee but also the TBT Committee. A solution may be for the measures to be notified to both committees but the Climate Change Committee would consider any climate measures (with perhaps a representative of the TBT or SPS Committee as appropriate on the Climate Change Committee).

[6]   By way of example, between 1995 and 2007, a total of approximately 245 specific trade concerns were brought to the attention of the SPS Committee. During this time, only 28 requests were made for formal consultations under the Dispute Settlement Understanding. Of these, five disputes were subsequently heard by a Dispute Panel. The number of trade concerns is as cited in a summation paper by the Secretariat: WTO Secretariat, Specific Trade Concerns – Note by the Secretariat (2007), WTO Doc. G/SPS/GEN/204/Rev.7.

- *Mitigating climate change as a legitimate objective*   Any such agreement could specify clearly that reducing GHG emissions as well as adapting to climate change are legitimate policy objectives from the perspective of the WTO. While such objectives are likely to be within the scope of GATT Article XX(b) and (g), there is no benefit in having any uncertainty on this issue in relation to Article XX or to any other WTO agreements to which Article XX does not apply. Again, specifying these matters would increase certainty and reduce the cost of dispute settlement. Further, it would possibly enhance flexibility by providing Members with greater certainty about the types of measures that are permissible.

- *Non-aggression Clause*   The Climate Change Agreement could include a provision prohibiting any unilateral trade measures (including border tax adjustments) based on climate policies for a particular period of time. Zhang, for example, argues that based on the length of time the US is taking to put in place climate measures, the peace period should be at least ten years.[7] Such a Non-aggression Clause would be particularly important for developing countries which lack both the resources and the institutional capacity to take broad-reaching climate action in the near term.[8] Further, as discussed in Part III, unilateral measures can negatively impact international relations since they may be viewed as based on idiosyncratic or colourable (that is, disguised protectionist) claims about climate change. A Non-aggression Clause could therefore reduce the negative effects of such measures on international relations and increase the perceived fairness of the trading system.

- *Procedural (risk management) review of measures*   The agreement could specify that in any dispute about the legitimacy of a measure, the panel will look at the process by which the decision was made to ensure that it meets some minimum threshold for procedural standards. It could list the factors to be taken into account such as international standards and IPCC determinations. In this sense, the

---

[7]   Zhong Xiang Zhang, 'Climate Change Meets Trade in Promoting Green Growth: Potential Conflicts and Synergies' (15 July 2009). Available at SSRN: http://ssrn.com/abstract=1511982.

[8]   Note that a Non-aggression Clause is different from the Peace Clause discussed earlier in that the Non-aggression Clause would entail not taking unilateral action against other members while the Peace Clause would involve a commitment not to challenge the measures of other members.

Climate Change Agreement might be similar to the SPS Agreement except that the provisions of the Climate Change Agreement would relate directly to the procedural nature of the decision. Such a procedural review would tie into the domestic and international accountability of the process as it would increase the transparency of the decision-making process. Such transparency would hopefully reduce the scope for successful protectionist pressure by concentrated interests and reduce error costs by increasing the information to decision-makers.[9]

- *Climate subsidies*   The agreement should include an environmental exception for subsidies. As noted in Chapter 7, there is some debate about whether Article XX may apply outside the GATT to other agreements such as the SCM Agreement. However, there are valid efficiency reasons for using subsidies to encourage and provide incentives for certain actions to address climate change (including research and development) but also to encourage other aspects (such as implementation of new technology) where first-best instruments such as pricing are not politically feasible.[10] The use of subsidies should be clearly legitimate provided they are not protectionist. More ambitiously, the agreement could follow the example of the Agreement on Agriculture and schedule existing or potential levels of subsidies and establish a schedule for reduction of the levels of those subsidies.[11]

- *Substantive review of measures*   The risk from merely having procedural review of measures is that members will engage in empty proceduralism – that is, they will go through the motions of the procedural steps without changing the substantive outcome. The transparency that comes with the procedures only helps to the extent that there are effective domestic accountability mechanisms. Some mixed form of review may be more useful, taking into account other indicators of the necessity or legitimacy of the measures such as their consistency with international norms or practice. However, as was noted in Chapter 10, while greater use of substantive review reduces

[9]   Robert Howse, 'Democracy, Science and Free Trade: Risk Regulation on Trial at the World Trade Organization' (2000) 98 *Michigan Law Review* 2329.
[10]   A. Sykes, 'The Questionable Case for Subsidies Regulation: A Comparative Perspective' (Stanford University School of Law, Law and Economics Research Paper Series, No. 380, 2009).
[11]   Howse, *supra* note 3.

the risk of empty proceduralism, it entails potentially increased error costs.

- *PPMs* The agreement could also set limits on the scope for measures to address PPMs. The legitimacy of measures which take into account PPMs in other countries is currently highly controversial. As noted in Part II, it is not clear to what extent PPMs are incorporated into the tests under either the substantive provisions of or the exceptions to the GATT. An explicit agreement as to the ability of countries to take PPMs into account in their measures could greatly reduce trade conflicts. Given that the limits on PPMs could be set within an agreement dealing specifically with climate change, there is the possibility of establishing a baseline or threshold for the use of measures based on PPMs. However, the disadvantage of a WTO-based climate change agreement as opposed to a non-WTO negotiated agreement addressing trade and climate measures (discussed further below) is that the WTO climate agreement would probably have to incorporate some notion of equivalency or sufficiency of action from another agreement. For example, the agreement could specify that measures could not be based on PPMs where the target Member is in compliance with its international commitments on climate change (this may not be known until the end of any given commitment period). The difficulty is that such a provision requires that there be meaningful commitments from another forum that are acceptable to the Members. If not, it would probably be costly and time consuming to attempt to develop an acceptable definition of when PPMs are permissible within a WTO-based agreement.

The advantages of a WTO agreement on trade and climate change would be that there would be lower enforcement costs since the parties would have information on what domestic measures are acceptable under WTO rules. There would be clearer grounds on which to establish that a particular measure was permissible, potentially reducing both the number of challenges and the cost of each challenge. Further, the processes and rules under the Climate Change Agreement could allow for national variation (enhancing the flexibility of the WTO arrangements) through, for example, a committee of experts which understands the potential scope for variance in policy. The greater certainty would enable countries to take climate action which accords with their national context.

The obvious difficulty with a WTO Climate Change Agreement would be the negotiating costs. It would take a long time to negotiate such an agreement given the conflicting interests of the Members and the information required to specify some of the terms of the agreement. It may be, however, that this concern can be reduced by a staged approach – that is, attempting to get agreement and implementation of the less contentious elements of the agreement first rather than waiting for complete agreement. The list above is ranked from the least contentious to the most contentious elements – that is, it is likely to be less contentious to establish a committee composed of members and possibly experts to initially hear and attempt to settle climate disputes than it is, for example, to obtain agreement on the appropriate scope of strictures on PPMs.

The negotiations lead to another concern about a WTO Climate Change Agreement. The legitimacy of any rules depends on the negotiating process and who is involved in the process. The WTO negotiations have the benefit of the WTO process and the norm of consensus decision-making. While it may not be free of power dynamics, it may be preferable in this regard to the use of the dispute settlement process. It allows the decisions to be made by the Members rather than panels or the Appellate Body, which may have different preferences from the Members. Further, it does not depend on the ability of parties to take advantage of dispute settlement or remedies, which, as noted in Chapter 10, is problematic for developing countries. It allows developing countries to increase the power of their voices by combining as blocs in negotiations, as they have done in the past and are doing in the Doha Round. Finally, negotiations over a climate change agreement could incorporate development policies in a more comprehensive way than could be done through dispute settlement, increasing the actual and perceived fairness of any such arrangement.

16.2.3 Changes to Existing Rules and Procedures

Short of a new Peace Clause or WTO Climate Change Agreement, there are some changes that can be made to existing WTO rules that would help meet the goals set out in this book of addressing climate change, deterring protectionism, and furthering development. These rule changes could include:

● *Changes to Article XX*   Article XX(b) and (g) could be modified to more explicitly provide for climate measures as a legitimate objective. Such a change would be more standard-like than a rule-like Peace Clause. In one sense this standard-like form makes it easier to negotiate as the Members do not have to debate the details of the wording to such a great extent. However, it will still be difficult to negotiate as it depends on trust by the members in panels and the Appellate Body distinguishing legitimate from illegitimate climate measures. It will also require agreement on whether these measures would have to be 'necessary', or simply 'relate to' the objective of addressing climate change, or whether there would be some other standard.

- *Addition of an Article XX type exception to the SCM Agreement* Howse notes that the non-actionable subsidies category could be revived but with some changes.[12] It would be connected to instruments listed in a multilateral agreement (the Kyoto Protocol or presumably its successor); the subsidy would have to be connected to the goals of the Kyoto Protocol (based on scientific and other evidence); and it must be consistent with the principles of non-discrimination and transparency. Howse argues this change may be possible through an interpretative understanding, although the potentially significant implications of the changes may make this politically infeasible.

- *Changes to the burden of proof or standard of review* The Members could also make changes to the Dispute Settlement Understanding that would take issues relating to climate change into account. There could, for example, be particular rules addressing the standard of review in the case of climate change issues or the burden of proof in the case of uncertainty. As noted above, the standard of review currently is somewhat unclear. Under Article XX, it has both substantive and procedural elements. A mixed form of standard of review is likely to be desirable. However, greater clarity of the approach panels are to take to climate measures would be helpful. There is also an on-going issue about how panels treat minority scientific opinions.[13] It would be useful to obtain greater clarity on what evidence is required in order to allow members to adequately prepare for challenges.

These changes would hopefully provide panels and the Appellate Body with greater direction on how to decide any WTO challenges to climate measures. They may aid in reducing the costs of challenges (as there is greater certainty as to the rules) and error costs. These changes may be

---

[12] Ibid.

[13] See, in the health context, Tracey Epps, *International Trade and Health Protection: A Critical Assessment of the WTO's SPS Agreement* (Cheltenham, UK and Northampton, MA, USA: Edward Elgar, 2008).

beneficial to the extent that they are easier to obtain agreement on than a more general agreement or a broad Peace Clause. They would, however, continue to provide panels with considerable discretion, which allows for flexibility but raises concerns as to errors by inexpert decision-makers.

The concern is, of course, that it may be too difficult not only to obtain a new agreement on climate and trade measures but also to formally change existing rules. Members may be concerned that, with such changes, decisions would be left in the hands of panellists and would therefore be unpredictable and difficult to control. Whether or not these substantive changes are possible, more procedural changes may make a considerable difference to avoiding or resolving challenges. If there are no substantive changes, these procedural changes would exist beside the current evolving rules (which, as noted in this book, do currently provide considerable scope for action on climate change). These procedural changes could include:

- *Notification*   As we have discussed through the concept of a new climate change agreement, it may be useful to have a process through which Members would notify others of climate measures which may have trade impacts so that other countries can take early action (including negotiations with the Member taking the measure).

- *Climate Change Committee*   Like the SPS Committee, a Climate Change Committee could take on the role of helping with early resolution of disputes about the WTO legality of climate change measures. It could perhaps give a preliminary opinion on WTO legality. Such a committee may help settlement and may be particularly helpful to developing countries lacking the resources or expertise to address these measures.

- *Procedural changes through decisions*   More controversially, the Appellate Body could make changes to the evidentiary and procedural rules concerning challenges related to climate change. The Appellate Body has made statements in recent decisions that signal that it is sensitive to the scientific and other types of uncertainty that lie at the core of climate policies. For example, in *Brazil – Tyres*, the Appellate Body pointed to the need to be sensitive to the uncertainty about the effectiveness of different instruments as well as the need to view instruments as part of a package of measures.[14] The Appellate Body could make further moves in the direction of recognizing the

---

[14]   See Chapter 9 for a discussion of the *Brazil – Tyres* decision.

specific concerns with policing climate measures while remaining within the current language of the agreements.

The fairness of changes either to existing rules or to procedural rules through interpretation depends in part on the fairness of the dispute settlement process. Uncertainty may allow developed countries to engage in greater protectionism. Uncertainty combined with the cost of litigation and the difficulties with remedies may hinder developing countries from challenging measures. The greater certainty from the changes may therefore make developing countries more willing to challenge colourable climate measures, thereby forestalling or reducing the incentive of developed countries to take such measures.

16.2.4   Multilateral Trade and Climate Agreement

The alternative to taking action through the WTO would be to obtain an agreement on trade rules and climate policy through a different multilateral process such as the UNFCCC process. This agreement could be a stand-alone agreement on the connection of trade and climate measures or it could be within a broader climate agreement such as the post-Kyoto negotiations. Like the WTO agreement, the non-WTO agreement could set out a list of permissible measures or set a standard for legitimate actions. In either case, a form of dispute settlement mechanism would have to be established.

The benefits of a non-WTO process relate to the frame of negotiations. Discussing trade and climate change within the WTO may preference the trade perspective to too great an extent. If it is trade negotiators and specialists discussing the relative merits of hindering trade versus providing space for climate action, there may be a risk that the agreement will be shaded towards trade at the expense of the environment. A non-WTO process may allow a greater range of specialists to be involved in the negotiations and to set the direction for the relationship between trade and climate measures. This balance between trade and climate concerns may also relate to the dispute settlement process. While the WTO dispute settlement system is in many ways very successful, at its core it may be unable to deal with the uncertainty at the centre of climate change, even with the greater certainty provided by a new agreement. Moreover, the membership of panels and the Appellate Body may consciously or unconsciously prioritize trade interests over the environment. A non-WTO dispute settlement body may not have these predilections.

However, the efficiency of a non-WTO agreement may be low, depending on the nature of the enforcement mechanism. Given that the dispute

settlement arrangement will have to address the legitimacy of trade measures, the efficacy of the dispute settlement process will depend on whether
the agreement sets rules or standards. If the agreement sets detailed
rules, the dispute settlement body will have an easier time of settling the
legitimacy of a particular measure. However, the more standard-like the
agreement is, the more difficult it will be for the dispute settlement system
to determine whether the measure is permissible. It will require a more
sophisticated infrastructure. The probability of a non-WTO agreement
containing a dispute settlement mechanism of the same type of sophistica-
tion as that of the WTO seems low. The DSU is a unique and complicated
arrangement that reflects a balancing of interests that would be difficult to
replicate.

Further, the fairness of the non-WTO agreement will depend on how
the negotiations are conducted. Both the WTO and the non-WTO processes will have high negotiation costs, as can be seen from both the
on-going WTO Doha Round of negotiations and the recent Copenhagen
meetings under the UNFCCC. The length of time to complete these negotiations and the costs depend in part on the number of parties involved as
well as the range of issues included in the negotiations. In some respects,
the non-WTO negotiations may be more difficult and costly if the trade
and climate measures are bound up with negotiations over caps and other
matters. Perhaps the main factor pointing towards a greater likelihood of
conclusion of negotiations on trade and climate measures is that there may
be a greater sense of urgency within the non-WTO negotiations to obtain
agreement. However, again the recent Copenhagen negotiations provide
an illustration of the difficulties entailed within these negotiations.

16.3 BRINGING TRADE AND CLIMATE ACTION TOGETHER

There is therefore a range of possible solutions to improve the status quo
in relation to the connection between trade and climate measures while
supporting achievement of the goals highlighted here of addressing climate
change, deterring protectionism, and furthering development. Each has its
advantages and costs. Many countries will be reluctant to adopt aggressive
climate change policies for fear of competitive impacts and leakage. There
are measures countries can take to protect against the adverse competitive
impacts and leakage (such as BTAs) but these measures are risky under
existing trade law and can be politically divisive. Countries will be reluctant to adopt significant climate policies in conjunction with such measures protecting their competitive position if there is a significant risk that

the protective measures will be challenged and found inconsistent with WTO rules. Some greater certainty of WTO rules is required to ensure that countries have the space to take climate action and that the likelihood and costs of disputes are reduced. The difficulty will be in determining the best process by which to bring these changes about fairly and efficiently.

The best approach is a staged process within the WTO, at least in the short term. The WTO has the infrastructure to examine trade and climate disputes but requires some adaptation to make it fairer and more efficient. Stern notes that 'the building of an agreement is so urgent it will have to be carried out with existing institutional structures.'[15] He points mainly to the UNFCCC process but, given its recent disappointments (in particular, the Copenhagen Accord), it seems that at least some movement through the WTO processes will be necessary. Probably the least controversial and most beneficial would be to institute a clearer, more focused process for notification and settlement of disputes prior to the panel stage. Based on the model of the SPS Agreement, this process would consist of a require-ment of notification and the submission of any disputes to a climate com-mittee (composed of members and potentially at least assisted by experts) focused on these particular issues. Such a process should go a long way to fostering confidence and respect for climate measures and improved panel decisions even without formal changes to the rules. Moreover, the Appellate Body should continue on its current path of attempting to find a more nuanced approach to trade and environment issues, recognizing the nature of the underlying uncertainties.

In terms of a broader agreement, the best case would be to have a multi-lateral agreement specifying some consensus about when climate measures can legitimately impact trade and when trade measures can be used against countries which are not taking action on climate change. The UNFCCC seems an obvious place for such an agreement given the history of multilat-eral agreements in other areas with trade provisions such as the Montreal Protocol. However, because of the interests involved in the broader discus-sion of limits on emissions and funding for developing countries, it will be difficult to obtain any agreement on trade measures through this process beyond a Peace Clause which seems likely to increase conflict rather than promote peace. There may be an opportunity to break the process into smaller segments and get agreement on a sectoral basis, although this has tended to be rejected through the UNFCCC approach.[16] It may then

---

[15]   Stern, *supra* note 1 at 200.

[16]   See S. Barrett, 'Climate Treaties and the Imperative of Enforcement' (2008) 24 (2) *Oxford Review of Economic Policy* 239 (arguing for sectoral agreements).

be that the WTO is the best place for an agreement relating to trade and climate change, although we recognize its limitations. Designing a staged approach may allow agreement to evolve over time towards a more comprehensive agreement, while allowing some progress within the existing WTO structure.

Whatever the process used, progress is essential. The key theme of this book has been that the goal is not to address climate change per se or to increase economic growth as an end in itself. Both are important to enhancing social welfare – improving the lives of people now and in the future and protecting the environment. There are ways of mitigating climate change and deterring protectionism to the benefit of all. We need to build on the many positive developments in recent WTO jurisprudence. There is much to gain from taking advantage of the synergies between trade rules and climate measures and much to lose if we do not.

But see also C. Hepburn and N. Stern, 'A New Global Deal on Climate Change' (2008) 24 (2) *Oxford Review of Economic Policy* 259 (arguing that a multilateral deal with a world target is necessary).

Index

SPS Agreement (Application of
    Sanitary and Phytosanitary
    Measures) 78, 143, 170, 255
Staiger, Robert W. 25, 28, 30, 34
standards
    defined 31
    international, and TBT Agreement
        77–80
    setting of 63–64
static efficiency 86
Stavins, Robert N. 9, 49, 52–54, 58,
    188, 190, 201, 210
Steenblik, Ronald 235
Steger, D. 169
Stephenson, John 122, 125–128, 137,
    140, 141, 171, 206
Stephenson, Matthew 171
Stern, Sir Nicholas 5, 18, 249
    Stern Review 124–125
Stewart, Richard B. 194, 195
'sticks' *see* negative incentives ('sticks')
Stiftung, Friedrich Ebert 78, 120
Stigler, George J. 21
Stiglitz, Joseph E. 41, 43, 110
subsidies
    actionable 40, 114–117
    adverse effects, tests for 116
    Climate Change Agreement,
        proposals for 257
    definitions 108–112
    and externalities 103–105
    limitations/drawbacks 107–108
    market-based determination 111
    non-actionable 117–118
    objectives of policies 104
    prohibited 40, 112–113
    reasons for restricting 118–121, 162
    reasons for subsidizing 103–108
    reducing, for environmentally
        harmful industries 57
    remedial provisions 164, 165
    specificity requirement 114, 115
    values, subsidizing 105–106
Sugathan, Mahesh 235, 237, 239, 243
sulphur oxides 84
Summers, Lawrence 178
Sunstein, Cass R. 46, 53, 65, 106, 190,
    194, 197
Sweden, carbon tax introduced in 89
Sykes, Alan O. 20, 21, 25, 26, 34, 66,

103, 105, 107, 108, 111, 113, 115,
    117, 146, 165, 168, 257
synthetic fertilizers, tax on 91

Tamiotti, Ludivine 59, 235, 236, 237
Tarasofsky, Richard 200
taxes
    addressing of climate change 83–91
    and border tax adjustments 127–129
    carbon *see* carbon taxes
    direct 130
    energy 84, 90
    and environmental efficiency 53
    'gas guzzler' on cars 75
    GATT Article III.2
        'directly competitive or
            substitutable' products 96–99
        generally 91–92
        'like' products 92–96, 130
        'not similarly taxed' 99–100
        product-related distinctions 75
        'so as to afford protection'
            100–101
    indirect 130
    institutional framework 101–102
    internal 137
    'like' products 92–95
taxes in excess of those applied to
    95–96
    market-based and non-market-based
        mechanisms 86
    and non-discrimination 91–101
        GATT Article III.2 (first sentence)
            92–96, 101
        GATT Article III.2 (second
            sentence) 92, 96–101
    prior-stage indirect cumulative 135
    revenue-neutral 54, 90
    upstream or downstream 85, 93–94,
        99
TBT Agreement (Agreement on
    Technical Barriers to Trade) 143,
    199, 250
    and international standards 77–80
    linkages between trade and climate
        change 38, 39
    regulations and domestic emissions
        trading 81, 82
technical regulations, and TBT
    Agreement 77, 78

Printed and bound by CPI Group (UK) Ltd, Croydon, CR0 4YY

23/04/2025

14660988-0004